THE SIBLING SOCIETY

THE SIBLING SOCIETY

ROBERT BLY

⁂ *Addison-Wesley Publishing Company*

Reading, Massachusetts   Menlo Park, California   New York
Don Mills, Ontario   Harlow, England   Amsterdam   Bonn
Sydney   Singapore   Tokyo   Madrid   San Juan
Paris   Seoul   Milan   Mexico City   Taipei

Library of Congress Cataloging-in-Publication Data
Bly, Robert.
    The sibling society / Robert Bly.
        p.   cm.
    Includes bibliographical references and index.
    ISBN 0-201-40646-2
    1. Culture.   2. Popular culture.   3. Social values.
    4. Intergenerational relations.   5. Youthfulness.   I. Title.
    HM101.B6165   1996
    306—dc20   95—42630
                                                                                CIP

Jacket design by David High
Text design by Diane Levy
Set in 10.5-point Stone Serif by Pagesetters, Inc.

1 2 3 4 5 6 7 8 9-MA-0099989796
First printing, March 1996

Contents

Introduction

I'T'S THE WORST OF TIMES; IT'S THE BEST OF TIMES. THAT'S HOW we feel as we navigate from a paternal society, now discredited, to a society in which impulse is given its way. People don't bother to grow up, and we are all fish swimming in a tank of half-adults. The rule is: Where repression was before, fantasy will now be; we human beings limp along, running after our own fantasy. We can never catch up, and so we defeat ourselves by the simplest possible means: speed. Everywhere we go there's a crowd, and the people all look alike.

We begin to live a lateral life, catch glimpses out of the corners of our eyes, keep the TV set at eye level, watch the scores move horizontally across the screen.

We see what's coming out of the sideview mirror. It seems like intimacy; maybe not intimacy as much as proximity; maybe not proximity as much as sameness. Americans who are twenty years old see others who look like them in Czechoslovakia, Greece, China, France, Brazil, Germany, and Russia, wearing the same jeans, listening to the same music, speaking a universal language that computer literacy demands. Sometimes they feel more vitally connected to siblings elsewhere than to family members in the next room.

When we see the millions like ourselves all over the world, our eyes meet uniformity, resemblance, likenesses, rather than distinction and differences. Hope rises immediately for the long-desired possibility of community. And yet it would be foolish to overlook the serious implications of this glance to the side, this tilt of the head. "Mass society, with its demand for work without responsibility, creates a gigantic army of rival siblings," in Alexander Mitscherlich's words.

This book is not about siblings in a family; we'll use the word *sibling* as a metaphor. We'll try to make the phrase *sibling society* into a lens, bringing into focus certain tendencies, habits, and griefs we have all noticed. Adults regress toward adolescence; and adolescents—seeing that—have no desire to become adults. Few are able to imagine any genuine life coming from the vertical plane—tradition, religion, devotion. Even graduate students in science are said to share this problem. The neuroscientist Robert Sapolsky writes:

> *My students usually come with ego boundaries like exoskeletons. Most have no use for religion, precedents, or tradition. They want their rituals newly minted and shared horizontally within their age group, not vertically over time. The ones I train to become scientists go at it like warriors, overturning reigning paradigms, each discovery a murder of their scientific ancestors.*

Perhaps one-third of our society has developed these new sibling qualities. The rest of us are walking in that direction. When we all arrive, there may be no public schools at all, nor past paradigms, because only people one's own age will be worth listening to.

There is little in the sibling society to prevent a slide into primitivism, and into those regressions that fascism is so fond of. Eric Hoffer remarked:

> *Drastic change [has produced] this social primitivism . . . a new identity is found by embracing a mass movement . . . [the] mass movement absorbs and assimilates the individual . . . [who] is thereby reduced to an infantile state, for this is what a new birth*

really means: to become like a child. And children are primitive beings—they are credulous, follow a leader, and readily become members of a pack. . . . Finally, primitivism also follows when people seek a new identity by plunging into ceaseless action and hustling. It takes leisure to mature. People in a hurry can neither grow nor decay; they are preserved in a state of perpetual puerility.

The society of half-adults, built on technology and affluence, is more highly developed here than in any other country on earth; but in other parts of the globe the same tendencies are growing fast. We can't be definitive, but we can glance at some of its characteristics.

It is hard in a sibling society to decide what is real. We participate in more and more nonevents. A nonevent transpires when the organizer promises an important psychic or political event and then cheats people, providing material only tangentially related. An odd characteristic of the sibling society is that no one effectively *objects.* Some sort of trance takes over if enough people are watching an event simultaneously. It is a contemporary primitivism, "participation mystique," a "mysterious participation of all the clan."

Kierkegaard once, in trying to predict what the future society would be like, offered this metaphor: People will put up a poster soon saying *Tonight John Erik will skate on thin ice at the very center of the pond. It'll be very dangerous. Please come.* Everyone comes, and John Erik skates about three inches from shore, and people say, "Look, he's skating on thin ice at the very center of the pond!" A lecturer says: *On Friday night we will have a revolution.* When Friday night comes, the hall is filled, and the radical talks passionately and flamboyantly for an hour and a half; then he declares that a revolution took place here tonight. The audience pours out into the street, saying, "Tonight we had a revolution! Tonight we had a revolution!"

Nonevents are now a regular national feature. Millions watch them—Tiny Tim being married on Johnny Carson's "Tonight

Show," CNN reporting the Grenada invasion, elaborate celebrity efforts such as "We Are the World." In a recent nonevent, Diane Sawyer interviewed Michael Jackson and Lisa Marie Presley, implying a promise to confront the dark secrets of Jackson's past, and a promise that she herself would be an adult in her concern for the truth. She was not an adult that night, and the hidden event was a marriage of Sony and ABC.

It's HARD FOR JOURNALISTS OR ORDINARY PEOPLE TO GET AWAY from envy when they look at a leader. Every detail of a president's life is used to discredit him. President Clinton has his faults, but no other American president has been put in the stocks so soon and left there so long. Recent biographies of Franklin Roosevelt mention how careful journalists at that time were not to photograph him when he was moved from his car to a wheelchair. It wasn't an attempt to hide failings, but to give him some place of dignity in his leadership.

The *American Spectator* carries ads offering pins that say "It's a Bird . . . It's a Plane . . . It's Hillary, Nix the Witch in '96," or a bumper sticker for $3 reading "Newt's Mom Was Right." Journalists and ordinary citizens join together in this mixture of envy and aggression. Adam Gopnick, in his piece on recent journalism, remarks:

> *In the past twenty years, the American press has undergone a transformation from an access culture to an aggression culture. . . . Aggression has become a kind of abstract form, practiced in a void of ideas, or even of ordinary sympathy. . . .*

One sad result of this habit of envy and aggression is the utter discouragement and bitterness of voters, who move into an adolescent place in relation to the duties of citizenship.

It IS HARD TO BE AS POPULAR AS WE ARE SUPPOSED TO BE. THE superego or Interior Judge has altered its requirements. An Interior

Judge that once demanded high standards in art, in writing, and in ethics now requires early success, at twenty or twenty-two. Those insistences on early success have devastated the art world.

The French writer Giles Lipovetsky says, "The superego presents itself under the guise of demands for fame and success which, if they are not achieved, unleash an implacable storm of criticism against the ego." The Interior Judge remains authoritarian and brutal, but it no longer asks the citizen to be honorable, disciplined, and noble; now it wants its owner to have public gratification. We could say the superego wants everyone to appear on talk shows, the very act that it would have forbidden as vulgar a hundred years ago.

The Interior Judge's changed requirements, paradoxically, give the media much more power than they have ever had before; and the media's accidental conferring of fame can become highly dangerous to the unwary. A recent example is Robert O'Donnell, the man who became famous for bringing Baby Jessica out of the well in Midland, Texas. He enjoyed his fame in the beginning, being interviewed and feted; but later he, or more accurately his superego, could not reconcile himself to the loss of attention that followed. He lost his job and then his family; developed migraine headaches; and finally, last year, killed himself.

Psychoanalysts describe the Interior Judge as they see it operating in youngsters now with terms such as "terroristic"; like a mad bomber, it can't be talked out of its demands. People in cultures of the past, and still in many cultures today, were able to reason with their conscience, talk to it, get a relaxing of admonitions, a forgiveness of sins. But the new Interior Judge hijacks the teenager and shoots all potential rescuers. The hangdog look, the druggy and disheartened mood, the lack of grace in body movements, the stammering in speech, are caused not by laziness or by being spoiled but by a constant humiliation administered by this new Judge.

Most adults have been slow to grasp how perfectionist the changed Interior Judge of their children is, and how savage. The Judge is more perfectionist than ever, but now there is not enough fame or popularity in the world to satisfy it. For parents to try to encourage the development of their children is natural, but now there is something desperate in it for both parents and children. If a teenager is not invited to the dance, she may try suicide. A high school boy, scoffed at, may retreat behind his computer for ten years.

That is how the picture looks among the advantaged. In the other half of society we see the absolute despair of young black men, who don't need an Interior Judge to tell them they have no chance of finding a good-paying job, or any job. They have the longing and the wanting and no legal possibility of satisfying it. As we all know, one out of three young black men are in the criminal justice system in some form. Their despair is beginning to resonate through the entire culture; that is why suburban children want rap music.

In the past, an authoritarian Judge demanded obedience to parents, insisted on sexual "purity," and, one could say, advocated high morals. The Interior Judge no longer uses Jesus or Gandhi to keep its bearings, but must shift instead to Barbra Streisand or Michael Jackson or a television anchor. For the one who fails to become successful and well loved, punishment is swift and thorough. Self-esteem receives a battering from inside, everyone feels insignificant and unseen, until, in desperation, we finally agree to go on a talk show and tell it all. Once that moment is over, and universal love has not poured over our heads following the program, we fall still farther. Sadly, longing for perfection in ourselves is, in the phrase of one observer, "perfectly compatible with indifference toward others."

Why has the Interior Judge become so brutal and terroristic? We can say that advertising from a child's earliest years has so influenced the greedy, desirous part of the child's soul that the resisting force, the Judge, has to enlarge itself in order to combat the inflamed wanting. The Interior Judge, moreover, can no longer rely on outward authority in its battle against impulse. Having to resist without help from the parents or teachers, it has to do it all alone, and so it naturally moves toward a primitive, humorless savagery, well expressed in grunge rock, action movies, and piercing of body parts.

The idea that our Interior Judge has changed its demands from requiring us to be good to requiring us to be famous is very sobering.

If the superego, detached from verticality and stretched out across the horizontal plane, truly has changed, it means that consumer capitalism's dependence on stimulating greed and desirousness has changed something fundamental inside the human being, a result that Freud never anticipated.

IN A SIBLING SOCIETY, IT IS HARD TO KNOW HOW TO APPROACH one's children, what values to try to teach them, what to stand up for, what to go along with; it is especially hard to know where your children are.

THE SIBLING SOCIETY

Part One

JACK, THE BEANSTALK, AND THE HALF-ADULT

CHAPTER ONE

The Woodstock Moment

MICHAEL VENTURA HAS SAID THAT AT SOME MOMENT IN 1956, when Elvis Presley let his pelvis move to the music on the Tommy and Jimmy Dorsey show, all the parents in the United States lost their children in a single night.

The first Woodstock thirteen years later signaled a change in American culture. Some unjust severity had been overcome or by-passed. Fundamentalist harshness, Marxist rigidity, the stiff ethic of high school superintendents, had passed away. People greeted each other, clothed or naked, in delight, feeling that a victory of human-ness had taken place.

With the help of rock music, young men and women felt freed from a parental or institutional tyrant, the one with a thin nose, a black coat, and steel-rimmed glasses, the one who had told them in grade school to sit down, to behave, to repress sexual impulses, to hold their bodies stiffly, to salute the flag and stand up when a teacher enters the room. The popular heroes of the late 1950s, James Dean, Elvis Presley, Marilyn Monroe, and Jack Kerouac, all took part in that struggle to loosen everyone up, and were loved for it by the older brothers and sisters of the Woodstock young. At Wood-stock, the high school students won. What had they won? A battle against what Jules Henry in 1962 called "the Indo-European, Islamic,

3

Hebraic impulse-control system." That's a mouthful, but it says it well.

All of us who lived in the 1950s saw so many lives destroyed by repression, by fear, by internalized superintendents, by shaming, by workaholism. By 1969, it felt as if human beings were able for the first time in history to choose their own roads, choose what to do with their own bodies, choose the visionary possibilities formerly shut off by that "control system."

Elvis was a part of what women had longed for, not militaristic, not rigid in feeling, not exclusionary toward mothers and young women, but lighthearted, open to impulses rising from below his belt, playful, and yet grounded in sexuality, heavier than Peter Pan, more human than the stiff-faced old grandfather who wound clocks. Young women felt themselves losing some of their Doris Day rigidity, their shame over their own sexual impulses. Why shouldn't a young woman make love with a man she found attractive, any man? Why shouldn't she encourage pornography to help loosen up the males? Why shouldn't she give up her mother's stuff about waiting until the ring is on the hand before having fun with zippers?

Schools had taught for centuries "the Indo-European, Islamic, Hebraic impulse-control system." The impulse-control system smelled of limitation; schools stank of it. The Indo-European, Islamic, Hebraic impulse-control system reeked of the bald, the severe, the cabined, the icebound, the squat, the cramped, the dinky, the narrow, the scanty, the roped-in, the meager, the bad, the tame. Woodstock, on the other hand, smelled of the grandiose, the footloose, the grandiloquent, the lofty, the radical, the bountiful, the prodigal, the free-spirited, the free-speaking, the free-tongued, the unconditional, the escaped, the unbuttoned, the cut loose, the exonerated, the unreined, the good, the princely, the escaped.

In 1962 Jules Henry interviewed a number of high school students for his book *Culture Against Man*. Repeatedly he heard them say that they liked whichever parent let them do what they wanted. "What the children talk about most is whether the parent 'lets me' or

'doesn't let me.' What permits impulse release is 'good' and anything that blocks it is 'bad.' "

What is cause and what is effect is hard to know, but some
fathers—and some mothers—gave up their strictness in the late
1950s and early 1960s. One could say that teachers and parents and
certainly the popular media gave up defending "the Indo-European,
Islamic, Hebraic impulse-control system" which subscribed to a
certain asceticism for the young, postponement of pleasure, hard
work, no fooling around.

When the Englishman Geoffrey Gorer visited the United States,
he noticed the extraordinary desire of American grown-ups to be
loved. They didn't seem to feel it necessary to love in return; rather,
to be the object of love was all that was required. How could one be
more clearly worthy of love than to agree to whatever your children
want?

The movie *Mrs. Doubtfire* provides a clear example of this. As it
begins, the father, played by Robin Williams, is already so far advanced along the permissive route that his "let's all be funny" party
actually precipitates divorce; the reluctant wife is then left to stand
alone for superego values. (The scriptwriters make her a lawyer.)

Why would fathers, in particular, suddenly want love so much
from their children? Jules Henry guessed that the American workplace had become more cold and barren than it was in the nineteenth century. A man received little fellow-feeling there, and
needed more of it at home. Those years saw the "unmasking of a
masculine hunger for emotional gratification." "Deprived in his
work life of personality aspirations, the American father reaches
deeply into the emotional resources of his family for gratifications
formerly considered womanly—the tenderness and closeness of his
children; and his children reach thirstily toward him." Perhaps the
fathers didn't feel enough loving support from the "village" (now
transmuted into the suburb), or perhaps they missed love from their
grandparents, or had become conscious of how little love their
remote fathers gave them. For whatever reason, many fathers in the

late 1950s gave up their traditional setting of limits, and in return asked for new sorts of love from their children—at a price. The children soon saw they had been put into power. As divorce became more common, and custody remained with the mothers, the children's power increased. The father began being permissive when the children visited on weekends, formerly a time when children would be required to take on tasks as members of a family. But if the father isn't in the house, obviously he can't require the children to do homework, or any of the tasks they find onerous.

By 1980 most high schools were being run by their own students, and that has not changed. Schoolteachers all over the country will testify to that. If teachers ask for more homework, the students refuse, and the school board—mostly parents—usually sides with the students. Contemporary schoolteachers tell hundreds of such stories. One story that a teacher of advanced algebra told will stand for many. This teacher realized that one of his students had stopped attending class. He called the parents: "I thought you ought to know that your son has dropped out of Advanced Algebra." He had made many such calls over the years, and expected to hear, as he would have in the past, "What did you say? He hasn't said a word about that to me. I'll talk to him. If he began the class, he'll have to finish it."

But now the reply is different. In nine out of ten calls, the parent—father or mother—says, without anger or urgency, something like "We've brought him [or her] up to make up his own mind and make his own decisions. So I think we have to respect that."

That's the end of the algebra class. If a student acts up, and the "behavioral problem" is brought to the attention of the parent or parents, they usually want the student to be turned over to the school psychologist. The psychologist will have to do the tough work of listening, establishing requirements, and so on.

All over the country, the old structures of the impulse-control system have loosened: the superego took its hands away from the throats of young people, or so it seemed, and the whole nation relaxed, felt less depression, endured less repression. The Beatles said something, happily, about living in a yellow submarine.

Yet something went wrong. How did we move from the optimistic, companionable, food-passing youngsters gathered on that field at Woodstock to the self-doubting, dark-hearted, turned-in, death-praising, indifferent, wised-up, deconstructionist audience that now attends a grunge music concert? That is the question we need to answer.

CHAPTER TWO

Jack, the Beanstalk, and the Giant with a Large Appetite

In the days of King Alfred, there lived a poor woman, whose cottage was situated in a remote country village, a great many miles from London.

She had been a widow some years, and had an only child, named Jack, whom she indulged to a fault; the consequence of her blind partiality was, that Jack did not pay the least attention to any thing she said, but was indolent, careless, and extravagant. His follies were not owing to a bad disposition, but that his mother had never checked him. By degrees, she disposed of all she possessed—scarcely any thing remained but a cow.

The poor woman one day met Jack with tears in her eyes; her distress was great, and, for the first time in her life, she could not help reproaching him, saying, "Indeed, dear son, you have at last brought me to beggary and ruin; I have not money enough to purchase food for another day—nothing remains for me but to sell

We'll use here texts from the first full version of "Jack and the Beanstalk," as it was published in London in 1807. Iona and Peter Opie chose this version to include in their book *The Classic Fairy Tales*.

my cow. I am very sorry to part with her; it grieves me sadly, but we must not starve."

For five minutes Jack felt a degree of remorse, but it was soon over, and he importuned his mother to let him sell the cow at the next village. As he was going along, he met a butcher, who enquired why he was driving the cow from home? Jack replied, it was his intention to sell it. The butcher held some curious beans in his hat; they were of various colors, and attracted Jack's notice: this did not pass unnoticed by the butcher, who, knowing Jack's easy temper, thought now was the time to take advantage of it, and determined not to let slip so good an opportunity, asked what was the price of the cow, offering at the same time all the beans in his hat for her. The silly boy could not express his pleasure at what he supposed so great an offer: the bargain was struck instantly, and the cow exchanged for a few paltry beans. Jack made the best of his way home, calling aloud to his mother before he reached the house, thinking to surprise her.

When she saw the beans, and heard Jack's account, her patience quite forsook her, she kicked the beans away in a passion—they flew in all directions, some were scattered into the garden. The poor woman reflected on her great loss, and was quite in despair. Not having any thing to eat, they both went supperless to bed.

Jack awoke very early in the morning, and, seeing something uncommon from the window of his bedchamber, ran downstairs into the garden, where he soon discovered that some of the beans had taken root, and sprung up surprisingly: the stalks were of an immense thickness, and had so entwined, that they formed a ladder nearly like a chain in appearance.

Looking upwards, he could not discern the top, it appeared to be lost in the clouds: he tried it, found it firm, and not to be shaken. He quickly formed the resolution of endeavoring to climb up to the top, in order to seek his fortune, and ran to communicate his intention to his mother, not doubting but she would be equally pleased with himself. She declared he should not go; said he would break her heart, entreated, and threatened, but all in vain. Jack set out, and, after climbing for some hours, reached the top of the bean-stalk, fatigued and quite exhausted. Looking around, he found himself in a strange country: it appeared to be a desert, quite barren: not a tree, shrub, house, or living creature to be seen; here and there were scattered fragments of unhewn stone, and, at unequal distances, small heaps of earth were loosely thrown together. Jack seated himself pensively upon a block of stone, thought of his mother, and reflected with sorrow on his disobedience in climbing the bean-stalk against her inclination: he concluded that he must now die with hunger.

THIS TALE SOUNDS LIKE THE STORY OF A CONTEMPORARY mother with her teenage son who is "indolent, careless, and extravagant," with no fatherly limitation on him. But it also has a third element: the overwhelming energy of the Giant, whose headlong greed eventually dominates the lives of both mother and son.

Something in this pattern of energies—a parent, a child, and a third presence in the house that seems barbarous—is familiar.

The physical landscape of the Giant's territory suggests regression to a barbarous state, a time before sculpture or cities:

. . . it appeared to be a desert, quite barren: not a tree, shrub, house, or living creature to be seen; here and there were scattered fragments of unhewn stone, and, at unequal distances, small heaps of earth were loosely thrown together.

It's clear that we are now in "the other world," the place where all time is present time, where all historical periods exist together, and certain actions take place over and over.

The Giant, whom the boy is about to meet, will be a serious enemy. Sociologists, who ordinarily inhabit only the physical world, will probably bail out of the story at this point. Marxists will insist that the Giant is the patriarchy, or perhaps he represents all landlords. I enjoy saying that, too, but it isn't quite appropriate here. We need to catch a glimpse of something the Marxists, for all their attentiveness, do not see. From the point of view of contemporary culture, we can speculate about why we have moved, in only thirty years, from the gladness of the "free" Woodstock to the terrorized schools full of guns.

"Jack and the Beanstalk" is one of those prophetic stories that appear, God knows from where, perhaps from residual memory of cultures in the past that have also suffered a falling back like ours.

In the 1807 version of "Jack and the Beanstalk," which we are quoting here, and which is probably closer to the oral original than the more elementary versions published later, we find an amazing conversation that has been left out of almost all later versions. It is a conversation between Jack and an old woman. "Crone" is the mythological name for the old woman who has knowledge, in whose body the blood that once escaped as monthly flow has turned now into shrewdness, culture, wisdom, second sight. The Crone is familiar with death and doesn't mind these "heaps of earth."

> However he walked on, hoping to see a house where he might beg something to eat and drink: presently an infirm looking woman appeared at a distance; as she approached, he saw that she was old, her skin much wrinkled, and her tattered garments proved poverty. She accosted Jack, inquiring how he came there; he related the circumstance of the bean-stalk. She then asked if he recollected his father? he replied he did not; and added, that there must be some mystery relating to him, for he had frequently asked his mother who his father was, but that she always burst into tears, and appeared violently agitated, nor did she recover herself for some days after; one thing, however, he could not avoid observing upon those occasions, which was, that she always carefully avoided answering him, and even seemed afraid of speaking, as if there were some secret connected with his father's history which she must not disclose.
>
> The old woman replied, "I will reveal the whole story, your mother must not; but, before I begin, I require a solemn promise on your part

to do what I command: I am a fairy, and if you do not perform exactly what I desire, your mother and yourself shall both be destroyed." Jack was frightened at the old woman's menaces, and promises to fulfil her injunctions exactly, and the fairy thus addressed him:—"Your father was a rich man, his disposition remarkably benevolent; he was very good to the poor, and constantly relieving them. . . . Such a man was soon known and talked of. A Giant lived a great many miles off . . . he was in his heart envious, covetous, and cruel; but he had the art of concealing those vices."

The old woman then tells Jack how the Giant managed by lies to inveigle himself in the father's house; in fact, the Giant and his wife received a place to live.

One day a shipwreck off the coast drew all the servants out of the house to care for the survivors. The Giant chose that moment to act, and appeared in the library.

"The Giant then joined your father in the study, and appeared to be delighted—he really was so. Your father recommended a favorite book, and was handing it down: the Giant took the opportunity and stabbed him, he instantly fell dead; the Giant left the body, found the porter and nurse, and presently dispatched them. You were then only three months old; your mother had you in her arms in a remote part of the house, and was ignorant of what was going on. . . ."

She says that the Giant spared the boy's life, and the mother's, but made her swear to answer no questions on the matter, insisting on silence on this and other events. The mother and son escaped.

"Having gained your father's confidence, he knew where to find all his treasure: he soon loaded himself and his wife, set the house on fire in several places, and when the servants returned the house was burnt down to the ground."

The old woman explains to Jack that this is how Jack and his mother ended up living in a poor cottage. The old woman also mentions that it was she who secretly prompted Jack to take the beans in exchange for the cow, and she helped the beanstalk to grow high.

She closes her conversation with Jack by saying:

"I need not add, that I inspired you with a strong desire to ascend the ladder."

UNKNOWN TO JACK AT THE START, THERE HAS ALWAYS BEEN SOME large and cruel being in his story, behind the scenes, although very much involved in everything that has happened.

We can say that during the Woodstock period, a large and cruel being lurked just out of sight, and those listening to Crosby, Stills, and Nash did not see him. Perhaps the obvious brutality of the Vietnam War occupied all our attention. We saw brutality every day on television, and it distracted us from the invisible being nearby. The savage acts taking place overseas with their napalm and Christmas bombings were so engrossing that people's attention to dark things nearby faded; little energy was left to see beings close to us who were part shadow and part god. We recall how the invisible beings in *The Iliad* are both seen and unseen: they float down from mountain peaks and secretly aid either the Trojans or the Acheans.

Goya's canvas *The Giant* offers an image of a "god" such as this. The bottom of the canvas shows refugees, huddled in caravans like displaced or fleeing gypsies; there's a sense of suffering, hastily cooked meals, chaos, and poverty. Rising high above these preoccupied miniature people is an enormous being, two or three hundred feet tall, a giant that none of the human beings seems to notice. The painting hints at the human inability to see it even when it is close.

Who was this one who was just out of sight at Woodstock, and who later appeared at Altamont and Oklahoma City?

The Crone knows the whole story. She remembers that the Giant stabbed the benevolent parent inside his own study. We can say that the father was the Giant's first obstacle to his reclaiming of territory.

The library is important because books bring information about the Giant, so he likes to burn those down. When the father was dead, he set the house on fire.

Having gained your father's confidence, he knew where to find all his treasure: he soon loaded himself and his wife, set the house on fire in several places, and when the servants returned the house was burnt down to the ground.

The presence of the Giant in the house—in our psychic house—is connected with some other house being burned to the ground.

A FTER THE CONVERSATION WITH THE CRONE, JACK WALKS ON.

He walked until after sunset, and soon, to his great joy, espied a large mansion. A plain looking woman was standing at the door, he accosted her, begging she would give him a morsel of bread and a night's lodging. She expressed great surprise on seeing him, said it was quite uncommon to see a human being near their house, for it was well known that her husband was a large and powerful Giant, and that he would never eat anything but human flesh, if he could possibly get it; that he did not think anything of walking fifty miles to procure it, usually being out all day for that purpose.

This account terrified Jack, but still he hoped to elude the Giant, and therefore again he entreated the woman to take him in for one night only, and hide him in the oven. The good woman at last suffered herself to be persuaded, for she was of a compassionate disposition. She gave him plenty to eat and drink, and took him into the house. First they entered a large hall, magnificently furnished; they then passed through several spacious rooms, all in the same style of grandeur, though they appeared to be forsaken and desolate.

A long gallery was next; it was very dark, just light enough to shew that instead of a wall on one side, there was a grating of iron which parted off a dismal dungeon, from whence issued the groans of those poor victims whom the Giant reserved in confinement for his own voracious appetite. Poor Jack was half dead with fear, and would have given the world to be with his mother again, but that he feared could never be; for he gave himself up for lost, and now mistrusted the good woman. At the farther end of the gallery there was a winding staircase, which led them into a spacious kitchen; a very good fire was burning in the grate, and Jack, not seeing any thing to make him uncomfortable, soon forgot his fears, and was just beginning to enjoy himself, when he was aroused by a loud knocking at the street-door; the Giant's wife ran to secure him in the oven, and then made what haste she could to let her husband in, and Jack heard him accost her in a voice like thunder, saying "Wife, I smell fresh meat." "Oh! my dear," she replied, "it is nothing but the people in the dungeon." The Giant appeared to believe her, and walked down stairs into the very kitchen, where poor Jack was, who shook, trembled, and was more terrified than he had yet been.

At last the monster seated himself quietly by the fire-side, whilst his wife prepared supper. By degrees Jack recovered himself sufficiently to look at the Giant through a crevice; he was astonished to see how much he devoured, and thought he never would have done eating and drinking.

That's the way the African people, and to some extent people the world over, think of the United States. We don't have to assume that the Giant *is* the United States; and yet whatever meaning we get from this story will depend on how we understand the Giant.

Giants and witches populate many stories. Some giants are stupid but charming; those types, easily bamboozled because they are so tall, so far from the ground, can easily be deceived and manipulated by Tom Thumbs. In the Grimm Brothers story "The Raven," we meet three giant brothers who are important for the traveler because they have maps somewhere in their house that show how to get to the Golden Castle of Stromberg. The Giants haven't been asked about the maps for a long time. There's something archaic about all giants, prehistoric, earlier than cities, perhaps even earlier than laid walls, a detail our story hints at with the mention of unhewn stones.

The Giant who deals with Jack is not one of the charming ones; he eats people.

Our story takes place on two separate planes: the human plane on which Jack and his mother live in their cabin surrounded by some sort of village; and another, more ominous plane, at the top of the beanstalk, where a Giant and his wife live surrounded by stones and barren fields. There's some suggestion that this Giant lives in the brain, "on top of the beanstalk," since the head balances itself on the spinal cord—but it's only a suggestion.

The first rule for interpreting fairy stories—the same rule used in interpreting dreams—is that everyone in the story belongs inside one psyche. If, in a dream, the dreamer's car hits a large stone on a rainy road, we can say that the car represents the dreamer; but the stone also represents the dreamer, and the road somehow represents the dreamer as well. If we do that with our story, the beanstalk is inside us, the mother and son are inside us, and the two planes are inside us.

First Interruption: What Is the Giant?

A long-standing philosophical habit in the West is to take the Enlightenment view of human nature, which says that human beings are good and they only occasionally fall into evil behavior. That's the optimistic view. Some even in the West take the more somber view that emphasizes the aggressive animal base, the dark, instinctive substructure, which is older than our ego, that dark ground that is implacably reborn with every child. According to that view, our human houses are built over a rough, selfish, presocial animal ground. The substructure is powerful because it does not change. Any thought that two thousand years of Christianity and five hundred years of the Enlightenment had softened its crude and brutal nature had to be abandoned when the first photographs of the camps at Sachsenhausen and Auschwitz appeared. The photographs were a huge shock for Europeans, hardly bearable. Some

Americans perhaps did not feel it as deeply, because we ended World War II proud of the skill and discipline that helped win it. We seemed to ourselves to be a part of the Enlightenment; but the Europeans and, in a way, the entire world saw in the war the utter defeat of the Enlightenment.

George Steiner, born in Geneva, said:

My own consciousness is possessed by the eruption of barbarism in modern Europe. . . . This is the crisis of rational humane expectation which has shaped my own life. . . . It did not spring up on the Gobi Desert. . . . It rose from within, and from the core of European civilization. The cry of the murdered sounded in earshot of the university; the sadism went on a street away from the theaters and museums.

European civilization had not eradicated the understructure that the camps represented. The archaic brutality resembled a rough, thoughtless animal-being shrugging a small culture bird off its shoulder.

We can take the Giant to stand for our archaic, brutal underpinning. On our human plane, we live among sunlit windows with red geraniums on them; we live surrounded by cows and milk and kindness, by conversation and codes of politeness, by loving parents and cared-for children.

But on the second and older plane, which is firmly ensconced at the top of the beanstalk, at the base of the skull, there are stones that have never been shaped, piles of dirt loosely thrown together, and, most of all, appetites on a scale that is not human; there are immense hungers, and gigantic angers, and cages where people are kept to be eaten a little later. Children are especially favored as food there. And if a human being should wander into that instinctive plane, he or she had better be ready to hide.

That is what Anne Frank did; that is what we all do. Despite the controls that the church fathers laboriously laid out in their various councils to intensify the codes, and despite the various ideas of order that we make up in solitary rooms, we had better know, once we reach the top of the beanstalk, where the Giant's cookie jar is, and we had better climb in. Then, from inside the cookie jar, we can sing a little: "Irene, goodnight."

Our task in this chapter is to elaborate the picture of the Giant so we can see what we are facing in everyday life, and then to ask why facing that power is more difficult if the child is fatherless or motherless.

Brain researchers have established that each of us has a "tripartite brain"; each brain is really three brains. Like old Roman buildings whose foundations remain, even though covered by later cities, the earliest brains were not absorbed as we evolved, but added onto. The most primitive brain lies at the base of the skull and is a part of the brain stem: "This is the phylogenetically oldest part of the brain, its core or chassis, roughly corresponding to the basic structures of the reptile's brain." This brain, in human times, has become specialized for alarm, for response to fear, and for survival of the organism. Paul MacLean has said that the persistent trait of paranoia in us is probably caused by our inability to shut off the energy source to the reptile brain. MacLean, whose research is fundamental for this field, calls it the archicortex, or the reptile brain, and says of it that "when the psychiatrist bids the patient to lie on the couch, he is asking him to stretch out alongside . . . a crocodile." The crocodile, if asked to express its troubles in words, cannot do so, and the "inability is beyond the help of language training." When this brain is stimulated, it sets off alarms and prepares to face danger.

The second oldest brain is called the mesocortex. Mac-Lean calls it the old mammalian brain, and says that "the reptilian brain and the greater part of the old mammalian brain are folded like two concentric rings." The two infolded rings together form a large convolution, the so-called limbic lobe of the cerebellum. *Limbic* means "hemming in," and the term was coined in 1878 by the great brain mapper Paul Broca. The limbic system, then, is made up of the two older brains—the reptilian and the primitive mammalian. The paleomammalian brain is an inheritance from the lower mammals. It can be compared to a rhinoceros or a horse.

Investigations of the last twenty years have shown that the lower mammalian brain plays a fundamental role in emotional behavior. . . . It has a greater capacity than the reptilian brain for learning new approaches and solutions to problems on the basis of immediate experience. But like the reptilian brain, it does not have the ability . . . to put its feelings into words.

The primary distinction between reptile species and mammal species is the warm blood of the latter. The old mammal brain has some qualities we associate with warm blood: passion, intensity, jealousy, wildness, erotic obsession, greediness, ferocity, loyalty over years, anger, and artistic madness.

In this discussion we will call the oldest brain the survival brain, with its Alarm System, and we will call the old mammal brain the Feeding, Sexuality, and Ferocity System. We make excuses for the old mammalian brain, and French courts provided lesser penalties at one time for "crimes of passion." We know that a divorce court evokes both early brains: the lawyers, one could say, awaken the Alarm System, and the anger of the couple awakens the Feeding, Sexuality, and Ferocity System. Colin Turnbull, in his *People of the Mountain,* describes what happened to the formerly alert and generous Ik tribe when the English took away their tribal lands and moved them to a new and barren territory. The Feeding, Sexuality, and Ferocity System, uniting with the survival brain, overwhelmed all their codes of unselfishness, even their altruism toward children. The Iks grabbed food away from their own children, left grandparents to starve after stealing their food, dropped their dung on the doorsteps of neighbors, and so on. Turnbull was shocked to see how frail the "civilized tendencies" are; like Margaret Mead, he saw how easily intricately learned behaviors, essential to a "human" life, could be lost.

We know that either the Alarm System or the Feeding, Sexuality, and Ferocity System can easily overwhelm a child. What equipment does the child have to resist? When an infant's hunger instinct is frustrated, we can see the infant call into play the Ferocity System without a moment's hesitation. If the infant could accomplish what it wants at these moments, the mother and father would be burned to cinders, shit would be heaped on their bodies, the chair would evaporate, and much ferocity would still be available. The Feeding, Sexuality, and Ferocity System can overtake an adult as well. *The Tain* has several descriptions of what happened to the Celtic warrior Cuchulain when he went into his warrior mode. One summation reads:

> *His calves and feet turn in reverse position; one eye bulges out and one recedes into his skull. His hair becomes a tangle, and a jet of blood erupts straight up from his head and causes the atmosphere to fill with a red mist. In this condition he's difficult to defeat, but the same energy or rage that rises to defend the borders against his enemies can blindly turn against his own home and people.*

In LATE MAMMAL TIMES, THE BODY EVIDENTLY ADDED A THIRD brain. The development of the third brain, known as the neocortex, or new mammalian brain, may be connected to the invention of tools, or it may be a response to changed climatic conditions, or descent from trees. It takes the form of an outer eighth-inch of brain tissue laid over the surface of the old mammal brain. Its brain tissue is immensely elaborate and has millions of neurons per square inch. Observers speculate that it is capable through its circuitry of solving problems of immense complication. Some neurologists speculate that an intelligent person uses one-hundredth of its power; Einstein may have used one-fiftieth of its power. If the reptile brain is associated with cold, and the mammal brain with warmth, the third brain is associated with light. The parables of Christ and the advices of Buddha may involve instruction on how to transfer energy from the reptile brain to the mammal brain, and from the mammal brain to the new brain. The gold light around Buddha's head or a medieval saint's head may be an attempt to suggest the enormous light-giving power of the new brain.

When we enter the therapist's office, we enter with a crocodile and a rhinoceros. We prefer not to look behind us. Knowledge of these two old brains helps us to understand the sort of plane on which the Giant lives at the top of the beanstalk. We notice how fearful he is of any intrusion, and how enormous his appetite is.

> *By degrees, Jack recovered himself sufficiently to look at the Giant through a crevice; he was astonished to see how much he devoured, and thought he never would have done eating and drinking.*

THE SOURCE OF OUR GREEDINESS AND FEROCITY IS KNOWN IN other traditions as the *nafs*. In the Muslim and Sufi tradition, the word *nafs* simply means "soul." There are four levels of the *nafs*: the lower *nafs*, which is the "bitter soul"; then the blaming *nafs*, which blames itself and others; then the inspired *nafs*, which begins to hear; and finally the *nafs-at-rest*. One hears the *nafs-at-rest* in much classical Persian music. The lower *nafs*, the greedy one, is called the "al-nafs al-amara," or the bitter soul.

The term *nafs*, as understood today, refers primarily to the greedy soul. Another phrase used for it is the Commanding Soul, which implies that it is dictatorial and tyrannical. Dr. Javad Nurbakhsh of Iran, the head of the Nimatullahi Order of Sufis, says that the *nafs* basically commands its owner to do wrong.

> *The commanding nafs is that which has not passed through the crucible of aesthetic discipline, or shed the tough hide of existence. It actively resists all of God's creation. This nafs is of a bestial character that harasses other created beings and consistently sings its own praises. It always follows its own desires and grazes on the field of material nature; it drinks from the spring of the passions and knows only how to sleep, eat, and gratify itself.*

We can see how closely some of this description corresponds to ideas that Western scientists have worked out around the reptile brain and the old mammal brain. To say of the *nafs* that it "drinks from the spring of the passions" is precisely the way one would speak of the mammal brain. "It always follows its own desires" is right for the Feeding, Sexuality, and Ferocity System. It "knows only how to sleep, eat, and gratify itself." The reference to its "bestial" character refers to the Sufi belief that what we have inherited from the centuries in which we were animals are the claws and the teeth.

But the Sufi visualization adds several new and valuable elements: "It constantly sings its own praises." The *nafs* wants to be praised and respected as something more civilized than it really is. Movies and television series that come straight out of the *nafs*, such as *Forrest Gump* and *Twin Peaks,* present themselves as worthy of awards; and their writers insist their work is somehow an addition to high art.

The Sufis say that the *nafs* is utterly opposed to the spiritual intellect. Its main task is to move people toward selfishness and greed. Moreover, "the *nafs* itself claims to be God."

Claiming that it is God, the *nafs* expresses no fear of God. If we assume that the *nafs* is acting among us in the West, the assumption throws some light on the Western insistence that one can snap one's fingers at God, an attitude so astonishingly distinct from the attitudes of earlier generations.

The nafs *may, for example, command one to be a worshiper, and ascetic, a servant or a Sufi, solely for the purpose of being accepted by people, of being respected and praised by others.*

A certain Sufi master was devout in his behavior at prayers each day for years, always praying in the first row. One day, however, he arrived at the mosque late and had to pray from the back. He noticed that his *nafs* was irritated; soon the irritation penetrated his whole body. He realized it was the *nafs* who loved to pray in front, so it could feel the praise. After that he prayed "in secret."

One of the latent vices and secret maladies of the nafs *is its love of praise. Whoever imbibes a draught of it will move the seven heavens and the seven sublime realms for the very flutter of an eyelash. The symptom of this affliction is that when the* nafs *is deprived of praise, it falls into violence and laxity.*

Dr. Nurbakhsh lists several other qualities of the *nafs*. It is ignorant; it is quickly weary of all things; it is alive to the passions; it is arrogant and egocentric.

It considers important the least thing it has done for anyone, remembering it for years afterwards, being overwhelmed by its own kindness. Yet however great the favors others do for it, it places no importance on them, forgetting them quickly.

The brilliance of this visualization is that it adds to the scientific visualization a kind of personality.

"The very constitution of the *nafs* is founded on breach of etiquette." There's something funny about imagining a force whose very essence lies in breaking etiquette. The idea, however, makes us rethink the darker side of the American "freedom of manners," of which we were once so proud, but which is now shifting into gross rudeness between children and parents, between students and teachers, and even between people on the street, or people on the Internet.

The *nafs* is associated with the element of fire: "It is like a firebrand both in its display of beauty and in its hidden potential for destruction; though its color is attractive, it burns."

Christianity puts some of its knowledge of the *nafs* onto Satan, into whom we place the hatred of God. That attribution is valuable, and yet we could say it projects the energy far out in the universe, wherever Satan is. The Sufis maintain that the *nafs* is inside everyone, available at every second, as near to us as our fingernails.

Finally, the Sufis say that the *nafs* in a person may lie for years as inactive as a snake or dragon frozen on a mountain. The Persian poet Rumi wrote a poem about this possibility:

Listen to this, and hear the mystery inside:
A snake-catcher went into the mountains to find a snake.

He wanted a friendly pet, and one that would amaze
audiences, but he was looking for a reptile, something
that has no knowledge of friendship.
                                           It was winter.
In the deep snow he saw a frighteningly huge dead snake.
He was afraid to touch it, but he did.
In fact, he dragged the thing into Baghdad,
hoping people would pay to see it.
                                     This is how foolish
we've become! A human being is a mountain range!
Snakes are fascinated by us! *Yet we sell ourselves*
to look at a dead snake.
                          We are like beautiful satin
used to patch burlap. "Come see the dragon I killed,
and hear the adventures!" That's what he announced,
and a large crowd came,
                          but the dragon was not dead,
just dormant! He set up his show at a crossroads.
The ring of gawking rubes got thicker, everybody
on tiptoe, men and women, noble and peasant, all
packed together unconscious of their differences.
It was like the Resurrection!

He began to unwind the thick ropes and remove
the cloth coverings he'd wrapped it so well in.
Some little movement.
                        The hot Iraqi sun had woken
the terrible life. The people nearest started screaming.
Panic! The dragon tore easily and hungrily
loose, killing many instantly.
                                 The snake-catcher stood there,
frozen. "What have I brought out of the mountains?" The snake
braced against a post and crushed the man and consumed him.

The snake is your animal-soul. When you bring it
into the hot air of your wanting-energy, warmed
by that and by the prospect of power and wealth,
it does massive damage.
                    Leave it in the snow mountains.
Don't expect to oppose it with quietness
and sweetness and wishing.
                    The nafs *don't respond to those,*
and they can't be killed. It takes Moses to deal
with such a beast, to lead it back, and make it lie down
in the snow. But there was no Moses then.
Hundreds of thousands died.

(translated by Coleman Barks)

What name shall we choose for the *nafs* in English? Coleman Barks translates it as the "animal" soul. We might call it the "Insatiable Soul," or the "Giant Who Is Never Satisfied," or the "Dragon That Is Now Thawing Out."

THE GIANT IN "JACK AND THE BEANSTALK" RESEMBLES THE *NAFS* in his huge appetite, in the way he seems to control completely the plane on which he lives, and, most of all, in his vast power, suggested by the castle, the imprisoned human beings, the wealth, and his physical size. Jack's power is so small compared with the Giant's that confrontation is out of the question; the boy finds a small place and hides there. The Sufis say that approximately 97 percent of human beings in any nation are controlled by the *nafs;* every breath they take comes out of the *nafs,* all their acquiring and spending amounts to worship of the *nafs,* and their reason, or rational element, overwhelmed by the *nafs,* is reduced to making up excuses for people's improper and embarrassing behavior. A few of the people in any nation, perhaps 2 percent, are, while possessed by the *nafs,* also aware of it; some of them try to appeal to the *nafs* of the other 97 percent. These people—politicians—can get the masses to do what they want them to do. An example would be Reagan's suggestion to "vote for me and we'll get the government off our backs." That the *nafs* hates government would be a surprise to no one.

Rumi wrote:

The animal soul has given birth to all the fetishes.
A fetish made of wood is a little like a garter snake,
But a fetish made of energy is closer to a dragon.

To snap a wooden idol in two is extremely easy;
But to break a dragon is a task beyond our power.

My friend, if you're interested in the character of the insatiable soul,
Read an account of the seven gates of Hell.

Cunning evasions flow out of the insatiable soul
During every breath we take, and in that frail stream
A hundred Pharaohs and all their armies could drown.

Our effort here is to put clearly the odds that our "I" or neocortex faces when it tries to wrest governorship of the human organism away from the Alarm System and the Feeding, Sexuality, and Ferocity System well rooted in our archaic brains. It's like aware voters trying to wrest control of the country from the sleeping voters whom the *nafs* inspires. The chance of that happening becomes smaller all the time. Those awake are what Hebrew culture has always called the remnant. There are perhaps thirty-eight of them alive at any one time, none of them visible. They are probably people like Thomas Merton, sitting in a tiny cell somewhere writing about the connections between Buddhism and Christianity.

To these visions—the Western vision of the archaic brain and the Sufi vision of the *nafs*—we must add Freud's vision of the *id*. Freud imagined an *id*, or more accurately an *it* (for in German the term is "Das Es"), which is a vast underlying *unconscious*, with immense powers of forgetting and chaos, which sets itself against the frail "I" and the insecure "super-I" or superego for control of the organism. The *it* or *id* usually wins. According to MacLean,

Considered in the light of Freudian psychology, the old brain would have many of the attributes of the unconscious id. *One might argue, however,* that the visceral brain is not at all unconscious (possibly not even in certain stages of sleep), but rather eludes the grasp of the intellect because its animalistic and primitive structure makes it impossible to communicate in verbal terms. *Perhaps it were more proper to say, therefore, it was an animalistic and illiterate brain.*

All three visions work together very well. The Sufis say that control of the *nafs* requires tremendous discipline and cunning. Freud is pessimistic about any long-term victory of the ego. The absence of an executive function to settle disputes among the archaic reptile brain, the old mammal brain, and the more recent neocortex sets the stage for a never-ending struggle among all three. The result is a chaotic confusion on the battlefield as the three brains fight every second for control of consciousness.

We notice that the Alarm System has become highly mobilized in the sibling society. The growth of the militias and the National Rifle Association testifies to that. As one feels danger from the persistent violence, one sinks farther and farther back into the fantasies of the reptile brain. Then we can say that consumer advertising, particularly on television, overstimulates the *nafs* or the old mammal brain. The Feeding, Sexuality, and Ferocity System is ready to push aside all disciplines, all higher concerns, all difficult art, and require pleasure and excitement in each moment. The recent development of television and the media's emphasis on crime and violence help explain why these two old brains are having such an enormous effect in the new sibling society. The neocortex or new mammal brain is having a hard time, both in men and in women, getting any genuine space for itself. This is a relatively new situation.

Some readers may object that too much is being read into the beanstalk tale. It is a silly story made up for children, and its back cannot bear all this weight. One could also object that if the Muslim view of the *nafs* is so brilliant, then the Muslims should be better able to control brutality than they are. But the Sufis say clearly that the *nafs* controls all societies, even their own, and the current chaos of the Muslim world is a testimony to the realism of their descriptions. As for us, if we want to dismiss Freud and MacLean's research on the three brains and the idea of the *nafs* as silly nonsense, then we must find and name that secret road that has led American society in such a brief time from a moderately disciplined, moderately respectful culture to a culture in which twelve-year-olds shoot each other, Calvin Klein uses children for sexually explicit advertisements, and we overeat, and remain in a state of materialist violence. If anyone has a better explanation, I will be glad to hear it.

ACTUALLY, WHETHER OR NOT THE GIANT IS THE *NAFS*, WHETHER or not the Giant is the Feeding, Sexuality, and Ferocity System, or whether or not the Giant is the *id* is not exactly to the point. The story offers us a way of grasping that Jack has met some sort of enemy with more power than he has. The fascinating detail is that the human being in our story who faces that large male who wants to kill him is not a Beowulf or an Odysseus—that is, one armored, initiated, and experienced—but a small human being, a boy named Jack, who is, like so many of our children, a fatherless boy. Jack represents all men and women who live in a fatherless and, increasingly, motherless society.

LET'S RETURN TO THE STORY AGAIN, AND GO BACK A BIT TO THE moment when the Giant's wife brought Jack into the house:

> At the farther end of the gallery there was a winding staircase, which led them into a spacious kitchen; a very good fire was burning in the grate, and Jack, not seeing any thing to make him uncomfort-

able, soon forgot his fears, and was just beginning to enjoy himself, when he was aroused by a loud knocking at the street-door; the Giant's wife ran to secure him in the oven, and then made what haste she could to let her husband in, and Jack heard him accost her in a voice like thunder, saying, "Wife, I smell fresh meat." "Oh! my dear," she replied, "it is nothing but the people in the dungeon." The Giant appeared to believe her, and walked down stairs into the very kitchen, where poor Jack was, who shook, trembled, and was more terrified than he had yet been.

At last, the monster seated himself quietly by the fire-side, whilst his wife prepared supper. By degrees Jack recovered himself sufficiently to look at the Giant through a crevice; he was astonished to see how much he devoured, and thought he would never have done eating and drinking. When supper was ended, the Giant desired his wife to bring him his hen. A very beautiful hen was brought, and placed upon the table before him. Jack's curiosity was very great to see what would happen; he observed that every time the Giant said "lay," the hen laid an egg of solid gold. The Giant amused himself a long time with the hen, meanwhile his wife went to bed. At length the Giant fell asleep by the fireside, and snored like the roaring of a cannon. At day-break, Jack finding the Giant not likely to be soon roused, crept softly out of his hiding-place, seized the hen, and ran off with her.

He met with some difficulty in finding his way out of the house, but at last he reached the road in safety, without fear of pursuit: he easily found the way to the bean-stalk, and descended it better and quicker than he expected. His mother was overjoyed to see him; he found her crying bitterly, and lamenting his fate, for she concluded he had come to some shocking end through his rashness.

Jack was impatient to show his hen, and inform his mother how valuable it was. "And now, mother," said Jack, "I have brought home that which will quickly make you rich without any trouble: I hope I have made you some amends for the affliction I have caused you through my idleness, extravagance, and folly."—The hen produced them as many eggs as they desired; they sold them, and in a little time became very rich. For some months Jack and his mother lived happily together.

The divine hen or goose is usually associated with sun energy, radiant life, spiritual power, a generous ally. The divine bird, we are told, once belonged in Jack's parental house. The Giant, then, has a lot of stolen property.

The detail that the Giant snored "like the roaring of a cannon" gives us a little pause. Most of all, we notice how much protection the feminine gives to Jack, even after his mother is no longer present to protect him. In the presence of the Giant, the feminine protects. This theme appears in hundreds of fairy tales; sometimes the woman is the Giant's daughter, sometimes his sister, sometimes—as in our story—his wife. The story would not go forward without her. Clearly, she has trickster energy; she hides the human being, whether a boy or a girl, and a little lying is all right for her. Her help often lets her in for verbal or physical abuse from the Giant, particularly after his favorite objects begin to disappear. It happens over and over.

So the story says that Jack, after this very light brush with the large male, carries the divine hen down the beanstalk and sets up life again with his mother. The reconciliation with the mother is very much a pattern in current society, for in the fifty years since 1945, the number of homes in which the father is the dominant energy has declined steeply. The father, when present in an American home, can no longer rely on the old deference to him. The culture doesn't automatically offer the father the prerogatives he enjoyed in the paternal society, his jurisdiction has become limited, his authority lessened; he lacks moment and consequence these days. We don't have as much *father* as we used to have. For some that is fine, better than fine; others suffer withdrawal; still others feel the world is coming to an end.

Second Interruption: Where Have All the Parents Gone?

THE LOUDEST SOUND IN NORTHERN EUROPE AT THE END OF THE nineteenth century was the sound of the door closing when Nora in Ibsen's *A Doll's House* left her husband to live alone. But now the loudest sound is of men leaving, several million in the United States. Nothing like this has been seen before. During the 1940s, the wartime draft pulled American men out of the house; but there was some feeling of sacrifice and nobility about that, and it was not voluntary. What can this voluntary leaving mean? Mothers are also leaving.

Some English caretakers of elephants on the India subcontinent reported in July of 1995 that mother elephants in India were, for the first time, leaving baby elephants behind. So much forest cover has been destroyed that an elephant herd apparently feels anxiety in the long trek to the next forest cover; and mothers abandon baby elephants, who are then found wandering by themselves.

DURING OUR EIGHTEENTH CENTURY, THE AMERICAN FATHER WAS thought of as the stone and roof-pillar of the family. The Puritan household in 1750 was set up so that it paralleled the Puritan State. Older men ran both. The service involved, for many fathers, more power than love; and it would be wrong to be sentimental or nostalgic about those families. We are talking not of the wisdom of father-power but merely of the extent of it. If we look at a family in, say, Salem, Massachusetts, in 1750, the father was the Navigator in social waters; he was the Moral Teacher and Spiritual Comforter; he was the Earner, who brought in the income and kept the family alive; he was the Hearer of Distress as well; cares were brought to the mother and then to him. People imagined the family as a Hebraic unit, as if the children were all children of God, and the house a tiny house of Abraham.

But this arrangement soon faltered. When the West opened up, fathers and prospective fathers headed there. Many factories opened in New England. The father's eyes turned outward toward opportunity, factories, and long days; and the mother became the sole confidant of the children. Susan Juster and Maris Vinoskis say, "The transition from the father to the mother as the primary socializer and educator of young children was completed by the nineteenth century."

For a time during the mid-nineteenth century, then, mothers become the sole center of the family. Many devotional meetings took place in the family, the heat of devotion entered the house, and the mothers taught inclusiveness, compassion, and self-restraint. We can feel the reality of such households in Mark Twain's novels. Mother was the Navigator in social waters, the Moral Teacher and Spiritual Comforter, and the Hearer of Distress. In most families the husband remained the Earner.

The mother's position changed again in the early twentieth century. She lost power when the selling industry succeeded in inserting itself between her and the children. She could no longer provide the emotional tone of the house, and pass on the tastes in books or music that her parents had given to her.

For centuries in the West, the young had learned music through hearing—even learning—folk ballads, Bach, Mozart, opera, polka tunes, dance music that the previous generations had loved. The music industry soon saw that huge profits would flow from urging each generation to have its own music. Media heroes such as Elvis, Prince, Michael Jackson, and Madonna became, through the very number of eyes trained on them, people with that mana that comes from the attention of millions. The parents didn't stand a chance. These people were a thousand times more exciting than one's parents. The siblings "understand" the new music; and soon that's all they hear. Six- and seven-year-olds are now listening to rap music that spouts active hatred of women. In fact, our children get most of their values from music, videos, and films, and even though we regret that situation, we have not yet found a way to change it.

Mothers and fathers still do teach some values, such as empathy, discipline, helpfulness, honesty, and community responsibility, but by and large the parents are overwhelmed. Business's maneuver to substitute themselves for the parents has worked. Like the German *blitzkrieg*, it took place so fast that no one could stop it. Most mothers remain in the house, but they have, like the fathers, the feeling that they are disposable.

Psychology HAS BECOME A LIVING, MANY-WINDOWED SUBMA-rine that enables psychologists to examine huge fish, sea vegetables, and half-blind worms on the floor beneath the unlit emotional sea; its discoveries have been one of the great glories of the twentieth century. And yet these discoveries have terrified parents by showing them how many mistakes they will certainly make. Parents felt a shock when they realized that the "bad kid" turned bad not because of some "seed" inside him but because the parent had fed him as a child from a stock of bad food that grandparents had cooked. Millions of parents now realize that to raise children without damaging them is impossible.

The sense that one could be responsible for "what is wrong" with one's children, because of one's own childhood, produces deep anxiety. Virtually every parent feels it now; but the great mass of parents had not felt this terror until this century.

Eighteenth- and nineteenth-century American parenting went along on old tracks like those toy trains for which the crossings and tunnels and red-painted stations never changed. It was agreed that fathers shouted at regular times. If children, particularly sons, didn't do their work, or were rude, they were beaten; that was understood. Sometimes fathers sexually abused the children; that may not have been understood, but it was not challenged. Children had nightmares regularly, and dreamt of killing their parents; that was understood. Having these parent tracks laid out is what Marion Woodman calls being an "unconscious father or an unconscious mother." One didn't think much about what to do.

Parents in general have become less unconscious, and that is a great blessing. And yet the doubt and guilt that parents feel have flowed in from the truth-telling of the great psychologists. No one is to blame here. Yet we know that the fear of doing wrong as a parent while still remaining a child oneself has been contributing to the fleeing of the fathers. Many mothers would flee, too, if they thought they could.

The English lawyer and writer Owen Barfield noticed a change in the English and American mind over the last eighty years. Some spot in the brain that used to hold the substance called responsibility now holds the substance called guilt:

> Are people feeling guilty nowadays? Well, if I were asked to lay my finger on one of the most striking differences between the social climate of Europe and the West as it is today and as it was, say sixty years ago, I think I should have to specify the presence in it almost everywhere of a vague, uneasy feeling of guilt. There is an atmosphere of guilt. . . . Responsibility is food for the will, guilt is food for the feelings only . . . confused feelings of guilt tend to beget paralysis rather than energy.
>
> Those who are old enough to remember the years between the wars will recall the skillful use Hitler made of just that paralysis in the '30s, when even young people, who were in their cradles at the time it was signed, were somehow made to feel guilty about the unjust provisions of the Treaty of Versailles.

He then refers to the cross-blaming that goes on at all levels of our society:

> Feelings of guilt tend to turn rather easily into feelings of hatred and contempt. We may feel a bit guilty ourselves, but we are very sure that

a whole lot of other people are much more guilty, and probably ought to be destroyed.

In the sibling society we can see the deep bitterness between the right and left wings in the country, and the deep bitterness between men and women. Neither gender can stand the sense that it may be guilty of bad parenting, which it did without knowing any better.

In her essay "But Where Are the Men?" Ruth Sidel correctly links the phenomenon of fathers leaving the house with economic realities. Layoffs that began in the 1970s continue and sharply rise. The media concentrate on deadbeat dads—and that's understandable—"and yet virtually no one blames an economic system that deprives millions of workers of jobs."

American business made a decision some years ago to be "competitive" in the fast market as opposed to keeping promises to workers or supporting their communities. From 1973 to 1991, the average hourly wage for production and nonsupervisory workers steadily fell. "From 1980 to 1993, the Fortune 500 companies shed more than one quarter (4.4 million) of all the jobs they had previously provided. Meanwhile, during that same period, these companies increased their assets by 2.3 times, and their sales by 1.4 times." The major CEOs increased their annual compensation by 6.11 times. We know all these figures, and they are heartbreaking. To fathers, and mothers, they are devastating.

We know that "the unskilled black man has little chance of obtaining a permanent job that would pay enough to support a family. He eventually becomes resigned to being unable to play the traditional father role, and rather than being faced with his own failure day after day, year after year, he often walks away."

Unemployment among Native Americans—there are roughly one million—ranges between 45 and 55 percent, but it reaches 80 percent in some areas and in some seasons.

Andrew Kimbrell remarks that the purportedly " 'patriarchal' industrial production system began by destroying fatherhood" in England through the form of enclosures, which amounted to abolishment of common pastures, ordered by the courts, that drove men into the factories. The patriarchal system's destruction of fatherhood continues in the United States: here it is free hours that are "enclosed." In 1935, the average working man had forty hours a week free, including Saturday and Sunday. By 1990, it was down to seventeen hours. The twenty-three lost hours of free time a week since 1935 are the very hours in which the father could be a nurturing father, and find some center in himself, and the very hours in which the mother could feel she actually has a husband.

MANY JUDGES, SOCIOLOGISTS, AND LAWMAKERS MOREOVER have regarded fathers as insignificant in the family structure throughout the last hundred years.

Decisions by judges to award custody to mothers both reflects the idea of the nonimportance of fathers and deepens it. At the same time, we know that many nineteenth-century fathers abandoned their families to go west, and many contemporary fathers abandon the family emotionally by working fourteen hours a day. For whatever reasons, fathers are becoming scarce: "Fathers are vanishing legally as well as physically. About one-third of all childbirths in the nation now occur out of marriage. In most of these cases, the place for the father's name on the birth certificate is simply left blank."

Katha Pollitt, an otherwise bright columnist, said: "Why not have a child of one's own? Children are a joy; many men are not."

Misguided government decisions contributed to the exile of fathers from distressed families. AFDC money was granted to single mothers only if no man was living in the house. Daniel Patrick Moynihan, in his famous book of 1965, *The Negro Family: The Case for National Action*, warned that this practice was causing devastation in the black community; but he was mocked and demonized by observers on both the right and the left, by both blacks and whites. His warning that the fatherlessness would spread to the white community was correct. Fatherlessness now stands at 60 percent and rising in the black neighborhoods, and 35 percent and rising in white neighborhoods.

I think it is important to recognize that these mistakes in judgment do not amount to a conspiracy against men. It is simply that no one thought it out. The father seemed so pervasive, so constantly present, that no one grasped how swiftly that might change.

Our vision of the family as an ecological system remains now at about the same level as our vision of the natural system in the nineteenth century, when no one really understood the way all elements in a long-growth forest, for example, depend on each other. If human beings remove one element—pine trees or squirrels—out of a deep growth forest, much also changes. Seeding may depend on the squirrels. Some abusive fathers need to be taken out of the family, but there hasn't been much discrimination between kinds of fathers. The solution some sociologists have proposed to solve the problem of anger by removing fathers has had a serious effect on human culture as a whole, an effect we now see in the aggression of fatherless gangs among the disadvantaged, and the presence of depressed and passive youngsters among the advantaged.

A similar mistake may now be in the making in relation to mothers. Alvin L. Schorr and Phyllis Moen, representing thousands of marriage counselors and sociologists, foolishly say: "The presence or absence of both parents per se makes little difference in the adequacy of child-rearing or the socialization of children." Such nonsense means that mothers, too, are now considered nonessential. Throughout these last four decades, mothers have felt increasingly unvalued, both by the male culture and by some spokeswomen of the women's movement, who could have been their champions; the morale of mothers is low.

MICHAEL VENTURA BELIEVES THAT THE ABANDONMENT BY PARents of their children is a worldwide phenomenon.

*Children born at the end of the Second World War behaved with
shocking force in the '60s. Sometime around 1965, family disciplines
that had been in force for centuries suddenly dissolved. This didn't
happen just in America. It also happened in countries without TV,
affluence, rock & roll, or racial tensions. In China, a tidal wave of
youth calling themselves "Red Guard" created a "Cultural Revolution," a dogmatic stripping-down of their society on a scale surpass-
ing any social upheaval in the West. . . .*

*In Cambodia, at almost the same time, almost the same thing
happened in form and scale, but far more murderously. . . .*

*. . . A paradigm of family life that has existed everywhere for mil-
lennia, is breaking down everywhere at the same time. A mass change
is occurring on a fundamental, unconscious, compulsive level of the
human psyche, for reasons that are neither personal nor national.
Both affluence and poverty are producing basically the same dissolu-
tion of families.*

*Something that everyone agrees (on the surface, at least) is essen-
tial, something as basic as family, is being destroyed everywhere, by
everyone, as though by some unconscious general consensus—and no
one knows why.*

Gᴌᴀɴᴄɪɴɢ ᴇᴠᴇɴ ʙʀɪᴇꜰʟʏ ᴀᴛ ᴛʜɪꜱ ʜɪꜱᴛᴏʀʏ ᴏꜰ ꜰᴀᴍɪʟʏ ʙʀᴇᴀᴋᴜᴘ,
we can deduce that Jack's situation, as an unprotected child, is going
to be representative of our children for a long time. We may as well
get used to the dilemma he faces, because millions of sons and
daughters already face it.

Among boys, one could say that if the son is released from the
oedipal struggle with his father, he will find somewhere in his life a
really big male energy that wants to kill him. Mary Pipher, in *Reviving Ophelia,* her study of adolescent girls, points out that they are not
doing well either. Even inside the house, adolescent girls feel unparented. They are often literally unfathered, and they tend to reject
their mothers, which sometimes leads to running away. They want
to be parented but will not accept the mother's values. If a young girl

experiences rape, she may—amazingly—blame the parents more than the rapist. Such misplaced anger testifies to their deep need—as deep as Jack's—for protection. They need it and deserve it, but many adolescent girls are not receiving it.

L<small>ET'S</small> <small>ENTER THE STORY ONCE MORE</small>. A<small>FTER THE FIRST ENCOUN-</small>ter with the Giant, mother and son live well for two or three years. They have money. They do all right. At the end of that time, the hen gets sick, or stops laying the golden eggs. In one version mother and son kill the hen by reaching in to get the gold a little ahead of time, like credit cards, I suppose. The hen dies and the two become poor again. Soon Jack, against his mother's will, prepares to climb the beanstalk a second time.

Jack, finding that all his arguments were useless, pretended to give up the point, though resolved to go at all events. He had a dress prepared, which would disguise him, and with something to discolour his skin, he thought it impossible for any one to recollect him. In a few mornings after discoursing with his mother, he rose very early, put on his disguise, changed his complexion, and, unperceived by any one, climbed the bean-stalk. He was greatly fatigued when he reached the top, and very hungry. Having rested some time on one of the stones, he pursued his journey to the Giant's mansion. He reached it late in the evening, the woman was standing at the door as usual; Jack accosted her, at the same time telling her a pitiful tale, and requested she would give him some victuals and drink, and a night's lodging. . . .

At last she consented, and as she led the way, Jack observed that every thing was just as he had found it before; she took him into the kitchen, and hid him in an old lumber-closet. The Giant returned at the usual time, and walked in so heavily that the house was shaken to the foundation. He seated himself by a good fire, saying, "I smell fresh meat"; the wife replied it was the crows, who had brought a piece of carrion, and laid it at the top of the house upon the leads.

Jack, secure in his lumber closet, watches now as the Giant orders bags of gold and silver coins to be brought to him. He counts each coin, and his old greed is palpable.

The gold was put up as the silver had been before, and, if possible, more securely. The Giant snored aloud; Jack could compare his noise to nothing but the roaring of the sea in a high wind, when the tide is coming in. At last Jack, concluding him to be asleep, and therefore secure, stole out of his hiding place, and approached the Giant, in order to carry off the two bags of money; but, just as he laid his hand upon one of the bags, a little dog, whom he had not perceived before, started out from under the Giant's chair, and barked at Jack most furiously, who gave himself up for lost; fear rivetted him to the spot— instead of running he stood still, though expecting his enemy to awaken every minute.

Jack finally seizes both bags and escapes down the beanstalk. Evidently quite a bit of time has passed, and he finds his mother at a neighbor's house, apparently dying. She revives; and with the new gold, the cottage is repaired and well furnished, and the two live happily with each other for another spell.

For three years Jack heard no more of the bean-stalk, but he could not forget it; though he feared making his mother unhappy; she would not mention the bean-stalk, lest it might remind him of taking another journey. Notwithstanding the comforts Jack enjoyed, his mind dwelt upon the bean-stalk, he could not think of anything else, it was in vain endeavouring to amuse himself.

Jack now climbs the beanstalk a third time, and has once more disguised himself so completely that the Giant's wife does not recognize him. At last she hides him in a copper pot. The Giant eats a great supper; when finished, he commands his wife to fetch down his harp.

Jack peeped under the copper-lid, and soon saw the most beautiful harp that could be imagined; it was placed by the Giant, he said "play," and it instantly played of its own accord, without being touched. The music was very fine, Jack was delighted, and felt more anxious to get the harp into his possession, than either of the former treasures. The Giant's soul was not attuned to harmony, and the music lulled him into a sound sleep. Now therefore was the time to carry off the harp, and the Giant appeared to be in a more profound sleep than usual. Jack quickly determined, got out of the pot, and took the harp. The harp was a fairy; it called out loudly "master! master! master!" The Giant awoke, stood up, and tried to pursue Jack, but he had drank so much that he could not stand. . . .

Jack runs to the beanstalk, with the Giant after him.

The moment Jack set his foot on the bean-stalk, he called for a hatchet; one was brought directly; he soon reached the ground, just at that instant the Giant was beginning to come down; but Jack with his hatchet cut the bean-stalk close off to the root, which made the Giant fall into the garden—the fall killed him. Jack's mother was delighted when she saw the bean-stalk destroyed; he heartily begged his mother's pardon for all the sorrow and affliction he had caused her, promising faithfully to be very dutiful and obedient to her for the future. He proved as good as his word, and was a pattern of affectionate behaviour and attention to parents. His mother and he lived together a great many years, and continued to be always very happy.

In other versions, Jack marries and moves into his own house, remaining on good terms with his mother.

That's the end of the story for Jack and his mother; but I think it's clear that as a nation we have not arrived at that part of the story yet. We don't know how to steal "gold" back from the Giant. As a people, we have no idea what to do about greed in general, nor the Giant, nor the television that eats more and more of our lives each day, nor the increasing hunger for new goods that children and adults feel. The message of television is always appetite, and as Marshall McLuhan said, "The medium is the message."

There is no evidence that business or the advertising industry will back off; no evidence that most parents, addicted themselves, have the will to prevent addiction of their children; no evidence that we will keep guns away from children. Children in the inner cities are hiding in the closet now, exactly like Jack.

Freud talked optimistically in 1899 of cultural progress in Europe. He used as a metaphor the Dutch farmers' laboring to reclaim land from the sea by building dykes, and then desalting the ground, so that grain fields now stand where there was once only sea. Freud noticed that the European "I" had been reclaiming territory from the *id* or the lower brains for centuries. Civilization means that the ego or the "I" is increasing its control. But he lost his optimism during World War II.

During his lifetime the German nation, long a leader in Europe in this type of transcendental reclaiming, suffered an enormous setback: a barbaric "sea" reclaimed farms, pastures, barns, gardens, villages, schools, and churches once thought secure. Great artists signed on as Nazis; thousands of German doctors participated in obviously vile experiments; the most religious people in Europe, the Jews, and the most intuitive people, the Gypsies, were wiped out with the complicity of hundreds of thousands of grown-up and well-educated people. That time—from 1933 to 1945—was the first reclaiming of civilized ground; our culture is the second.

The Giant shows himself differently in each of his visits, but when he arrives, the change can be felt. The teenagers in our inner cities are expressing the presence of the Giant, who is, fundamentally, opposed to life. He is the one who stabs people in the library and eats children. We are drawing nearer to what Freud called "the pure culture of the death instinct." The presence of the death instinct makes the faces of teenagers and their movements, even on subways, utterly different from the bodies of men and women forty years ago.

The story reminds us that the Giant eliminates the father first, which our society has already accomplished. The mother and children, spared for a while, are in great danger. Children particularly have to hide. Jack, representing the new brain, has to hide and let the two old brains decide how life is to proceed.

The Giant, from the human point of view, means isolation and deprivation. We don't realize that when we put a computer or television in a child's own room, we are sending that child to be alone with the Giant.

As a culture, we still don't know how to steal from the Giant; we allow the Giant to continue stealing from us. As a culture, we remain stuck in that frightful scene in which the Giant is eating and Jack is watching from his hiding place. Many people work for the Giant. Instead of working toward removal of guns, for example, we go up to the cupboard where the children are hidden, call the Giant over, and say "Here they are!" Our story ends with Jack being eaten.

CHAPTER THREE

Swimming Among the Half-Adults

IN MANY WAYS, WE ARE NOW LIVING IN A CULTURE RUN by half-adults. Fraternities used to be the main exhibit of half-adults, with their half-realized pornography. In the computer Usenet news group, where digital images are stored, 83.5 percent of the pictures are pornographic. The half-adults, twenty to thirty years old, don't try to protect children from the files. Serious participation in politics is at an all-time low; Congress allows corporations to meet air quality standards by lowering the standards. We are always under commercial pressure to slide backward, toward adolescence, toward childhood. With no effective rituals of initiation, and no real way to know when our slow progress toward adulthood has reached its goal, young men in our culture go around in circles. Those who should be adults find it difficult or impossible to offer help to those behind. That pressure seems even more intense than it was in the 1960s, when the cry "Turn on, tune in, drop out" was so popular. Observers describe many contemporaries as "children with children of their own."

"People look younger all the time." Photographs of men and women a hundred years ago—immigrants, for example—show a certain set of the mouth and jaws that says, "We're adults. There's nothing we can do about it."

By contrast, the face of Marilyn Monroe, of Kevin Costner, or of the ordinary person we see on the street says, "I'm a child. There's nothing I can do about it."

People watching Ken Burns's *History of Baseball* remarked that faces of fans even in the 1920s looked more mature than faces of fans now. Looking at those old photos, one sees men and women who knew how to have fun, but they had one foot in Necessity. Walk down a European street these days and you will see that American faces stand out for their youthful and naive look. Some who are fifty look thirty. Part of this phenomenon is good nutrition and exercise, but part of it is that we are losing our ability to mature.

ADOLESCENTS ARE SEPARATING OFF AS A GROUP. WE KNOW THAT the duration of childhood and adolescence has been lengthening over the past several decades. During the Middle Ages, the stage of youth was virtually ignored; a peasant child of seven joined the workforce. At Plymouth Colony, a child was considered a small adult at the age of eight. Children were asked to be aware of the group. There was no real time for adolescence then. From the community's point of view, an adult is someone who knows how to preserve the larger group of which he or she is a part. Today's adolescent, by contrast, wants his or her needs gratified now, and seems not to notice that he or she is living in a complicated web of griefs, postponed pleasures, unwelcome labor, responsibilities, and unpaid debts to gods and human beings.

Adolescents have generally refused to accept the larger goals of their elders. That attitude is proper to adolescence, which is a sort of larval stage. A problem develops, though, when people remain in adolescence long past its normal span.

Animal adolescents, if we can use such a phrase, are always in training, and they soon become tuned to their group. Among apes and chimps, for example, young ones often feel responsible for the others, as we have learned from the famous story of the traveling baboons. That troop, guided by older baboons, and with a few younger ones going ahead as scouts, was moving through the jungle on a random trip to new ground. One young baboon came upon a tiger waiting, quietly, for the main troop to arrive. The young baboon threw himself on the tiger—he had no chance of winning that battle—and the ethologist who witnessed it realized that the baboon had sacrificed himself to save the troop members following behind. We know, too, that certain human communities—such as the Inuit and the Australian Aborigines, who live in harsh areas—produced, when their culture was intact, juveniles who knew how to preserve what had nurtured them.

We all recognize that our emphasis on individualism in the West has dimmed whatever instincts Western youth might have had to preserve the troop. For some time now our own spark of life has often been more compelling, more important to us, than the flame of the larger group.

American movies in the late 1950s vividly brought forward an old theme of adolescence: the impulse not to defend common projects, common stories, common values. James Dean and Marlon Brando played the roles of young men who demonstrated this rebellion, and the theme began to have an edge on it. "What are you rebelling against?" a Brando character is asked. "What do you have?" is the witty reply. But with that reply the baboon troop is gone.

Human beings often struggle to preserve a given cultural group through the stories it holds in common, its remembered history or fragments of it, and certain agreed-on values and courtesies. A gathering of novels, plays, poems, and songs—these days wrongly called "the canon," more properly "the common stories"—held middle-aged people, elders, and the very young together.

That most adolescents these days reject the common stories is no surprise. More often than not, they reject them without having read or heard them. When adolescence lasts only three or four years, the youths' refusal to support the commonly agreed on novels and poems does not affect the long-range commitment of the group to this reservoir; but now, as American adolescence stretches from age fifteen or so all the way to thirty-five, those twenty years of sullen

silence or active rejection of any commonality, in literature or otherwise, can have devastating results. One can say that colleges and
universities are precisely where the gifts of the past are meant to be
studied, and absorbed, and yet those very places are where the
current damage to the common reservoir is taking place. Men and
women in their twenties take teaching jobs, and if they are still
adolescent in their thirties, their hostility to the group's literature
and to the group itself becomes palpable.

We know it is essential to open the cabinet of common stories to
include literature from other cultures besides the European, and to
include much more women's literature than the old reservoir held.
That is long overdue. But inclusion, one could say, is a job for adults.
When the adolescent gets hold of it, a deep-lying impulse comes
into play, which says, "I'm taking care of people my age, and that's
it! My needs are important, and if the group doesn't survive, it
doesn't deserve to."

English departments have always had Wordsworth-killers and
Lawrence-killers, but a change has taken place. At Modern Language
Association conventions, papers whose language excludes everyone
but the postmodernist sibling are now presented.

One sees much sibling behavior, too, in corporate offices and
computer vocations. "We have our computers and that's all we care
for. Helping the group is for someone else." The rule for siblings of
any age is "Take care of your own; go along and get along."

Hostility toward the larger group can now be found even at the
grade-school level. A third grader says: "I don't have to obey you!
You're nothing but a teacher!" A friend who drives a school bus has
noticed a significant change in children during the last few years.
"Grade-school kids now," she says, "have less respect for other
people, less respect for others' property, and less respect for their
own property. One sixth-grade girl whom I asked to close the bus
windows at the end of the run last week closed one, and that done,
said, 'That's not my job. Fuck you!' "

As parenting becomes less effective, children become more savage
and uneasy and less able to feel a part of any dignified group. It is

natural, then, that they look for respect, and self-respect, from their peers.

P EOPLE OF ALL AGES ARE MAKING DECISIONS TO AVOID THE DIF- ficulties of maturity. Freud maintained in *Civilization and Its Discontents* that human beings feel a deep hate and a deep love for civilization. Civilized behavior demands repression and restraint, in the face of which, of course, the instinctual energies know they will not be satisfied.

One way to outwit the demands that civilization makes is to set up a sibling society. To make all the necessary changes is hard, but once they are made, most of us can then avoid the painful tasks of the civilized adult. When enough people have slid backward into a sibling state of mind, society can no longer demand difficult and subtle work from its people—because the standards are no longer visible. Without the labor of artists, for example, to incorporate past achievements—in brushwork, in treatment of light, in depth of emotion, in mythological intensity—people with some talent can pretend to be genuine artists. Their choices seem to be to cannibal- ize ancient art, or to create absurdly ugly art that "makes a state- ment." They don't ask themselves or each other for depth or intensity, and most contemporary critics pretend not to miss them.

Another way of outwitting the demands of civilization is to make sex a plaything for regressed adults. Sex loses its grandeur and its fate. In past eras, some societies said: "If you agree to accept the painful labors of parenting implicit in pair-bonding, then you can have regular sexual release. Otherwise, no." We know of successful cultures that have allowed great sexual freedom, but the youngsters are not abandoned after the initial sexuality; they have the support of the entire tribe, which knows how to bring about adult behavior.

The person who decides to omit the difficult labors of becoming civilized receives, in return, permission for narcissism, freedom from old discontents, and a ticket to the omnitheater where fanta- sies are being run. One could say that the greedy and lazy part of the soul obtains permission to do as it wishes. Thousands of other siblings in other countries will cover for that person, just as troops support each other in a retreat.

Emily Dickinson said:

I think the Hemlock likes to stand
Upon a Marge of Snow—
It suits his own Austerity—
And satisfies an awe.

The experience of austerity and the experience of maturity are connected.

That men are in essence boys has long been a theme with women, but the boyishness used to be endearing. Now it feels dangerous to those nearby. As the supply of adult men lessens, fewer daughters grow up experiencing the adult male presence, so they choose a mate without reference to any standard of maturity. Some women speak with surprise of a lover: "He looked so good at first—he let his feelings show, he didn't have all these hard edges that the corporate clam-men have, he talked about his childhood, he made me feel needed, wasn't afraid to say he is scared." Then what? "All of a sudden he doesn't do his share, he leaves his clothes everywhere. He quits his job because there's 'too much hassle,' and he doesn't try for another; if I tell him I'm feeling sad or lonely, his eyes look somewhere else in the room. Then I feel like a mother! An unsuccessful mother, at that. And as soon as that happens, he doesn't make love much anymore: we end up as brother and sister. That's it. It's over." Women are shocked to learn how many men are helpless, vulnerable, isolated, and depotentiated by longing.

Women, as well, are directed by society to be young, even immature, physically and emotionally. There are women who can offer advice in adulthood, but they are seldom visible.

MANY YOUNG MEN NO LONGER ARRIVE AT THE OEDIPAL WALL. In the old paternal society—often unhealthy, particularly in the son-father rivalry—a son, around age twelve or fifteen, would hit the oedipal wall. It still happens. Perhaps the father assumes the right to tell the son what to do, perhaps he arrogantly orders others around and does nothing himself, or he belittles the son: "You never do anything right!" "Why don't you get off your ass and do something?"

When the son in such a family gets angry and climbs the oedipal wall, he finds his father already there—at the top. The two wrestle. Sometimes one falls off, sometimes the other. Kafka's great story "The Judgment" describes a son who fell off. The son, living in an apartment alone with his aging father, loses the battle decisively. The father humiliates him; and the father suddenly seems so tall that he can touch the ceiling. As the story ends, the son rushes down the stairs and vaults over the bridge rail into the Vltava River, whispering, "Dear parents, I loved you all the same." If he lives through such a fight, the son acquires considerable confidence simply from having faced the father. Sometimes that earned confidence gives him the energy to become adult.

Freud gave structure to this turmoil by using the Greek story of Oedipus, who, as William Stafford said, "won so well he lost." Freud gave class, one could say, to the rough battle by naming it after a Greek hero. Psychologists after him have written extensively and well of the oedipal wrestling.

The amazing fact is that thousands of young American men in recent decades have never reached the oedipal wall at all. If the father is physically absent, or even only emotionally absent, the wall is difficult to see or experience. A son may come near the wall and then curve gracefully back toward the mother. This curving back toward the mother's comfort is repeated so often in contemporary families that we must look at it.

The German analyst Alexander Mitscherlich sensed that in North America the old love-hate relationship of son to father is fading. The typical American son's attitude, he said, "includes a non-respect for the father which is associated with very little affect indeed." "Very little affect indeed" describes unmistakably the emotional flatness we see now in young men.

A young man studying to be a doctor remarked that he had very little feeling for his father—he "didn't know him"—and many of his friends were in the same boat. He complained that he couldn't find his anger; and he wondered if the absence of his father made his anger remain unconscious. He added: "And when I do feel anger, there's so much pressure from peers for it to be there that I don't know if it is valid or not. My girlfriend chose the day of my graduation from medical school to tell me she was leaving me. She said many hurtful things to me; but all I could think to do was to comfort her." His comforting was good, but something was missing from his response.

Sons who have a remote or absent father clearly can receive no modeling on how to deal appropriately with male anger, what it looks like, what it feels like, what it smells like, how to honor it, or let it go, or speak it without hurting someone. Such sons are usually so frightened of anger that they repress it entirely. Others, with no better modeling, become violent. Few sons in a city culture learn to fuse instinctive aggression with the pleasure of hard physical work. Few sons now share a toolbox with their father. The son experiences the father only in the world of longing.

When the son used to meet the father on top of the oedipal wall, their mutual anger sometimes had the sorry result of fistfights or even murder. But with many fathers absent, millions of males linger passively in a dangerous, frightening, and inarticulate fantasy world. Such a person is not free of aggression; he tends to radiate an aggression that is diffuse, nondirectional, inconsolable. The names of some rock bands describe this situation very well. They call themselves Suicidal Tendencies, Porno for Pyros, Crash Test Dummies, Revolting Cocks, Hole, Urge Overkill, and Arrested Development. Some of the late Kurt Cobain's lyrics certainly reveal inconsolable anxiety. The Beatles' affectionate lyrics are replaced by gangsta rap. The artist Bruce Nauman's early images of woods and fields are replaced by dead horses and guns, and by video installations that pour out hostile words over and over to the museum-goer. Nauman's 1984 neon sign says: "Play and Die," "Suck and Die," "Come and Die," "Know and Die," "Smell and Die," "Fall and Die," and so on.

CAN WE SAY THAT DAUGHTERS NO LONGER HIT "THE ELECTRA wall"? Freud's attempt to set up the Electra complex—the love of the father and rejection of the mother—as a counterpart to the oedipal story was not completely convincing. The complementarity of the genders is not that cut and dried. Both genders need to learn to stand on their own, independent of their parents. The daughter has to disidentify, as psychologists say, from the mother's personality, and the son has to disidentify from the entire gender. Some succeed and some don't. But to disidentify is not at all the same thing as to repudiate.

Daughters today often find themselves not with too much mothering but with too little. Some interrupt their movement to adulthood by their felt need to ask others—other women, older men, lovers—for mothering. Some valiantly try to mother themselves, splitting into a small girl and a mother. Still others become pregnant at fourteen deliberately, hoping to receive some sort of mothering from their child soon to come.

SOME ELEMENT IS MISSING AMONG THE REASONS GIVEN FOR EXtended youth. We know that our culture extends adolescence; that the rarity of emotionally present fathers is a factor; that adulthood offers fewer economic incentives than it used to; that the emphasis on slenderness and youth holds back a majority of us, particularly females, in youthful states; that children find their help less essential to the community; and so on. But it is hard to get a job in India, too, and yet that doesn't seem to bond Indians to adolescence;

American fathers were absent in wartime without evidence of excessive failure of adulthood among their sons or daughters. Another element—I suspect the overuse or wrong use of the neocortex—is involved. That would help explain why the infantilization is deepening in a culture increasingly driven by electronics.

As a species we are large brained and large skulled. We know that evolutionists envisage a long struggle between the movement toward a larger head and the limitations of the pelvis, whose bones limit the size of the head. The large head, as it is and has been, makes birth an intensely painful experience for the human female: "In sorrow thou shalt bring forth children," God said to Eve.

Despite that limitation, the human brain is large at birth, and the skull enlarges greatly after birth. At birth, the rhesus monkey, for example, has a brain that is already 65 percent of its final size; the chimpanzee brain is 40.5 percent of its final size; but the human baby's brain is only 23 percent. That means that three-quarters of the skull growth takes place after birth. Another puzzling detail is that the skull sutures on a typical ape close within a year or two after birth, but the human skull sutures remain open until age thirty-five or so. There are several other puzzles, including the absence of brow ridges (which in the ape develop during the last month of gestation), the absence of body hair (which in the ape develops during the last month), and, strangely, that human babies are born with big toes not able to rotate, a trait that apes develop, again, in the last month.

These matters came into closer focus when a professor of human anatomy at Amsterdam, Louis Bolk, published a series of papers, collected in 1926, pointing out that the fully grown human being has an astonishing resemblance to the eighth-month fetus of a chimpanzee. He listed twenty-five traits of adult humans, including the flat face, that exist only in the fetal stage of apes.

During the final month in the womb, many finishing traits are experienced, among them the DNA order to start closing the skull sutures, thereby limiting the size of the adult skull. One way for human beings to achieve a head size larger than allowed by normal ape development would be to omit the last month, to allow the baby to be born early, slipping past several limitations. Many adult apes have a protruding or long jaw. The protrusion is tied into a skull frame that requires a relatively low dome. If the baby is born before the jaw lengthens, a high dome is more likely.

Louis Bolk suggested that this skipping of the final month is exactly what human beings do. It has certain benefits, such as open sutures and the possibility of a high forehead, and certain disadvantages, such as less mobile toes, a naked skin basically without hair, and so on. We can feel immediately that much is at stake here. Some loss of self-esteem is likely, as appeared also when Galileo suggested that the sun does not revolve around the earth. Bolk summarized his position in these words:

> *If I wished to express the basic principle of my ideas in a somewhat strongly worded sentence, I would say that man, in his bodily development, is a primate fetus that has become sexually mature* [einen zur Geschlechtsreife gelangten Primatenfetus].

He expressed surprise that a fetuslike being could reproduce itself, but such a being is apparently what we are. We are a species that literally holds onto youth. The word *neotony*, which means something like that, was coined by J. Kallmann in 1905. By emerging from the womb early, human beings have a higher skull; and we notice that human beings of all races, as a result, have a curiously flat face, sometimes even a flat nose. These are traits of the chimpanzee fetus. Not all evolutionists accept Bolk's theory, but it explains characteristics of the human baby that no other theory can explain. Among American scientists and writers who accept Bolk's ideas are Stephen Jay Gould, who discusses the reality of neotony in *Ontogeny and Phylogeny*, and Paul Shepard. The Swiss writer Konrad Lorenz is an advocate as well.

Let's summarize the main points of Bolk's ideas.

One way to talk of the mystery of the large brain is to suppose that the human being at some point interrupted itself during its own womb development and emerged, unfinished, about a month early. The human fetus as it exists now has skipped the final finishing. A chimpanzee, which by contrast remains in the womb for the full term, is, when born, already integrated into its forest environment. The little ape, we could say, became finely tuned to forest life in the womb. Its large toe became capable of rotation, and hair grew all over its body. When the human being decided to take away the elaboration achieved in the final month, and so to undo the fine-tuning, the whole situation was thrown into chaos.

The trade-off, however, is substantial. The human skull, which is now born with the sutures still wide open, can continue to expand, providing space for an enlarging neocortex. In other words, the unfinished human has a greater chance of ingenious evolutionary adaptation to a changing environment than does a finished, or fine-tuned, fetus. We do notice that the human infant's head is startlingly large compared with the rest of its body. Paul Shepard has remarked:

> *Infantilizing is one of the means by which increased brain size evolved. . . . This "foetalizing" or "infantilizing" not only stretched the duration of immaturity, but modified the adult as well. During immaturity, there were fewer "fixed" action patterns, more flexibility. . . .*

Apparently the plan was that the new baby-person would solve with its immense neocortex some of the challenges that the well-developed ape, which fits into a niche in its environment, solves through its built-in instinctual responses: "Man is programmed to *learn* to behave, rather than to react via an imprinted determinative instinctual code."

Konrad Lorenz declares that humans' constant curiosity is related to the trade-off: "Human exploratory inquisitive behavior—restricted in animals to a brief developmental phase—is extended to persist until the onset of senility."

What we have, then, for human beings is a hairless, helpless,

chaotic, large-headed baby, whose neocortex *must* grow to make up
for its body's infantile, hairless, arm-waving incompetence.

W E HAVE RECEIVED MUCH FROM THIS TRADE-OFF, BUT IT WORKS
only so long as the neocortex does its intended job of checking out
the leaves, insects, snakes, and other animals with immense care.
That's partly what the hunter-artists in the Dordogne caves were doing. Because the human brain lacks an "imprinted determinative instinctual code," its neocortex turns with avidity to the natural world;
the human child becomes fascinated very early with all the animals—
butterflies, ants, grasshoppers, chickens, horses, cats, or dogs—
around it; with all animal sounds, which it will imitate with delight;
with rain, snow, thunder, gravity, sunlight, wind. This is called playing. Thoreau continued doing so all his life. His aunt, who admired an
ethical man named Dr. Chalmers, complained, "Henry will stand for
six hours watching frogs hatch, but he won't read the biography of
Dr. Chalmers!" When Thoreau was dying, a neighbor said to him,
"How do you stand with Christ?" Thoreau said, wittily, but truthfully
for him, "A snowstorm is more to me than Christ." Thoreau appears
to be showing a loyalty to the immensely curious neocortex that his
ancestors had worked so hard to develop.

Thomas Hardy's wonderful novels always begin with his aware-
ness of the weather, the dampness or dryness, the season. The Japanese require every haiku to include one detail that reveals the
season. Opening flowers belong to spring. Basho said:

The temple bell stops,
but the sound keeps coming
out of the flowers.

This is the neocortex doing its stuff.

The frightening thing, for us in the industrial world, is that the
neocortex may not reach its maturity—and the human being with
it—*unless* it wraps itself intricately, intensely, in the sense world,
and draws the sense world in around it, seeing, smelling, hearing,
touching, weighing, tasting. Soon after an infant is born, for exam-

ple, the neocortex learns to its amazement about gravity; having been upside down in the womb, it finds gravity a great surprise. And it has much else to learn. The hours and hours that children, until the last few years, spent playing outdoors are hours in which the brain receives the food it wants. Wordsworth said that the growth of men and women goes not from childhood to adulthood but from childhood to *nature* to adulthood. Without a time of immersion in nature, a person, he believed, would be a child all his or her life.

> *My heart leaps up when I behold*
> *   A rainbow in the sky:*
> *So it was when my life began;*
> *So it is now I am a man;*
> *So be it when I shall grow old,*
> *   Or let me die!*
> *The child is father of the Man;*
> *And I could wish my days to be*
> *Bound each to each by natural piety.*
>
>   ("My heart leaps up when I behold")

>   *. . . Well I call to mind*
> *('Twas an early age, ere I had seen*
> *Nine summers) . . . 'twas my joy*
> *To wander half the night among the cliffs*
> *And the smooth hollows, where the woodcocks ran*
> *Along the open turf. . . . Oh! when I have hung*
> *Above the raven's nest, by knots of grass*
> *And half-inch fissures in the slippery rock*
> *But ill sustained, and almost, as it seemed,*
> *Suspended by the blast which blew amain,*
> *Shouldering the naked crag; Oh! at that time,*
> *While on the perilous ridge I hung alone,*
> *With what strange utterance did the loud dry wind*
> *Blow through my ears! the sky seemed not a sky*
> *Of earth, and with what motion moved the clouds!*
>
>   (from "The Prelude")

Television is stealing the neocortex's observation time and giving a little useless information in return. A child who watches three to four hours of television a day from the age of two loses thousands of hours of playtime, which means that he or she suffers a serious loss in the neocortex.

It is the neocortex, with its vast love of light, insects, and other creatures, that brings fieriness to the girl or boy; and that love is also liveliness and heat. In the industrial society, human beings are more deeply cold each year, dumber, and increasingly open to miscellaneous information produced by anonymous entities. Some schools now accept free computers, with the understanding that students will in turn accept commercials and newscasts prepared by the vendor.

WHEN THE NEOCORTEX CANNOT DO ITS OLD WORK, A TRULY new element has entered human life. What if the neocortex no longer interacts with plants and animals but only plays with its own inventions? The neocortex of the Internet fanatic is no longer figuring out how to remain warm in this climate; he is not curious about mound-building ants or how past cultures did things. He is curious about his own curiosity. Deconstructionists no longer read Thomas Hardy to glimpse the ominous forces that distort human hopes; but instead the neocortex is curious about how far it can go in making up a language that will undermine all Hardy's meanings. The neocortex becomes analytical about analysis, or inquisitive about inquisitiveness.

The too-early-born, helpless, and hairless human baby without its old instinctual patterns of adaptation requires a long time in which to be nourished and protected by family—and that is not happening. The extended family is gone for most; playtime outdoors has been replaced by television and computers indoors. Grown-up people have no time, and decline the hard work of parenting. Students in return decline the hard work of learning Latin or studying any literature or discipline that isn't attached to the immediate moment. Millions of children and adults decline the hard work of figuring out how to give delight and entertainment to themselves and others, and do not immerse themselves in the details of nature. Some grade-school teachers say they have to force their second graders to go outdoors.

The experiment in which the new brain substitutes for the old instinctive patterns by its devoted study of plants, weather, snow-flakes, beaver ponds, ant heaps, and birds is not working. If the new brain cannot do its work, which is to study animals, wind, thunder, stones, and feathers in detail, it cannot feel safe. Not feeling safe, the boy or girl feels utterly unable to confront the "ills that flesh is heir to," and finds a way to numb the fearful mind and the emotions. Contemporary teenagers find themselves metaphorically moving back from the eighth month to the seventh month. The neocortex, as the inventors of LSD noticed, sees amazing things; but it doesn't see the real things. Old and young become "acid heads" or "Internet heads."

Built in to us is a tendency to regress in time of trouble. One regression—skipping the last month of pregnancy—does not make the other regression—into childishness or drugs—inevitable. And yet it is likely that, preserved somewhere inside the vast DNA information reservoir, is a knowledge that to regress in some way is human. As neotonous humans, we resemble a train stationed in Pittsburgh whose wheels are wild to get to New York, but before leaving, it backs up to Chicago. We see countryside going by as we back away from New York. In Chicago some trains break down and we never do begin the journey toward our goal. Some trains just continue to back up.

When we look at animals, we don't feel that to regress is mouse-like, nor that to regress is wolverinelike. On the contrary, wolverines, mice, herons, and wolves seem to accept without difficulty the sacrifices required of them as parents. Among birds, sometimes the male sits on the eggs, sometimes the female. Among wolves, sometimes the male wolf endures the endless irritating play of the cubs, sometimes the female endures it; sometimes both become thin in their felt need to give food to the cubs first. Extreme conditions such as enforced zoo life can destroy such habits, but flight from parental maturity is rarely seen in the animal kingdom.

The strategy of putting the new brain in charge of checking out the environment paid dividends for a long time. So long as the neocortex could follow with its marvelous intensity the sensual and natural life all around it, ice floes and boa constrictors, the human child managed to become relatively adult. But today we are lying to ourselves about the renaissance the computer will bring. It will bring nothing. What it means is that the neocortex is finally eating itself.

SOMETIMES POEMS SHOW THE NEOCORTEX DOING WHAT GIVES IT vigor—scanning the natural world for every trace of life that will help us tune to the environment in the absence of programmed responses. Brains in that situation are rigorists, as described in the title of Marianne Moore's poem:

Rigorists

'We saw reindeer
browsing,' a friend who'd been in Lapland, said:
'finding their own food; they are adapted

to scant reino
or pasture, yet they can run eleven
miles in fifty minutes; the feet spread when

the snow is soft,
and act as snow-shoes. They are rigorists,
however handsomely cutwork artists

of Lapland and
Siberia elaborate the trace
or saddle-girth with saw-tooth leather lace.

One looked at us
with its firm face part brown, part white,—a queen
of alpine flowers. Santa Claus' reindeer, seen

at last, had grey-
brown fur, with a neck like edelweiss or
*lion's foot,—*leontopodium *more*

exactly.' And
this candelabrum-headed ornament
for a place where ornaments are scarce, sent

to Alaska,
was a gift preventing the extinction
of the Esquimo. The battle was won

by a quiet man,
Sheldon Jackson, evangel to that race
whose reprieve he read in the reindeer's face.

Pablo Neruda wrote a book of poems called *Residencia en la Tierra*, or *Being at Home on the Earth*; there, and in his later book *Odes on Simple Things*, he makes a lovely union of physical objects and his brain:

Ode to My Socks

Maru Mori brought me
a pair
of socks
which she knitted herself
with her sheep-herder's hands,
two socks as soft
as rabbits.
I slipped my feet
into them
as though into

two
cases
knitted
with threads of
twilight
and goatskin.
Violent socks,
my feet were
two fish made
of wool,
two long sharks
seablue, shot
through
by one golden thread,
two immense blackbirds,
two cannons,
my feet
were honored
in this way
by
these
heavenly
socks.
They were
so handsome
for the first time
my feet seemed to me
unacceptable,
like two decrepit
firemen, firemen
unworthy
of that woven
fire,
of those glowing
socks.

Nevertheless
I resisted
the sharp temptation
to save them somewhere
as students
keep
fireflies,
as learned men
collect
sacred texts,
I resisted
the mad impulse
to put them
in a golden
cage
and each day give them
birdseed
and pieces of pink melon.
Like explorers
in the jungle who hand
over the very rare
green deer
to the spit
and eat it
with remorse,
I stretched out
my feet
and pulled on
the
magnificent
socks
and
then my shoes.

The moral
of my ode is this:
beauty is twice
beauty
and what is good is doubly
good
when it is a matter of two socks
made of wool
in winter.

Part Two

INSIDE FAMILIES

CHAPTER FOUR

The Adventures of Ganesha: A Hindu Story

PEOPLE ARE NOTICING THAT THE OEDIPUS STORY IS BECOMING less and less applicable in our present society. It doesn't describe current father-son relations. Not only do young men not want to kill their father; many have never even met him. Father-longing is beginning to replace father-anger. That longing is palpable in maximum-security prisons, as well as in kindergartens, where small boys tend to hold onto the trouser legs of any man who enters the room and don't want to let him go.

Father-hunger is often accompanied by a sense of the son's increased responsibility for his mother: "You are the man of the house now." Sons, in the absence of protective adult males, appoint themselves to be their mother's guardian.

A myth still current in India describes this guardianship in story form: the son at the door of his mother's chamber.

Ganesha

Once upon a time, the great Goddess Parvati, the Daughter of the Mountains, enjoyed her own sacred place inside her house. It was a bath and a bedroom and a place for her ceremonies. Nandin the bull guarded the door for her, particularly when she was bathing. One day her husband, Shiva, the Lord of the Dance, arrived unexpectedly from a long period of ascetic meditation in the mountains, pushed Nandin aside, and went into the room. The Daughter of the Mountains stood up embarrassed. Later she thought to herself, "I need a servant of my own, a man of some substance, who will obey me and no one else. I want a man who will not separate himself from me by more than the width of a hair."

She said to Shiva, "I want a son." And went on: "When you have conceived a child, you can return to your yoga, great lord. I will bring up the son and you can be a yogi. I yearn painfully for the kiss of a son's mouth; and since you took me for your wife, you should give me a son. Your son will not desire marriage for himself, if you like, so you will not have grandsons and descendants."

In the Bridhaddana Purana, Shiva says:

"Daughter of the mountain, I am not a householder, and I have no need for a son. This wicked group of gods gave you to me as a wife, but a wife is surely the greatest fetter for a man who is without passion. Besides, children are a noose and they are like the stake that keeps one from roaming. A householder needs a son and wealth; he needs a wife in order to obtain a son, and he needs sons in order to make offerings to the ancestors when he himself is dead. But if I do not die, goddess, why do I need a son? Where there is no disease, what's the point of medicine? Come, you are a female and I am a male. Let us enjoy being the causes from which children arise, and let us rejoice in the pleasures between men and women, forgetting about children entirely."

Parvati does not accept his answer, and she decides to create a son on her own. The next time she has her bath, she takes some rubbings from her skin, or, other versions say, unguents from the marriage bed, and creates a son. The Shiva Purana says:

As she was thinking in this way, she rubbed some of the dirt from her body and created a young man who possessed all good qualities:

handsome, well-bodied, sturdy, well-adorned, and very brave and strong. She gave him many garments, many ornaments, many blessings. "You are my very own son. You belong to me as no one else does."

After some time, Shiva returns from his meditation practice on a mountain. The Shiva Purana says:

Shiva, who indulges in every form of play and is expert in all, arrived at her door. Ganadhipa [Ganesha], not knowing he was the lord Shiva, said, "You cannot enter without my mother's permission. She is taking her bath. Where are you going? You must leave." And after he said this he picked up his staff and pushed Shiva back. Then Shiva, seeing all this, said, "You are such a fool! Don't you know who I am? I am none other than Shiva!" But then Ganesha beat him with his staff, and Shiva, who is skilled in all forms of play, became enraged and said, "What a fool! Don't you even know that I am Shiva, the husband of Parvati? Little boy, I am going into my house, why do you block my way?"

The Skanda Purana says:

Ganesha struck the great lord with his axe; but the great lord, raising his trident, struck off Ganesha's head, which fell to the ground. When Parvati saw that her son had fallen to the ground in this way, she began to cry loudly. And when Ganesha collapsed on the ground there arose a great lamentation throughout the whole world.

The Shiva Purana says:

Astonished at this, Shiva took his son's head in his hand and said sweetly to the goddess, "Do not cry, lovely Parvati, though you grieve for your son. No grief is greater than that for a son, but nothing so withers the soul. Stop your sorrowing. I will bring him back to life. Goddess, join his head onto his shoulders." And so Parvati joined that head on as he had told her to do, but it did not join properly.

Shiva said to his attendants: "Go in the northern direction and whatever person you meet first, cut off his head and fit it onto this body."

The attendants go north, and the first being they meet is an elephant. The attendants cut off the elephant's head.

Shiva, using his magic powers, now joins the elephant head to the boy's body, and after holy words and appropriate water and ritual, Ganesha comes to life as though "he had awakened from sleep."

That's the story.

Some Commentary

Parvati, the Daughter of the Mountains, and Shiva, the Lord of the Dance, have a long history together. Still earlier, each for centuries had their own worshippers. Parvati has associations with the independent Lady of the Beasts, known throughout the Mediterranean and often described in Babylonian and Hittite mythology. On seals she is pictured standing between two wild goats whose forefeet are lifted, or standing between two subservient lions. The Greeks associated this energy with their goddess Artemis. Most observers agree that she must have been a favorite of the early hunting culture, for it is always wild animals she has as her allies. She is powerful in herself; she seems to have no consort in archaic times.

Shiva goes just as far back in prehistorical life. Alain Danielou's book *Shiva and Dionysus* details the association between Dionysus and Shiva, and connects both with the Celtic god Cernunnos, who, we recall, wore a set of antlers on his head. Both Cernunnos and Shiva are connected to meditation and asceticism; Cernunnos is shown in meditation posture on the ancient Celtic silver bowl called the Gundestrop Cauldron. Shiva became an immense deity in India, and remains so. Like Parvati, his association is with mountainous territories, extravagant behavior, wildness.

It is possible that after humans moved from the hunting to the agricultural stage, which soon involved city life, the two divinities were brought together. We find the mythological material about

Shiva and Parvati recorded in the ancient Puranas. These English translations are taken, with slight changes, from Paul Courtright's fine book *Ganesa, Lord of Obstacles, Lord of Beginnings*. We see the two in our story living inside a house, doing domestic things, like the people who worship them, though each keeps a separate nature.

In the Western tradition, the closest story we have describes the situation of Penelope and her son Telemachus while Odysseus is away. There are many parallels. Odysseus has been gone for much of his son's life. (Alix Pirani says, with a sigh, "It is the job of the father to be absent.") He, too, spends years encountering dangerous forces—and gathering strength. After ten years, he returns to Ithaca and smuggles himself back into his own house.

Telemachus in a certain way has also been the guardian of his mother's bedroom. Dozens of suitors live at the palace, eating all the food and demanding that, since Odysseus is likely lost, she choose one of them as her wife and bed partner. Telemachus is her only male ally. She puts the suitors off by tricking them: she promises she will marry one of them when her tapestry, on which she works all day, is done; but at night she stays up undoing what she has created in the day. This is lovely, and gives a hint that she, too, is a great goddess who can create and uncreate. Her power is enormous, like Parvati's.

When Odysseus at last arrives home, we have a meeting of two complementary mythological forces, that of Odysseus, who wanders and deals with dangerous divinities, and that of Penelope, who stays at the center and creates; to that degree, the scene is parallel to the moment of Shiva's return to Parvati.

The two stories part ways now, however. Telemachus has already left the house to find his father, and so, on his father's return, a reconciliation has been prepared. And the two of them, with Penelope's help, dispose of the suitors (all are killed), and we settle down to a ritual group of three—Odysseus, Penelope, and their son—a situation very like Shiva, Parvati, and their son Ganesha. It parallels the Father, the Mother, and Jesus during the European Middle Ages. Earlier the Catholic Church had exiled the feminine element; and the trio became Father, Son, and Holy Ghost. But the worship of Mary grew during the Middle Ages so that by the year 1200 the family of Father, Mother, and Jesus was together again. Europe could not sustain that vision, and it fell apart once more during the Reformation, although in India the vision has remained firm. Ganesha is fanciful, forgiving, greedy for sweets, powerful, and fond of humans, and millions of people in India, rich and poor, pray to him every day.

Our task here is not to continue comparisons on the theological level but to relate the theme of the son guarding the mother's bedroom, common in both Telemachus and Ganesha, to the society that we see around us in the United States.

I think the Ganesha story is a blessing. It fits our current society more closely than the Oedipus story, which we're all tired of anyway. Women in the United States are re-securing some of their sovereignty; and that is very good. Sons often feel more weight now in their relationship with their mothers than with their fathers. That fact stands as a testimony to a profound change.

Through the details of the Ganesha story we can sense the complicated feelings that some sons of single mothers and absent fathers have, feelings we rarely see pictured in paternalistic literature and art.

In the Oedipus story the father dies, killed by the son; the mother hangs herself when the truth is known; and the son regrets his entire life and puts out his eyes with a hat pin. If that's what the patriarchy was really like, it's a wonder we didn't leave it earlier.

In the Ganesha story, the father can and does live, and the mother keeps her sovereignty and in fact creates a new god. The mother goes on with her life as well, and the son continues to live. As the distinguished poet and scholar, the late A. R. Ramanujan remarks, the son is "restored to proximity with his mother, though not to intimacy." The story brings in fresh viewpoints, and it may model new father-son and mother-son relationships that allow continuity and "proximity."

Thoughts on the Story

THE MOMENT GANESHA'S HEAD FELL, PARVATI'S GREAT CRY ROSE: "a great lamentation arose throughout the whole world." This lamentation reminds us of Demeter's inconsolable weeping when Persephone disappeared into the underworld, carried off by Pluto. Greek women in ancient times repeated this ritual each year, acting out their grief in a private and yet communal way, walking in groups along the river. Women grieved so for days. The lamentation, according to contemporary accounts, worked to heal losses suffered by women, including losses of daughters by death or by marriage, or, inwardly, the death of their own "girl" when the women themselves reached the age of marriage.

When Parvati sees that her son has been restored to life, she too uses her power, and declares that Ganesha shall be raised to the level of a god and given important tasks. He becomes the god in charge of removing obstacles, so he is a god that helps all human endeavors. He is the God of Obstacles and of Categories. There is a statue of him in most Indian houses, for he is a favorite god. He helps all beginnings. Usually he has a paunchy stomach, suggesting how fond he is—being still a boy in some ways—of sweets. He has four arms, and sometimes his toenails are painted red. The elephant represents the greater cosmos, the macrocosm, all that is beyond the moon and stars. The boy's body represents the small cosmos, the microcosm. The statue, then, says that a human being has in his or her person the entire cosmos, with all its spiritual energies and powers.

The doorkeeper myth gives a place for the mother's grieving. Every mother wants her son to receive a "new head," and yet so much that was sweet and delicious in their past together is gone when the new head is placed. When the boy does receive a new head, he somehow is part of the universe in a deeper way than before. He has shifted from the maternal realm to the social world.

The Ganesha story is not to be taken literally. It does not say to fathers, "Cut off your son's head." It does not mean violence between father and son. One could say that the gods do things so that human beings do not have to. The story is about working through the father's competitiveness with the son, and the son's attachment to the mother, without anyone getting killed, and without the affectionate feelings being destroyed. The myth also recognizes that something is cut away, and a new identity or head has to be taken from the unknown world of wild/tame things.

MANY A SON IN OUR CULTURE FEELS HE HAS BEEN APPOINTED TO stand where he already is: at that dangerous, luminous, liminal, threshold place between the world and his mother's bedroom, between the intruders and her bath, between the world of ten thousand things and her privacy. But we recognize too that the son's sense that he has to guard his mother's bedroom door is often a fantasy on the son's part.

A child's fantasies when living alone with his mother will be different from a child's fantasies when two parents are present. There are boys in the United States who now find themselves standing at the entrance of their mother's holy sanctum that is redolent with perfumes, silk clothes, mysterious laughter, and godly, attractive smells. The world outside is full of uncertainty around where the father is, who he is, and why he is not here.

If both parents are in the house, the boy still feels the mystery of the mother's room, but he doesn't have to do anything. It's as if the father's presence performs the protection. The son of the single mother receives a task he is too young to perform.

The fantasies around this task are highly disturbing to the young man. He has to protect the mother and take over the job the father would have had. In *East of Eden* James Dean played such a son, agonized over a "bad mother" who had vanished when he was young and who has now become the madam of a whorehouse. James Dean, alone, contacts and confronts the mother. This task is a little too complicated for a boy that age; moreover, the doorkeeping task inflates a son in a dangerous way, especially if he appoints himself a doorkeeper too early.

Even boys raised in two-parent homes remember the magical feeling of their mothers' bedroom—a curved dressing table, a mirror facing the room, and on the dressing table arranged perhaps shepherd boy and girl figures, jewelry boxes holding pins, rings, brooches, and the perfume bottles, the powder boxes, the dozen scents all mingling together.

If the father dies and the mother remarries, the son accepts the task in a deeper way. One could say such a son is guarding the door behind which his real mother and father conceived him. It will be anguish for him to see a stepfather or boyfriend enter that sacred room—real or symbolic—where he was conceived.

In most houses (despite what Freud interpolates from the Oedipus story), the son isn't lustful himself—he doesn't want to sleep with his mother, which would violate his parents' bedroom in a parallel way—but he does want to preserve the sanctity of that ritual place from any new intruder. There's a lot of anguish and possibility of failure here, for son or daughter.

From the mother's point of view, her bedroom is more than a bedroom. Like her bath, the bedroom is a ritual place where she guards the mysteries of the feminine. Those perfume bottles, and powder boxes, the mirrors, and the small shepherd and shepherdess figures in china or the New Age goddess emblems are representatives of the female divinities. Moreover, the bedroom is where she prepares to receive the future generations passing through her. Her room is the sacred place where the yang and yin forces, the overbright and the overshrouded, meet. A meeting place for such spacious forces needs to be honored with appropriate grace and some fierceness. If the father is gone, whom can she ask to do that but the son?

AND HOW DOES LIFE GO FOR SONS WHO ARE DOORKEEPERS OF their mother's holy bedroom? In many single-mother houses—with no blame to the mother—the son can do nothing but pull the pillow over his head and live with the knowledge of his repeated failures to keep intruders out. In more familiar terms he feels himself to be "the man of the house," a knight defending the castle, but he can't get the drawbridge to stay up.

The mysterious mood of the mother-protecting son (who fails) is penetrating the entire culture, in ways we don't understand.

A mother told me a story that suggests how deeply the son feels the doorkeeper impulse. She was very conscious of the way her son might feel about a man other than his own father in the house, and so for years she never met a lover in the apartment. She was very surprised when her son, at twelve, gave her as a birthday present a plaque that read:

Good Girls Go to Heaven.
Bad Girls Go Everywhere.

"Where shall I put this?" she asked. "You could hang it on your bedroom door," he replied. A few months later he said in an affectionate way: "Are you gay, or just a nerd?" He must have had a longing to test his powers.

Young boys with an absent father tend to remain doorkeepers through the latency period from age five to ten, and many sons then enter adolescence with that curious flatness and hopelessness that we sense in so many young men. James Dean's face looked as if he had failed at something that was dear to women; he is not James Cagney, who looked like a father-puncher, nor John Wayne, whom some women admired as they might admire a prize ram. James Dean carried the charm of a young man who had died—or fallen—in some fight for women. Trying to protect his mother's sacred space was possibly his battle, and even the failure to do it successfully would register on his face as a radiance perceptible to some. Elvis Presley is a second example of a movie-star doorkeeper. He was a mother's boy, but not the nice choirboy that white families knew. Rather, he was a doorkeeper who had learned sexual moves from rhythm-and-blues performers. He mimicked what went on in his mother's room on the other side of the door. His hip movements, so wicked and boyish, resembled the deceiving partridge's flapping walk to direct attention away from the eggs. He draws all attention to himself with his pelvic dance so that no one would think of going through the door.

It appears that no genuine father ever showed up on the doorstep and pushed Elvis away. He looks like a son who was never *seen* by an elder in a mentoring way. Certainly Colonel Tom Parker never *saw* who he was. Young women saw him; his mother saw him; but when you watch Elvis Presley, you're looking at a boy that no older man ever blessed with his eyes. We remember the swingset he always kept at Graceland. Elvis's daughter would swing in it, but the biographers say that when she wasn't there, Elvis occasionally took shots at the swing set. In Elvis's world, the missing father never came back from the war; Elvis kept holding the door of his mother's bedroom until, numbing his pain with drugs, he died of his terminal adolescence—which to him felt like old age.

THOSE WHO FIGHT WITH INTRUDERS, AS GANESHA DID, SOME-times win, sometimes lose. One young man told me the story of his doorkeeping: His own father, whom he didn't know, was long gone. When he was ten or so, his mother's lover moved in. Later the boyfriend became abusive to the mother, and she threw him out with all his stuff. That night the boyfriend returned and kicked in the door. When the ten-year-old son went downstairs in the morning, he found the mother gone and the man lying in bed, drunk, with a bottle of whiskey and a .44 lying on the floor near the bed. "I went in the kitchen and brought back two knives to kill him," the son said, "but I knew I wasn't strong enough." He went to the window and motioned to a cop to come up, but the policeman said he could do nothing without a warrant.

"What did you do?" I asked him. "I went upstairs and told my uncle to hold my sister," he replied. "Then I went to the kitchen and found the Crisco. I heated it in a frying pan, and then I brought it into the bedroom and threw it on his face."

What happened then? "Well, I had to hide out at my grandfather's for three weeks or so. He came back the next morning with some blisters on his face, but he never bothered my mother again."

This is a horrible story, but we find variants of it everywhere in our culture now.

Another man said that when he was a boy, he often heard his mother downstairs screaming because the stepfather was beating her. One day he called the stepfather up the stairs and then pushed him back down.

Both doorkeepers survived the test, at considerable risk to themselves and some damage to the perpetrators. Events like this happen all over the United States every day.

We have been told that Bill Clinton, as a boy of fourteen, intervened with his stepfather. David Maraniss reports: "Billy stormed into his parents' bedroom one evening when he heard his stepfather yelling at his mother, demanded that Roger stand and face him, and ordered Roger never to strike his mother again." The abuse slowed, but continued for a while. His intervention was a good doorkeeper tactic, and clearly the most powerful act he took as a boy; it gave him confidence that many milder sons lack. He also must have learned that his support will come from women, and that most men are not to be trusted.

It is invigorating to fight one's stepfather, if the fight is just, but the victory doesn't bring as much treasure as a battle with one's father. A son says: "He looks like me. And so I win some battles with myself if I win a battle with him." Yet even to start it, even to shout about an injustice, makes the son feel that an event has taken place. When the son fights his own father, tells him to go to hell, rages at him, something is accomplished by the act no matter what the father says back to him. The son still wins. He said the brave thing, did the brave thing, and the self-assertion toward his father helps center all his life.

Receiving a New Head in Our Culture

WHEN A YOUNG MAN IN OUR CULTURE ARRIVES AT THE END OF adolescence, the river of secularity typically carries him over the waterfall and he's out in the big world. The speakers at his high school graduation will say, "The future belongs to you." But the speaker doesn't mention to whom the student belongs. He belongs to nothing; he belongs to the river; he belongs to the trash at the bottom of the waterfall. He belongs to light beer, and sitcoms about bars, and forgetting. In ten years his muscles will be looser than they were at graduation, and high school will be very nearly his last experience of form. Whether he graduated from an eastern college or not, went to law school or not, he will find around him a group centered on the acquisitive instinct, by which I mean that impulse toward taking and consuming. Our country has adopted that impulse instead of some religious or mythological theme as a unifying theme.

Many economic and industrial forces have worked to create the sibling society. The son who drifts along in the commercialized, secular society, with no help from elders or community, no help in preparing for adulthood, goes usually one of three ways.

First, he may become a materialist, whether living in a trailer house in Montana or in a yuppie apartment in SoHo, and, the hunger never satisfied, becomes the angry white male or the angry black male.

Second, he may become a lightheaded spirit boy, which so many did in the 1960s, sitting in a zendo, flying to India to see the Maharishi, climbing towers at night, eating leafy vegetables, trying to embody the purity his mother would have had, had he been a better—he thinks—doorkeeper. It may be the road of purity, but he never becomes grounded in his own body.

Third, he may go the way of the alienated, empty "microphone fiends." For them, "everything has come under the anti-aura of the inauthentic, everything is already co-opted, already an act." They sit in basements, or they play video games for hours. They hardly know who their parents are. "There is a tendency to keep everything at a distance, to treat everything ironically, with no investment in one's investment."

AGAIN, THE GANESHA STORY IS NOT TO BE TAKEN LITERALLY. IT does not say to the father, "Cut off your son's head." Shiva is not human. The story says that if all goes well with a son, some large force *will* take off the son's head and give him a new perspective that leads to depth.

The boy's old head represented his infantile desirousness, his greediness for sweets, power, and maternal comfort.

Arthurian scholars speculate that when a young Celt presented himself to Arthur and was accepted into Arthur's group, he was ritually asked, "What do you want from Arthur?" The ritual answer was "A haircut." When, in the *Mabinogion*, Culwich, as the Celtic young man is named, enters Arthur's court, he rides his horse directly into the castle; so we know that some socialization is in order. Similarly, Ganesha's beheading resembles the cutting of an aspirant's hair. Middle Ages monks received a "tonsure" to mark their entry into monastic life.

Of course, the advertising industry is utterly opposed to ending infantilism. The ad companies want the boy's infantile desirousness to continue—he should keep his desire for fast food, for M&M's, for CDs, for filled refrigerators.

WHAT COULD A "SECOND BIRTH" MEAN IN OUR CULTURE? THE beheading of Ganesha and restoration of his head could be considered as an initiation. Initiation traditions ask that the young initiate "die," and then receive a second birth, which is symbolized by a new name. The name *Ganesha* is not given to Parvati's son until he has accepted the elephant's head, which in turn connects him to the wild. For us it means in part that the young man or woman is offered a way out of the meaningless consumer society. If the consumer society is determined to hold to literalness, if it continues to mock all initiation of boys and girls, slandering all ritual work as primitive, then we will have disappointed mothers whose sons remain dependent on them at forty; young women who have disappointments of their own, which we will discuss later, and who are also disappointed when they can't find a man adult enough to take on the responsibilities of fatherhood; and disappointed young men, who cannot struggle with their father in the real world or the symbolic world. Such a son endures an unfruitful suffering, which consists in never being able to move away from his mother's doorway. Such young men will waste much of their life before they receive the "new head" that gives them power over worlds.

We do not value initiation of young men or women, because we can't imagine invisible gifts anymore. Instead of listening to the passions of the gods, we watch utterly banal human beings on talk shows describe their degraded and repetitive brutalities toward each other. Talk shows are encouraging a massive regression to the literal state that should have been bypassed long ago.

Getting a new head is not the same thing as getting a new arm or a new leg, or a new aluminum hipbone. By the head we mean the entire nervous system. A new head means a whole new mode of looking at the world. To some extent, this new mode implies looking at the world in a way that is different from the way our families have looked at the world, and it implies a new mode of being looked at by others.

Many mothers and fathers feel disappointed in their sons these days. We could say that many American young men are no longer trying hard to be great teachers or great scientists or great pilots and then failing: they aren't trying in the first place. All over the country there are thirty-five-year-old men living with their mothers. Many don't want to marry and have children; it's too much hassle.

Businessmen don't try to be fair to their employees, students take the easiest courses, then plagiarize and expect approval if they are caught, administrators constantly steal money meant for the poor and find that natural. Doctors diagnosing a problem don't try to think their way through to the deeper life issues that cause illness, but administer the drug they have been told is appropriate.

In some punk rock now, as critics have reported, to play music without mistakes is seen as evidence of dishonesty and artificiality. Sloppy technique becomes evidence of honest expression.

As for artists, a learned discipline that might previously have led to a breakthrough is not attempted. Any one tradition is regarded as far too limiting. The artist then can become eclectic, imagine him- or herself as an honorary Native American, an honorary hippie, or an honorary Aborigine. A life of eclecticism usually means a life without the authentic. John Ashbery will provide fantasy poems, the Disney studios will provide fantasy deer, video games will provide fantasy death, and the Internet will provide fantasy friendship or fantasy sex.

It used to be the intent of those providing the first year of college to bring the student into a wholly new world. Often that happened. Sons of immigrants who had lived in a survival dog-eat-dog kind of frontier life found themselves suddenly amazed by philosophical talk, by religious passion, and sometimes simply by beauty. We can still feel that surprise in people like Sherwood Anderson, Kenneth Rexroth, and Willa Cather, who suddenly saw worlds, distances, horizons, and intensities of discipline of which their parents knew nothing. Gertrude Stein represented something like that in Paris, and passed on her surprise to Ernest Hemingway when he was a young man.

Now, as we know, colleges no longer provide such arrangements. Rexroth pointed out in the 1960s that our colleges and universities were becoming mere training grounds for corporations; they more and more resemble factories that turn out standardized parts, in this case standardized human beings. And since the 1960s, television has interposed itself between children and the world of depth so that the children receive so many snippets of philosophical thought, so many old rags used to wipe Michelangelo's face, that nothing they meet in college amazes them.

Receiving a new world of meaning today would involve complicated experiences far beyond reading a book on acceptable virtues. The act of beheading is chosen to suggest the difficulty of the enterprise; and the elephant, the oldest domesticated creature that is yet wild, is chosen to suggest how deeply the whole body would be affected. The "body-soul" needs to be changed in order to receive what Joseph Campbell calls "the inexaustible energies of the cosmos" that pour down toward human beings. Without gratitude to energies much greater than our own, there will be no new meanings. It could be said that we lack the imagination now to imagine any new power to whom we could be grateful. The procedure for young men and women would ask a reintroduction to the dangerous energies of nature, as some Native Americans still ask from their youth. The process is messy, and needs teachers, the out-of-doors, and lots of time.

We realize more and more that new meanings cannot be created entirely out of anger. Deconstructionist anger, postmodernist anger, some radical feminist anger such as Andrea Dworkin's, does not, even though it produces excitement, produce genuine justice. The "inexhaustible energies of the cosmos" cannot be called down by anger. They are called by extremely elaborate practices and stories.

In the inner cities, beheading is taking place without restoration. The father, as the Shiva story makes clear, has to participate in the restoration. If we and the television anchors could grieve over the young men at twelve killing each other and bystanders—by stopping all activity for ten minutes every day—instead of mechanically adding the numbers up, we might come closer to new meanings. If we could feel the grief young girls experience now because the feminine is brutalized, courtesy gone, grace utterly absent in high schools, genuine beauty eradicated by haste and analysis, empathy evaporated in the brutal songs they hear, we would be closer to the cry of Parvati. If we could realize the massive disrespect for the feminine that takes place every day, we could help one another to go "north," toward passion.

For grown men, serious change today usually means moving into expressiveness. It means leaving the tightly controlled, work-dominated, slavelike closed-mouthedness that has already de-stroyed their relationships with their families; it means they must move into expression of feeling, reconnection with nature, recon-nection with the feminine, reconnection with the deeper side of masculinity.

In daily life, without realizing it, we often meet ordinary people who have received new ways of being. Some of those are Alcoholics Anonymous people. Almost to a person, they feel amazed and grate-ful everyday for losing their old family perspective, which was an alcoholic perspective probably going back five or six generations. Once a week, they stand up in the AA meeting and say, "I am John, and I have a new head." Such people have to put it differently, lest they get inflated and find the old head fastened back on.

Our culture, particularly its rationalists among us, is so afraid of new meanings—or so full of despair at being unable to find them—that rationalist reporters make more and more fun of AA people. I bring this up to emphasize that a person with new meanings does not necessarily surface today as a great personality; he or she is more likely to live among the unseen. Perhaps this is because people either find a new perspective or they die.

When Mother Teresa went to New York after years of picking up the dying street people in Calcutta, she visited an an elderly Ameri-can woman in her Brooklyn apartment who was afraid to go out. Mother Teresa said, "Even in India I've never seen poverty like this." We have double poverty, from lack of money and absence of what we could call vertical passion.

If a young man or woman does not lose the head ritually, and if the drops of blood, metaphorically, do not hit the ground, then the blood appears magnified somewhere else—hallucinated, gigantic, on the television and movie screens. We go into a theater and see exploding body parts flying at us, severed heads flying past the screen and out.

WE KNOW THAT AMONG NATIVE AMERICANS ALWAYS, IN EACH tribe, in each family, parents never stopped longing for a new head for the son. It was the job of the elders to help the young ones receive that new head. In some Sioux tribes, the elders, after preparing a young man, would send him out on top of Bear Butte or some other isolated holy place with instructions like "Find some small cave, go into it, and stay there for three days without food or water." Sometimes a wild animal, such as an eagle, would enter the cave, and the boy would not be the same afterward. Poor Wolf, a Gros Ventre man, describes something similar that happened to him when he was a boy.

> *When I was seventeen years of age, I had the smallpox. I was left alone in a lodge, helpless, weak, and my eyes nearly closed. A bear came in and walked up to where I was lying. He sat down with his back pressed against me, and began to scratch his breast with his forepaws. By and by he got up and walked out of the lodge. Was I dreaming or had it really happened? While I was thinking it over, the bear returned, and while I trembled in fear, went through the same motions again, and then went off, leaving me unharmed. I thought surely the bear has had mercy on me. When my father came again, we talked it over and agreed that the bear had pitied me. After that I worshipped the bear, and in the dance I wore anklets of bears' teeth.*

Poor Wolf had received something amazing and new, and the only thing left to do was to throw away what he no longer needed. In his journal, he describes the numerous objects he had loved for years: a dried turtle shell, a muskrat skin, a mink skin, a crane's head, an otter's head, the long hair of the buffalo near the jaw, and a sweet-grass braid that represented a snake with two heads. "Such things as these I took out onto a hill, talked to them, saying, 'I do not need you anymore,' and threw them to the winds. For doing so, Crow Breast, the Gros Ventre chief, called me a fool." Crow Breast here represents the forces in our culture, both right and left, who resist all serious life-changing work. The left regards initiation as silly, and the right as an impediment to production.

To TAKE THE NEXT STEP WILL NOT BE EASY. AS THE CHRISTIAN movement for husbands called the Promise Keepers indicates, our first impulse as Westerners will be to return to literalness, strong father, and patriarchal, fundamentalist form. In the patriarchal trance, the sons keep the same heads as their fathers. The pull backward is powerful, but we can't go back, we will have to go through. Alan McGlashan has remarked that certain forces of chaos and darkness, visible in the Middle Ages, are pressing upward again; and he emphasizes that we need some way *other than war* for these forces to show themselves. The irrational forces are clamoring for recognition. In the contemporary world

> there is . . . for those who dare to look for it an unmistakable flavor of the sinister. What these adolescents are rousing is the sleeping urge to anarchy that hides not only in their hearts but in ours. And we must somehow make room for its reawakening demands. It is a task of enormous difficulty. To crush these anarchic impulses by superior power is to invite catastrophe.

But we must not indulge them naively, either. This is a task for ritual.

The violence of the beheading belongs to the world of myth. It does not belong to the human world, and it doesn't have to happen in the human world. We as modern people cannot "let the gods do it" because we tend to be ignorant of and hostile to the mythological world. There are some things "the gods can do for us," but only if we can imaginatively honor their world.

The sweetness of the Ganesha story distinguishes it from the

Greek story of the angry father-killer. In that story, the relationship of mother and son ends in deep bitterness, isolation, and despair. As we mentioned, the great Indian scholar Ramanujan makes a lovely distinction between proximity and intimacy:

> *The confrontation between father and son for the mother ends with the defeat of the son, followed by his restoration to the proximity of his mother, but not to intimacy with her.*

Every American mother I know continually longs for the post-adolescent son to be restored to some tenderness with her; but many sons, in the absence of elders and initiation, feel tenderness as too dangerous.

The sweet outcome we are talking of requires elders, ritual, and initiation. Ganesha remained in chaos while he carried his own head. Paul Courtright justly remarks, "With the second head comes order and harmony." Order and harmony arrive through the process of socialization, and the story says that socialization can be accomplished only by bringing the son into the resonance of initiation. That, in turn, requires ritual. When a young man does not receive the ritual called here a "new head," he is trapped in the horizontal world; he is exiled from order and harmony.

The father's absence is so pervasive in the sibling society that the mothers now carry an enormous burden; and mothers, no matter which community they live in, know how immense the burdens are that they carry alone. We know that the rituals we have, pitiful and unimaginative, are not working, because the boys are killing each other despite the mothers' care.

We have the possibility now of retrieving some parts of ritual—it is a gift that indigenous cultures all over the world are offering—the reintroduction of intelligent ritual centered not around patriarchal masculine doctrine but around ritual that both men and women can agree on.

Hindu culture has not solved many of its most serious problems, so we cannot consider it a model. Its treatment of women is often disgraceful. And yet we can learn much from it in the way it has preserved the vertical world and softened the relationships between fathers and sons and between mothers and sons.

When a Hindu son goes through the rite *upanayana*, the investiture of sacred thread, the teacher makes the son into a new person, "born again into a male world that is linked to the past through text, sacred speech and gesture. It is a necessity . . . that this process take place." It happens, one could say, at the very moment that the elephant head takes hold, and the son receives the power that accompanies it.

Through this rite, the boy is lifted out of the domestic realm and introduced to the world of the sacred, the world of ritual, the public realm of work and politics, the arena of judgment, discrimination, and discipline. The elders did that for his father and so on into the far past.

Among the Hindus, work in getting rid of greediness and infantilism is scattered among many adults besides those in the immediate family. Paul Courtright remarks that this "initiation work" leaves "the child with the feeling that the pains of maturation rest with forces larger than those of the mother and father."

The sibling society has lost so much ability to see mythologically that both sons and daughters wander in a flat landscape, where demons "flatter than stingrays" hurry between their feet. They do not become mature because they do not become lined up with their ancestors. They can't figure out how to look downward to depth or upward to the divine.

CHAPTER FIVE

The Wild Girl and Her Sister: A Norwegian Story

ONCE IN NORWAY, AT A TIME WHEN ANIMALS SPOKE AND *people still knew their way home, a king and a queen lived out in the country, happily surrounded by mountains and water, and only one thing was wrong: they had no children. The king accepted the situation stoically, but the wife did not. She would tell her story to passersby or to old women she met in the woods; and one day an old woman told her to bring a niece or a nephew into the house, and that would help the situation. So the queen did. She brought in a niece, a lovely girl about nine years old, and soon she could look out and see the girl playing about in the courtyard with the kittens or with a ball.*

One day when the queen looked out, she saw two girls playing there. The other was a black-haired, black-eyed sort of gypsy child. Apparently she and her mother had been walking through the country; the mother was probably waiting somewhere nearby. "Come on in here," the queen said to her niece. "You shouldn't be playing with trash like that." "But I like her," the niece said. "I don't care!" the queen said. "You belong to better people, and you shouldn't be playing with her." Later the gypsy girl said, "She wouldn't say that if she knew what my mother could do." It was only a few minutes before the niece went inside and said, "My friend says that her mother knows something that you should know." "What is it?" "She says that her mother knows how to get a baby."

A few minutes later, the queen arranged for her niece to invite the gypsy woman into the castle. The gypsy woman, also black-haired and black-eyed, and wearing a sort of ragged traveling dress, went in and sat down. The queen said, without any preliminaries, "You know how to get a baby. Is this true?" The gypsy woman replied, "We all have more to do in this world than listen to the things young girls say." She got up and walked out.

A few minutes later, the gypsy girl whispered to the queen: "I think that if you offer my mother a little Akavit or brandy, her tongue might wiggle more." The queen invited the gypsy woman back into the house, and gave her a chair and a little table. After some byplay and chatting and brandy, the conversation went better. The gypsy woman said, "If I understand this situation, you want to have a baby. Listen carefully! Take your bed out into the storehouse where there is a dirt floor. Bring a tub of water. Wash yourself and throw the bathwater under the bed. Then go to sleep. In the morning you will find two flowers growing below the bed. One will be white and beautiful, and the other more red and ugly. You're to pick the white flower, and eat it, and leave the other alone. Is that clear? Thank you for the brandy." Then she got up and left and took her daughter by the hand, and they both disappeared into the woods.

The queen was eager for the sun to go down. When night finally arrived, and all the maids and hired men were asleep, she did as the gypsy woman said. She washed herself and threw the water under her bed. As soon as she woke, she leaped to her feet and looked under the bed. Oh, two flowers were there, one white and brilliant, the other red and darker. She picked the white flower and ate it. It tasted good. I don't know how such things happen, but then her hand reached on its own and picked the other flower as well. And she ate it.

Nine months later, the midwife arrived and the housemaids were all excited. The queen lay in her big bed in the castle, ready to give birth—and a girl came out. As soon as she was born, she rode around the room on a wild goat and waved a huge wooden spoon. Her voice was already huge. She rode up and down, shouting "Mama! Mama!" and waving her big wooden spoon. The new housemaids all fainted, and the mother was so astounded that she couldn't speak. At last she said, "If I'm the mother of this child, God help us all!" The goat girl had some sort of raggedy hood over her head; edges of it hung down over her face and made her look very ugly. No one had ever seen anything like it. When the queen drew back, the goat girl said: "Don't worry, there's another one coming out soon, and she's a little blonde. You'll like her."

A second daughter was born, and sure enough, the queen really liked her. A few months later the queen tried to put the younger girl in a separate room, but the Sweet Girl wouldn't allow it. If the queen sent Tatterhood into some old attic room in the palace, or sent her out into the storehouse where the cod and the lefse were kept, the Sweet Girl would go there, too. She wouldn't allow anyone to separate her from her sister. And that's how they grew up. People talked about it for miles around.

THIS STORY CAN BE TREATED AS A TALE OF A GIRL IN ADOLES-cence. We know that before adolescence the wild part of a girl, the feisty, opinion-filled part, can remain connected with the more socialized "favorite girl" part. But around the fifth grade, trouble begins. After fifth grade, girls often split up with their old best friends. The question of popularity arises. If a girl is seen as a drag or a nerd, her girlfriends may abandon her for the friendship of more popular girls. Even worse, she may abandon herself. It's very difficult for a girl, particularly in our culture, to keep the two parts of herself in balance. The pressure will be to suppress the wild part, the "ugly part," and become utterly engrossed in attractiveness, femininity, passivity, and popularity. Mary Pipher, in her book *Reviving*

Ophelia, quotes Olive Schreiner, who in her autobiography, *The Story of an African Farm*, says: "The world tells us what we are to be and shapes us by the ends it sets before us. To men it says, work. To us, it says, seem."

Mary Pipher adds:

> *In America in the 1990s, the demands of the time are so overwhelming that even the strongest girls keel over in adolescence. The lessons are too difficult and the learning curve too steep for smooth early mastery. Strong girls manage to hold on to some sense of themselves in the high winds.... Soft- and hard-core pornography are everywhere. Sexual and physical assault on girls are at an all-time high. Now girls are more vulnerable and fearful, more likely to have been traumatized and less free to roam about alone. This combination of old stresses and new is poison for our young women.*

She talks of a young girl named Cayenne, who was in trouble.

> *Cayenne told me of a recurring dream in which she was asleep in her upstairs bedroom. She heard footsteps on the stairs and knew who was coming. She listened, terrified, as the steps grew louder. An old man leading a goat walked into her room. He had a long, sharp knife. Cayenne lay in her bed unable to move while he began slicing at her toes. He sliced off pieces of her and fed her to the goat. She usually awoke when he reached her knees. She'd be covered with sweat and her heart would be racing wildly. Afterward she was afraid to go back to sleep for fear the man would return.*
>
> *When she finished I asked her what she thought the dream meant. She said, "It means I'm afraid of being cut up and eaten alive."*

Two personalities live inside each young girl; and we see that the queen in our Norwegian story wanted to make one of them her favorite. But the Sweet Girl would not allow Tatterhood to be sent to a different room, and "they were always together."

One night when they were both about fifteen years old, everyone heard commotion and ruckus outside the castle. From the courtyard, shouts and cries and howls came up. Tatterhood felt frightened at all the noise and ran to her mother. "Oh," the mother said, "it's nothing. It's their night. The trolls get to leave their place in the mountains, you know, and this night is it. They come out and pester human beings and cause trouble and carry on. Pay no attention to them." She told the maids to close all the windows and to make sure the shutters were snapped shut tightly and the doors locked.

When Tatterhood heard the news, she pulled back the bolt on the main door, rode on her goat right into the mob of trolls, and hit them on their heads and backs until they rolled over, yelping and crying. She was having a good time, and shouted louder than they did. The Sweet Girl was very curious about the trolls, but still frightened, so she opened the shutter just a crack to peek out and, wham!—a troll going by at that moment grabbed her head, pulled it off, and in a flash replaced it with a calf's head. It happened so quickly that no one could prevent it. Tatterhood returned home, shut the door, and shouted: "Why didn't anyone take care of this? What kind of people are these?" She was furious at the queen and at all the maids.

Meanwhile, there stood the Sweet Girl, behind a chair, her hands and feet on the floor, lifting her head. She mooed in a pitiful way, and her large ears moved back and forth. When her father walked in and saw her, he fainted.

Now we have a mess. The beautiful daughter has lost her head and received a new ugly head. Boys sometimes say, "You're an ugly old cow." The story tells young girls that they need to put on either an ugly head or a false self. Those are the two choices.

We recall that the goddess Artemis had a bear clan in ancient Greece for young girls, who learned to behave like bears. These girls learned to walk unattractively, comically, heavily, like bears, and made fun of boys they passed; by that means they kept some privacy around themselves during that dangerous time when girls may give in to pressure for premature sexual activity. According to Mary Pipher,

> *In* Smart Girls, Gifted Women, *Barbara Kerr explains the common experiences of girls who grew into strong women. She studied the adolescent years of Marie Curie, Gertrude Stein, Eleanor Roosevelt, Margaret Mead, Georgia O'Keeffe, Maya Angelou and Beverly Sills, and she found that they had in common time by themselves, the ability to fall in love with an idea, a refusal to acknowledge gender limitations and what she called "protective coating." None of them were popular as adolescents and most stayed separate from their peers, not by choice, but because they were rejected. Ironically, this very rejection gave them a protected space in which they could develop their uniqueness.*

We could say that this calf or bear ritual is the ritual missing all over the contemporary West. The advertising forces would not want it to happen. Our culture, we could say, wants the girl after fifth grade—or before—to be utterly absorbed by the desire to be attractive to boys.

> *When things had settled down, and people had stopped fainting, Tatterhood said to her father: "Bring me a ship! I'll go up the fjord. I know where the trolls live. I'll bring my sister's head back myself. Hurry up! We're going to leave tomorrow!"*
>
> *The father said, "I'll arrange for a captain and some seamen." Tatterhood said, "Don't bother! I'll be the captain, I'll be the navigator. Just get me a ship. I'll need some food on board and some hay for my sister. Hurry up with it!"*
>
> *The next morning the ship was ready. The Sweet Girl was brought on board and placed below deck where the hay was. Tatterhood rode her goat onto the ship and trotted up and down the deck, waving her huge wooden spoon. The ship sailed off and soon headed up the fjord where the trolls lived.*
>
> *When she arrived, Tatterhood rode her goat up the mountain. There in a cave the trolls were at their usual stuff, singing and*

drinking and bowling and pushing each other around. Tatterhood could see on the wall her sister's head with its long golden hair. She didn't hesitate. She galloped through the cave on her goat, hitting the trolls right and left with her spoon, and shouting. Before they knew what had happened, she had grabbed the head off the wall and was back on her ship, sailing away before the trolls could reach the shore.

Then she put the Sweet Girl's true head back on her sister's shoulders, and her sister was her sister once more. They felt great merriment and affection for each other.

W<small>E DON'T KNOW HOW MUCH TIME PASSED, IN OUR WORLD,</small> before the Sweet Girl got her head back—perhaps three years. We don't know what the ritual of returning the human head involved. We can sense something serious even in this comical version in which trolls have to stand in for the gods.

Now that the head is back, what will happen in the rest of the story? We can guess from other tales of this sort that our story is probably heading for a wedding of four. Such a wedding happens at the end of the Russian story "Vasilisa the Beautiful," as well as in "Snow White and Rose Red." Marriage is not meant literally, but the emphasis falls on relationships inside the soul. The complicated soul is imagined as made up of four beings, two feminine and two masculine. Antonio Machado said:

How strange! Both of us
  with our instincts!
Suddenly we are four.

If there are two girls here or two sides of the feminine—one sweet and calm and in danger, and the other wild, sour, outrageous, and dangerous to others—there must also be two masculine sides, who will fit with the two feminines to make a foursome, a truly whole person.

On the way home, Tatterhood pulled in at the harbor of another kingdom. She tied up the ship and rode back and forth on her goat along the dock until people began to notice her. "Do you have a king in this place?" she asked.

People said, "Oh yes, we do. He's up there."

"Well, get him down here. I want to talk to him. Is he married?"

"Oh no, he is a widower."

"Good."

The king was informed of this strange scene, and on arriving at the harbor, he inquired politely what it might mean. "I have the most beautiful woman in the world on board this ship. She's my younger sister," Tatterhood replied. She called for the Sweet Girl to come up, and there she was, even more beautiful than before. The king was clearly smitten. "Well, what do you think?" Tatterhood asked. The king said, "I feel as if I've known her before; and I could imagine nothing more wonderful than that she would be my bride." "Good. That's settled," Tatterhood answered. The king continued, "Would it be appropriate if, in the absence of the father, I ask for her hand in marriage through you?"

"Not so fast," Tatterhood said. "This is not so easy as you think. I'm the older sister, and I have to be married first." She was a wild-looking thing, with a hood over half her face, which was sooty anyway, and bits of straw from the calf pen were hanging over her clothes, and she was still mounted on her big, smelly goat. The king said, "Is there anything I can do to expedite . . ."

"Do you have a son?"

"I do, but . . ."

"Never mind the buts, get him down here. If he's any good, I'll marry him. Don't let's waste time."

The son had just been taking fencing lessons. He looked about seventeen and wore an elegant coat with silver buttons and knee breeches. Before he boarded the ship, the king took him aside. "My son," he said, "I need some help from you. I have found the woman whom I wish to marry and which I, God willing, will marry tomorrow; and my request to you is that you agree to marry her sister, whom I will introduce you to now. I hope I've made myself clear."

Well, that's the way things are with kings and their sons, or at least

the way they used to be. The son stood a long time looking at
Tatterhood as she rode up and down the dock shouting at the mountains, and no one who knew him would have said that he looked
happy. However, he agreed.

Early the next morning, the wedding procession started off toward
the church, which was four or five miles away. The Hardanger fiddler
walked ahead, followed by the priest and all the neighbors and
townspeople. After them came the king and the Sweet Girl, riding on
elegant horses. Behind these two came Tatterhood on her goat and the
young prince on his beautiful horse. Tatterhood and the prince rode in
silence a long while. The groom looked depressed. Finally Tatterhood
spoke: "Why don't you say something to me?"

"What should I say to you?"

"You could ask me why I'm riding on this ugly old goat."

The prince pulled himself up and said, "All right, I can say that.
Why are you riding on that ugly old goat?"

"Because it isn't a goat at all!" And it wasn't. Suddenly she was
riding next to him on a handsome, elegant horse, and riding at the
same height as the prince, perhaps a little higher. Some time passed.
The prince said nothing. Tatterhood spoke: "Why don't you say
something to me?"

"What should I say to you?"

"You could ask me why I'm waving this ugly old spoon around in
the air."

"All right, I can do that. Why are you waving that ugly old spoon
around in the air?"

"Because it isn't an ugly old spoon at all!" In an instant she was
holding a silver wand. More time passed in silence. "Why don't you
say something to me?"

"What should I say?"

"You could ask me why I wear this raggedy old hood on my head
and all this soot on my face."

The prince replied: "I can do that! Why are you wearing that
raggedy old hood on your head and all that soot on your face?"

"Because it's not a raggedy old hood at all!" Suddenly she was

*wearing a golden crown, and beneath it a radiant, brilliant face, at
least as fine as her sister's.*

*Things were looking up now, and two handsome couples arrived at
the church door. No one had ever heard the fiddler play better, and the
priest was so excited that the wedding went on for hours. After the
wedding, people ate and danced and drank all evening and through
half the night; and the next morning all the food and beer would
appear again, no one knows how, and the celebration went on that
way for three days. Dancers danced, poets recited poems; even acro-
bats performed. I was invited as a storyteller. They gave me a bottle of
wine made in Napoleon's time, to share with you. But on the way here
it rolled out of my bag and broke, and I don't think we'll ever have
wine like that again in this world.*

I'M NOT SURE WE CAN SAY ANYTHING ABOUT THIS LAST PASSAGE
in relation to ordinary life. Tatterhood asks, "Why don't you say
something to me?" Millions of contemporary women address this
question to men. (Hundreds of young girls walk around with green
hair and ugly leather jackets and tattered jeans, but few speak to
them.) In this story, the man speaks and her lesson is that a man has
to see the ugliness or suffering and speak of it. If a person is limping,
it's important to say "Why are you walking with a limp?" Something changes when a suffering is brought up into language and
spoken, but permission needs to be given for the honesty: "Why
don't you say something to me?" "What should I say?" "You could
ask me why I wear this raggedy old hood on my head and all this
soot on my face." "I can do that! Why *are* you wearing that raggedy
old hood on your head and all that soot on your face?" "Because it's
not a raggedy old hood at all!" Some great gift is given to female
consciousness when people around a woman are able to speak
straight, stop beating about the bush, stand on the truth, so to speak.
The woman needs to have some mystery in herself brought up into
expression; and she knows when the time has come. When the man
responds to that need, he learns expressiveness, and that man,

whether we consider him to be inside Tatterhood or out in the world, or inside himself, helps bring about the change that Tatterhood outside or inside needs. That's as much as we can say about that odd conversation, and the transformations that follow it, because in truth it is a ritual conversation taking place in mythological space.

Mythological Commentary

The Norwegian story probably represents a ritual world as deep as the one the Hindus had and still have. What we see here as trolls were probably once an enormous spiritual force comparable to Shiva. We see in the story how well Tatterhood gets along with this enormous dark spiritual force, which has lost its name. The West has gone through a serious riddance of gods. When Christianity defeated the old religions in the West, the Shivas and Parvatis lost their place. Students of religion observe that defeated gods invariably turn into demons. Numerous trolls and goblins have been reduced to demons by the religious revolution. Tatterhood herself is probably more amusing than she would have been in the original tale. There is truly something fearsome about her, a truth hinted at in her mother's remark when she was born.

Moreover, the whole story unrolls because of a meeting with "gypsies," people who are at the edge of things and have mysterious knowledge. Tatterhood's future existence is symbolized not by the white, so to speak, Christian flower, but by the darker red, pagan, blood-colored flower, which in some versions of this story is also called an "ugly" flower. The mother is warned not to pick it or eat it.

Tatterhood knows ritually exactly how to get her sister's former head back. It's left to us to guess what energies poured into the Sweet Girl during that period in which her human head was gone and the head of what we might call an older divinity was resting on her shoulders.

The magical transformations toward the end of the story, goat to horse, spoon to emblem of power, caul to crown, are astounding. Some force has entered that was not apparent during the girls' childhood. We have the right to assume that the particular power that achieved the transformations must have come from the Sweet Girl, and was received during the time her original head was off.

The changes that Tatterhood herself goes through at the end are odd and do not offer themselves up for rational understanding. She needs the changes in order to be "married." The marriage is a religious or inner event of some kind—a marriage of east, west, north, and south; or a marriage of up, down, right, and left; or a marriage of earth, water, fire, and air.

We notice that our story is also, nakedly, a vertical tale; the underworld leaps up into it, and the story explodes beyond the timid boundaries that sociological or deconstructionist language sets for itself.

A lack of attention to the vertical world is, for a society, dangerous, and the beings below us in the underworld or above us in the heavens do not stop existing or playing just because we don't see them. When, on the appointed night, the dark beings burst out of their underground caves and come leaping into the castle courtyard, Tatterhood isn't afraid of them in the slightest. She rushes out on her goat and bops them on the head with a wooden spoon, laying them out right and left. One might say she's protected by the wild goat; and we recall that the goat was the main animal of Dionysus. The image we are given of her shows a fine balance: the goat clearly stands for the animal part of the personality, the so-called instincts, and it also stands for aggression and for the wildness that's somehow inherent in nature. As Gerard Manley Hopkins said, "There lives the dearest freshness deep down things." The detail of her tattery hood—a mysterious thing that she has on when she is born and doesn't take off until nearly the end of the story—has caught people's imagination for centuries. It is surely a reference to "the caul." The ancient world believed that when an infant is born with a caul, part of the lining of the afterbirth over the head, it means that the person is destined to be a powerful spiritual man or woman. In the Old Testament, Saul was born with a caul. That was a mark of his future royal state. We have to look at such words as *ugly*, then, in a couple of ways. In this case, *ugly* is a code word for spiritually beautiful, or great in spirit.

If the elephant relates Ganesha to the magnificent areas of male divinity, the cow's head relates the sister to the Great Goddess, to the Goddess of Life and Death. We know that Hera changed herself into a white cow, emphasizing her association with the moon; the cow is also sacred to Athena; and the moon goddess Io is a cow, as the goddess Brigit in Celtic mythology is a cow. Plutarch remarks that Isis is often pictured with cow horns, and the cow has to be considered an aspect of Isis. Isis's son at one point cut off her head and replaced it with a cow's head. Isis as a cow is the rain-bringing moon, as Osiris is the bull-sun.

"The inexhaustible energies of the cosmos," in Joseph Campbell's phrase, flow down to us through both "sisters," the meek sister as well as the flamboyant one. This is a surprise, and yet it fits the old tradition that it is the "stone the builders rejected" that becomes the cornerstone of the new temple, and, as the Taoists say, the divine energy is found best in the unnoticed and the small.

We'll leave this story here. We can see that it is at least as complicated as the Ganesha story. The story suggests that it's time for initiation reform for young women. We need to institute something like the Artemis bear-clan to protect young girls from the pressures of the junk culture or siblingism, and institute as well rituals to honor their associations with the divine world.

CHAPTER SIX

What Do Daughters Stand to Lose or Gain in a Sibling Society?

Traditional Stages

I'T'S UNLIKELY THAT A MAN OR WOMAN WOULD BE EXPECTED TO say anything authoritative about the other gender. The stages through which a girl moves on her way toward womanhood, and the possible effect the sibling society might exert on those stages, is something for a woman to write, who knows many times more about these matters than I do. And yet the questions are so important that I am unwilling to leave out this chapter. I will be guided in this piece by the work particularly of Jessica Benjamin and Jean Baker Miller.

The concept they want psychologists to grasp is how deeply the development of women is interactive, how much it is based on participation and affiliation.

TODAY WE KNOW MUCH MORE ABOUT THE BABY'S EXPERIENCES in the womb. Books such as *The Secret Life of the Unborn Child* make everyone aware of what many mothers have always known—namely, that there is much consciousness inside the womb. After several months, the infant is aware of everything the mother says or does; hears a great range of noises, centering most of all on the mother's heartbeat; and responds with kicks or movements of arms and legs to emotions that the mother expresses. The baby's body responds to sadness, to anger, to stories, to music, to individual words.

The baby already knows the sort of world she will be born into, and all the evidence suggests that this time in the womb is an ecstatic age for most souls. Surrounded and nourished, like a queen, the fetus destined to be female moves calmly, step by step. Some researchers compare the female's womb experience to a dancer ascending a spiral staircase; each step appears where it belongs (there are no sudden jumps or moves to the side), and after nine months, the girl emerges radiant and full of energy. The time in the womb has been her first experience of growing by being together, and she will never forget that.

THE NEWBORN GIRL BABY USUALLY FINDS HERSELF, DURING THE first eighteen months after birth, in a love affair with her mother. It is a love between two conscious beings. The baby soon recognizes her mother's face, and the emotions in it, and the two begin a dance together. The mother has a reservoir of voices that the baby can hear, and the baby changes her expression so as to elicit more of those sounds. Sometimes this ecstasy of likeness or participation floods both nervous systems. The baby soon learns to regulate her side of it, for when the intensity becomes too much, she will turn her face aside: she learns that she can do something, she is not helpless, she too has power.

Some psychologists, the Freudians among them, made a serious verbal mistake in settling on the term "object love" for the fascination a human being has for its mother or other beings. "Object love" implies that the baby is a subject, and the mother or another person an inert "object"—like a mineral. But both are subjects. The joy they feel is in the mutual subjectivities, the mutual participations.

Jean Baker Miller and her associates who work at the Stone Center for Developmental Studies at Wellesley argue that most accepted models for development of female babies are wrong. Some of those models were developed through the study of males; and the male principle is that growth occurs through a process of separation: "A Western bias of individualism and a 'Lone Ranger' ethic of meeting challenges underlies most psychological theories of the self." The new ideas say that females grow differently, through cooperative behavior. Jean Baker Miller remarks:

> *I think that the infant begins to develop an internal representation of itself as a kind of being that, for the moment, I will call by a hyphenated term—a "being-in-relationship."*

THE BABY DISCOVERS THAT SHE IS PART OF THE WORLD AROUND her. For example, if she is sad or happy, her mother's face may also grow sad or happy. It's important, then, for the parent to "mirror" the baby's emotions. The therapists around the English psychologist John Bowlby have developed a sentence about that idea, useful for both parents: "A blank face is a biological crime."

The girl baby then experiences exchanges, mingled feelings, participations in this early love affair with her mother. The father, although seen and delighted in, does not really, observers believe, at the start, affect this closeness. The baby girl often feels through her mother the enormous abundance and generosity of the world. The vital center in her solar plexus says "yes" to food, to affection, to excitement, to language, to closeness. This "yes" is the Good Breast. Of course, like everything else, the mother-daughter closeness has its dark side. The daughter also receives from the mother hunger, frustration, and abandonment. Melanie Klein named the experience of hunger, frustration, and abandonment the Bad Breast. In the child's magical thinking, the Bad Breast becomes the witch, who is cold, whose breasts are cold, who is isolated in some hut in the forest, dangerous, an eater, not a feeder. Such witch images are not patriarchal propaganda, but precise images of the child's experience of the Bad Breast. Young children love to hear fairy stories, because certain images help a girl or boy understand that what they have experienced around the good and bad sides of their mother is real, and they are not crazy.

The baby too has a dark or wild side. D. W. Winnicott and his students have put forward the idea that the infants of either gender want at some moments to utterly destroy the mother or whoever is caring for them:

> *It is a healthy thing for a baby to get to know the full extent of her rage. . . . If she really is determined she can hold her breath and go blue in the face, and even have a fit. For a few minutes she really intends to destroy or at least to spoil everyone and everything, and she does not even mind if she destroys herself in the process. Naturally you do what you can to get the child out of this state. It can be said, however, that if a baby cries in a state of rage and feels as if she has destroyed everyone and everything, and yet the people round her remain calm and unhurt, this experience greatly strengthens her ability to see what she feels to be true is not necessarily real. . . .**

At about eighteen months, the daughter begins to notice the father, or enters into play with him more deeply. Jessica Benjamin remarks:

> *Fathers' play with infants differs from mothers': it is more stimulating and novel, less soothing and accurately tuned. Fathers often introduce a higher level of arousal in early interaction—jiggling, bouncing, whooping. The father's novelty and complexity, as opposed to the mother's smoother, more contained play, have been characterized as an aggressive mode of behavior that "fosters differentiation and individuation."* . . .

---

* Writers on childhood, unable to find a neutral pronoun, use "he" or "she" interchangeably for babies. To stay with our subject, "he" was changed to "she" in the above passage by Winnicott.

The girl baby then, if she is welcomed by the father, enters into a passionate relationship with him for a time, perhaps from age one and a half to three. The daughter who experiences this idealistic love finds that it creates a deep resonance in her soul. Whether or not she can recall it later, the experience of loving and being loved by a loving masculine being settles inside her soul like a geological deposit.

If she receives only indifference, abuse, or neglect from a father, nothing will ever convince her later that the masculine is capable of nurturing. These two early loves, the first with the mother, the second with the father, enable her later to move in and out of gender fields with some assurance and ease.

And yet the drawback of the second love is that the daughter will tend to idealize the father and devalue the mother.

The question of "splitting," then, amounts to the perception that the father has intent and the mother has not. Jessica Benjamin puts this matter at the center of her book *Bonds of Love*:

> *No matter what theory you read, the father is always the way into the world. In some contemporary delivery rooms, the father is literally encouraged to cut the umbilical cord. He is the liberator, the proverbial knight in shining armor. The devaluation of the mother that inevitably accompanies the idealization of the father, however, gives the father's role as liberator a special twist for women. It means that their necessary identification with their mothers, with existing femininity, is likely to subvert their struggle for independence.*

Some say the daughter moves her desire in the father's direction because she has already sensed that in this world, or in this family at least, the feminine is valued less than the masculine.

The father seems to represent the way out, a fast river, the road into the great world outside the house, the mountain path that leads away from domesticity, a Saint George who kills the maternal dragon and says, "Follow me."

We know that the daughter has already received great assurance and support from the mother. At the same time, every child fears and desires a return to infant helplessness, a descent into womb waters.

What is the appropriate way, then, for a daughter to move toward the world?

Freud muddled this question disastrously when he developed the idea of "penis envy." What young women really envy is the avenue to the world. According to Jessica Benjamin,

> *little girls are seeking the same thing as little boys, namely, identification with the . . . representative of the outside world.*
>
> *. . . Even today, femininity continues to be identified with passivity, with being the object of someone else's desire, with having no active desire of one's own.*

Jean Baker Miller says that

> *the only thing women lack is practice in the "real world"; this, plus the* opportunity *to practice and the lifelong belief that one has the right to do so.*

We can feel how urgent this split is. A daughter sometimes feels it is a life-or-death matter—this getting to take part in the real world—and yet if she accepts her father's way, his confidence, his lack of fear, his hints about how to believe in the world, she is devaluing her mother and her own gender.

Around age three the daughter enters the exciting, competitive, forbidden, dangerous triangle. She may now claim the father, with whom she has developed a closeness, as hers. If she feels a special affinity with the father (the word implies chemistry), she will find the intrusions by her mother annoying. She may feel herself superior: "I understand him better than she does."

The time from three to five, then, means for the daughter, much turmoil, much jealousy of the mother, and usually much attraction to the forbidden parent. It is the model for all future triangles.

THE FAMOUS LATENCY PERIOD FOLLOWS THIS TURMOIL. JEALousy of the mother may diminish, and the brain feels a new infusion of energy as the daughter tries to figure out what goes on in the world. At this age, acute observations of the world—all its work and all its ways, its varieties of ambition and foolishness, those that Jane Austen brilliantly reveals in the center of her novels—begin. The father recedes temporarily to be a part of the furnishings, and the daughter may spend hours and hours figuring out how to distinguish herself from her mother. Benjamin and others remind us that she is not trying to break from her mother, and the classic images, clean breaks, and repudiation don't apply. The girl wants as much separation as will not damage the relationship, but no more.

Women grow, as Jean Baker Miller and her coworkers of the Stone Center for Developmental Studies at Wellesley College have said, by affiliation. Women's way is to live while encouraging others to live. Jean Baker Miller says: "I do think men are longing for an affiliative mode of living. . . . Men have deprived themselves of this mode, left it with women."

ADOLESCENCE PROPER BEGINS AROUND AGE TEN OR SO. DURING adolescence, the attraction to the father is, for many daughters, intense, bodily, riveting. There is some flirtation with the father, and there is the continuing struggle not to be overwhelmed by the mother's natural power. Some say that the daughter's main task in this stage is to renounce the father. For both son and daughter, the task is to renounce the forbidden parent without repudiating the gender. To renounce the actual father may be heartbreakingly difficult.

The boy, in his obsession with separation, may deny the reality of the one he is separating from (in this case his own mother); but the girl may deny the reality of her own self, in other words, deny her own passion and opinions. Carol Gilligan has spoken at length of the slump girls go into around age thirteen. Before that age, they tend to be feisty, full of opinions, ready to jump in. At about thirteen, many girls abruptly become vague; they say things like "I don't know" when asked for an opinion; they no longer raise their hands, they lose a voice. Observers offer several possible reasons for this change. Decline in self-esteem because of verbal criticism from other girls is one, a longing to attract boys is another, and a disappointment at their own perceived devaluation in the culture is a third. A few may feel that their alliance with the liberating father has failed.

A girl may have decided that her smartness will not help her in the task of affiliation or participation, which she feels important. If her own mother does not have an authentic self, creative, energetic, desiring what she desires, and acting on these desires, the daughter may fall into passivity, or put all her hopes for liberation and creativity on a boyfriend.

This loss of self can amount to loss of intent that in turn can lead toward submission to a dominating male. If she submits, she may begin to feel like "nature," which is traditionally submissive to "man." Jessica Benjamin dislikes the metaphor that women are like nature. It's too easy to say, and it explains the wrong things.

Women, like men, are by "nature" social, and it is the repression of their sociability and social agency—the repression of the social, intersubjective side of the self—that is at issue.

The self is found, then, or refound, by girls through remaining social in every way. Women do not so much separate from their mothers as *recognize* their mothers. The more active the mother is, the better, because the interaction of two active beings will have more desire and intent.

Somewhere inside herself a girl may sense that her mother's

source of power lies bound in her ability at self-sacrifice. In a certain way, self-sacrifice means exactly what it says, that the mother's "self," her intent, her creativity, her inventiveness, her power of intervention in the world, even her sexual desire, is sacrificed for the sake of family and children. Fewer and fewer young women want that power.

Or she can take her father, with his confidence in the world, as a model for outward power, but that will not work if he is absent, or abusive, or indifferent; in any case, it will lead to the split described earlier.

"The 'real' solution to the dilemma of women's desire must include a mother who is articulated as a sexual *subject*, one who expresses her own desire." Jessica Benjamin imagines the development of this sort of mother as the long-term solution of the gender split. She praises clarity of desire in a mother so the daughter can more easily re-identify with the feminine and the world of women while she is still moving outward and engaging the world.

We can point out one more way in which the girl's development at this age diverges from the son's. Her task, many now agree, is to accomplish the work of the affections, which is different from accomplishing the task of separation. Carol Gilligan and Eve Stern have pointed out the deep need in young girls for certain kinds of open space and solitude. Adolescent girls confide to their diaries; there is nothing comparable in boys of that age. Such girls will talk to the diary as if it were a person, and a unique union of affection and solitude comes into being. We recall Virginia Woolf's diaries, and Anne Frank's diaries. Girls often call their diaries "you." They continue affiliation, one might say, by making a loyal friend of their diary, to whom they confide feelings more than events or victories. At this age, girls are willing to accept the masculinity in their natures, much more so than adolescent boys, who tend to reject the feminine in their natures.

Perhaps another function of the diary is to help postpone (because it is an intimate confidante) premature sexual activity.

Losses for Daughters in the Sibling Society

Adolescent girls today are experiencing much difficulty. Mary Pipher remarks that teenage girls have traditionally labored to adjust to their parents' values. But most girls now have a separate and more difficult task—adjusting to the jagged, frightening, half-insane values of junk culture—obsession with popularity, demands for a thin body, for early sexual activity, for early use of alcohol and drugs, and so on.

The shallowness of relationship as pursued in the sibling society, the permission for interchangeable sex partners and "recreational sex," is in the long run damaging to women. Boys claim they feel stronger, but girls declare themselves to feel used, weaker, and abandoned.

In earlier extended families, girls were frequently surrounded with aunts, substitute mothers, and interested grandmothers, which we might call a motherline. Elizabeth Herron and Aaron Kipnis believe that the breakdown of the motherline has serious consequences for daughters. They say, "The narcissism of uninitiated women directly fuels a sibling society and colludes as well with the extended adolescence of men."

Young women tend to be more emotionally mature at eighteen or twenty than men their age, and it is difficult for them to find a partner who is adult enough to carry on a serious relationship, let alone a male adult enough to take on the job of parenting. Many women go along with the common male adolescent behavior, fall out of close touch with mothers, grandmothers, or any older women, and end as uninitiated as the boys.

The French feminist Elisabeth Badinter remarks that in Western culture "passion is headed for extinction." By passion she means high expectations between men and women and the risk of suffering. "Yesterday, their theme was the long process of conquest, strewn with pitfalls and resistance." "Both men and women dream of other things than heartbreak. But even if we wanted to, we could not experience it any more. The conditions for passion no longer exist, either from the social or psychological point of view."

Her statement needs some qualification, and yet we see evidence of the extinction of passion all around us. Those smoky scenes in movies during which the eyes promise each other twenty years of hopeless desire are no longer filmed. The great romantics, such as Clark Gable, shrink to boys like Kevin Costner.

Why should desire disappear, like the red wolf, the passenger pigeon, and the Irish elk, into extinction? We know that passion has always been associated with the overwhelming power of moral and social law. Lovers broke those laws to achieve passion. Badinter says, "By admitting that the heart is no longer *outside* the law, but *above* it, we have played a very dirty trick on desire." Romeo and Juliet, in contrast, prefer to commit suicide together rather than obey the law of their fathers.

Moreover, something has happened to time. Instead of lovers following "society time," requiring long periods of waiting, in which they brooded over each other, at a distance, looking up into the sky, lovers now obey a personal sense of time. A woman said, "We were immediately on very intimate terms. . . . We short-circuited the whole *waiting* period, the time when you find out, when you *dream* about the other, when you wait for him to look at you. Within three days we were already an old married couple."

So our hearts have become changed or mutant. The changed hearts no longer want the tortures of desire, and in a certain sense wouldn't know what to do with the old torments. "The resemblance model goes along with the eradication of desire."

What the sibling society offers men and women in relationship, instead of passion, is the resemblance model. Men are to become more like women, and women more like men. Elisabeth Badinter called her new book in French *L'un est l'autre (The One Is the Other)*. "We are less concerned to dominate and possess the other than to be loved, protected, consoled, understood, and forgiven. More than ever, the model of love is that of the mother for her child. . . . The archaic desire for a return to the maternal symbiosis has never been so strong, both in men and women."

The old relationship, difficult and full of treacherous and dangerous river crossings, was based on differences between men and women, a longing for elaborate adulthood, with codes of conduct that guided even the breaking of moral laws for the sake of intensity. But in the sibling society both men and women are more likely to want symbiosis, a merger of two beings, rather than an adult relationship in which the differences are a part of the dialogue.

We know that the word *passion* has many other meanings besides those intensities in relationships. Women have made it their important task to define and follow those other serious passions, such as the intensity of art, the practice of the essay and the poem, the protection of the earth, and the defense of suffering women all over the globe.

THE ENTIRE CULTURE'S LOSS OF ANY GAZE UP TOWARD SPIRITUAL goals damages both daughters and sons. Young women often have a passionate longing for spirit. When one enters a church, the vast majority of worshippers are women. Women constantly make pilgrimages, to the Black Madonna site in Switzerland, to Buddhist temples, to meditation centers. We've mentioned that many forces in contemporary culture work so as to break the motherline between daughters and grandmothers, but these forces also work to break the spiritline between women and the Virgin Mary, between women and Aphrodite, between women and Sophia.

Of course, the marketplace is especially dangerous for women's souls, because women *are* the market. They see their bodies paraded on billboards, ad pages, and television commercials, and presented not as intelligences, affiliations, or intents but as ordinary adjuncts to a greedy life.

We know that women paid a huge price in self-respect, in violence, in slavery, in shame, in the old paternal society. Almost no

woman in the world wants to return to that. But it is important to
see that the child-rearing arrangements which the new society has
worked out, including the one-parent house, are not supportive of
women's development either.

When no father is present, it is often more difficult for the daughter to move out into the world. The mother does the best she can,
and often does very well indeed. But many valuable community
contacts disappear if the father is not a part of the community; such
contacts may not be available to the mother. Sara McLanahan says
in *Growing Up with the Single Parent:*

> *In this book, we argue that growing up with only one biological parent*
> *frequently deprives children of important economic, parental, and*
> *community resources, and that these deprivations ultimately under-*
> *mine their chance of future success. . . . Children who grow up in a*
> *household with only one biological parent are worse off, on average,*
> *than children who grow up in a household with both of their biolog-*
> *ical parents, regardless of the parents' race or educational back-*
> *ground, regardless of whether the parents are married when the child*
> *is born, and regardless of whether the resident parent remarries.*

These are tough words, but to ignore such difficulties won't help.

The fatherless family experiences some gains. There is less terror-
ism from "toxic" fathers, whose right to brutalize family members
has been, and remains in some families, unquestioned.

But fatherlessness increases the daughter's risk of becoming a
teenage mother by a substantial amount. The risk of dropping out of
high school also increases, and the chance of going to college de-
creases. Early pregnancy and motherhood is a disastrous setback to
the young woman's need for open space and solitude.

Finally, we need to look at the young woman's loss in emotional
life if, for whatever reason, she has lived since birth in a house with
no father. We know that the first love affair (with the mother) will
still take place, but the second love relationship with the father—
from age one and a half to three—will not take place. With that
goes a deep base of affection for the father and, by extension, for

the masculine. Increasing difficulty between women and men in relationships and marriage may have some of its source in the increasing number of women who have not experienced an early noninvasive love relationship with the father.

The sibling society then, with its fatherlessness, its openness to junk culture, its encouragement of early and shallow sexuality, its destruction of courtesy, and its economic uncertainty has had a severe impact on daughters' souls. We need to do grieving about these losses.

CHAPTER SEVEN

What Do Sons Stand to Lose or Gain in a Sibling Society?

Traditional Stages

No matter how far back we go into the reaches of the past, sons have lived—except for particular periods of history dominated by devastating wars or natural catastrophes that have interrupted family life—in close proximity to their fathers and grandfathers. How close the relationship was is another matter. In African and Indonesian cultures, sons remain exclusively with mothers until they are six or seven; then the men, living together in buildings at the edge of the village, return and take the sons away to initiatory huts for a period extending from two or three months to their entire life. Such fathers, once they do intervene, offer tremendous attention to the boys, some of it helpful, some not. The aim of the initiation, some practices of which are stupid, some brilliant, some brutal, some mediocre and ineffectual, is imagined as a way to complete the development of the being from a neutral genderlessness to a state of genuine masculinity. It is meant to complete a process that was begun, but not finished, in the womb.

Research in recent years has found out many details about the production of a male or female baby from a neutral form. We know that if the fetus is marked to become male, at about the sixth week of pregnancy the fetus goes through something like 250 changes, which alter upper torso muscle, change some bone length, provide a

116

throwing ability in the arms, change the clitoris into a penis, change
the vulval tissue into the scrotal sac, and so on. Several books describe this process in detail, among them *Brain Sex* by Anne Moir
and David Jessel.

The route from the womb to this unknown, barely imagined place
called masculinity is a long one, and can be interrupted at hundreds
of points. It's almost as if men were an experimental species. The
smallest Aborigine group living in the desert, or the most tightly
knit Eskimo family living in the Arctic, has the same problems with
confused young males as we do.

Most observers consider our time in the womb a significant part of our life, even of our conscious life. We know that babies
hear a great deal while in the womb, and respond by differing
movements to the mother's voice and the father's voice, seemingly
dance a little to certain kinds of music; and some people say that
babies' bodies respond to different parts of speech, distinguishing
among a noun, a verb, and a preposition. The general belief is that
for most babies, the time in the womb is so satisfactory that it
borders on the heavenly. All is provided when it is needed, there is
no gravity; if the mother lives in a calm house, the baby feels calm;
in a safe house, the baby feels safe. The "oceanic feeling" is the
famous phrase through which one can compare one's time in the
womb to a later sense of being held in the safe hands of God, in
other words, with the so-called religious emotions of adulthood and
various kinds of blessings. Freud claimed he never felt the resemblance, but he listened carefully to men and women who did. The
first stage of a boy's life, then, as of a girl's, is this womb bliss, which
the baby leaves apparently with some reluctance.

After birth, most babies enter a joyful, even ecstatic,
love affair with the mother. For a while, the two in love are as close
as the mouth and breast. Observers believe the infant doesn't know

the difference; it's all one thing. Lovers later feel that way: "I can't tell who is making love to whom." The softness of the breast, the way the warm milk spurts in his face, the safety in the warmth, the smell, the big hands, the feeling of "rightness" are all part of this affair. It's like a love song. The song is only for you. It will never be quite this good again, but the first love affair teaches the boy how to receive. The nipple is inserted in his mouth; later he will have trouble with anything inserted. He wants to insert; the fear of homosexuality for many men comes to this. But in memory he still knows how to receive from this "early mother." Psychologists call this mother the pre-oedipal mother, which is a little silly, as if Europe were "pre-American." The big mother is the breasty mother, or the woolly mammoth mother, or the flooding mother. She is moorish, spongy. She is great.

There is another side to her, of course, already mentioned, using Melanie Klein's term, as the Bad Breast. For the hungry infant who isn't fed, she can become a witch, or she has fangs, and she doesn't come back when you cry, and she wants little boys to die. It's the beginning of dualistic thinking. It's not how she is, it's how we feel she is when we're in pain.

The Spanish poet Antonio Machado has left some magnificent lines evoking his early love for his mother, and hinting at its effect on his poetry and on his entire way of seeing. He said to a woman whose eyes were clear:

If I were a poet
of love, I would make
a poem for your eyes as clear
as the transparent water in the marble pool.

And in my water poem
this is what I would say:

"I know your eyes do not answer mine,
they look and do not question when they look:
your clear eyes, your eyes have

the calm and good light,
the good light of the blossoming world, that I saw
one day from the arms of my mother."

AT ABOUT AGE ONE AND A HALF, SO RESEARCHERS DECLARE, THE
son begins to switch his intense gaze over to the father. Mothers
have to be prepared for this. The rowdy play of the father suddenly
seems much more attractive. Probably before one and a half, the
infant boy sees the father as simply an alternative mother; but now
he feels strangely drawn to this different energy and different body
mood. The father throws him up in the air, or rolls around and
imitates a bear. The son knows that the vibrations of the molecules
here are different, and the boy sometimes gets high on this new
vibration too. A love affair with the father now starts; it will be one
of the most crucial events in his whole life, but he will not be able to
speak of it, because it takes place mostly before speech. It is a non-
competitive, ecstatic relationship with an idealized father.

Peter Blos, who has done his work on the fruitful Freudian model,
remarks that most Freudian analysts prefer to omit this love affair
and talk about the competitive, angry, conflict-ridden relationship
with the father later in adolescence. The adolescent boy can always
describe that one, with fire and vivid metaphors. But the earlier one
is lost. Blos noticed that when he was in long therapy with an
adolescent boy, the adolescent would speak of his current angry,
disparaging, contentious, cold relationship with his father; and
then when all that had been talked out and said, the boy would be as
if looking farther back, and then in silence would sob for a long
time. Because that earlier love happened before words, he has no
words to describe it; and the contrast between his joy then and his
loneliness now is so deep that he can only weep.

The noncompetitive love also served other purposes. Blos remarks: "The attachment to the father served the little boy—as it
does for all little boys—as an anchor which steadied him from
drifting into the powerful currents of his need for the pre-oedipal

mother." The "reengulfing" mother is another way to refer to the fear sensation that both boy infants and girl infants experience around the nourishing mother, a fear that their frail independence will be swept away in the tide pull back to the large and delicious mother.

For the boy, the love affair with the father produces amazing delight, if the boy can perceive that he is made of the same stuff as his father. If the mother says, "You and your father are both drinking from a blue cup; you are as alike as two peas in the pod," the boy, as Jessica Benjamin mentions, may cry out, "Mommy, say that again!" This sort of love has been named identificatory love.

The son, when twenty or so, may not be able to speak about his early father-love, ecstatic in its sweetness, but the memory remains held somewhere in his body as a source of grace that can lead to a profound gentleness later in his life. It can also be reexperienced in "a gathering of men." The media have made fun of men's events in the woods or out, but a gathering of men, particularly when it lasts a week, when the range of ages includes older men, and when some grief is encouraged, has a mysterious power for change in the man attending. A man who in daily life is given over to competitive business may be living in the mood he experienced when he was fifteen, competing with his father. When he feels around him dozens of men who are grieving or smiling, he may remember far down in his cells that earlier love for the father. He often goes home and calls up his father, and a change begins, very helpful for his marriage and his parenting.

It IS THOUGHT THAT WHEN A BOY IS ABOUT THREE YEARS OLD, identificatory love for his father begins to fade. He has felt two relatively untroubled loves, first with his mother, sweet and "right," next with his father, exciting and "right," and now the twosomes vanish and the number three comes in—a chaotic and anguished threesome. The boy still loves the mother, and feels that she belongs to him, but it becomes clear that this large man whom he adores has some claim on the woman he loves. Her behavior changes when the Big One is around. The changes feel life-threatening. Moreover, powerful sexual energies, earlier arrived, have deepened; his mother is someone who not only feeds him but is young and attractive. Europeans at the turn of the century found this assertion—that sex is present in three-year-olds—the one that they hated Freud most for. Freud would give his weekly lecture, required by his university post, every Wednesday night, but no one would come. He'd deliver his lecture to a single person, a male friend, every Wednesday night. After that he played cards every Wednesday night with this other man for the rest of his life. If sexual energy *is* present at three, the three-year-old boy feels sexual rivalry, a kind of mammal possessiveness and mammal jealousy, complete with fantasies of murder. Turmoil lives in the house. No one is safe. Freud recognized that the boy is a little Oedipus; he's a self-obsessed little Greek king who wants to sleep with his mother and knock his father out of the wagon, in any order. His nervous system is not yet big enough to accommodate these immense flows of feeling. Later, when he is twelve or so, he will encounter the same conflicting emotions again. Ideally, by that time he will be more skilled in dissembling, and more capable of enduring contradictory sets of emotions, but for now it is agony.

FROM AGE FIVE TO TEN, A BOY GOES THROUGH A PERIOD OF relative calm. Sexual energy is still present, but it gives in to latency. The mother's attractiveness is not so insistent. His mind grabs him, unfolds its hidden curiosities, and the social world fascinates him with its rules, its pecking orders, its possibilities for raising or lowering his self-esteem. He notices who is respected and who isn't. If women are not respected in the house, he notices that. If servants are not respected, he notices that. He begins to decide who he is, with very little evidence on hand. He switches between being Davy Crockett, to a colonel in the air force, to Superman, and being nothing but the pip-squeak the rest of the family thinks he is.

It's as if there is, for a few years, less obsessive jealousy, less murderous rage, so the ego finds fewer enraged instincts pounding on its door.

This is a time for the "I" to decide who it is. The boy's "I" tries to decide whether it is the same as everyone else's "I" or not. The governor or "I" tries to decide in which direction this ship is going to go.

It is thought that about this age, two "agencies" begin to develop in the child, male or female. One is an agency of prohibition, the other of aspiration. The agency of prohibition, which tells him not to do or say certain things, seems to be an internalized version of voices who have said no to him earlier. Often the male voices say the loudest no's. In the old days the mother said, "Just wait until your father gets home."

Freud called this figure the superego, or the Higher I. To many people, it seems like a "he," someone with steel-rimmed glasses, a thin nose, and cold eyes. The Freudian analyst Janine Chassaguet-Smergel summarizes much thought by saying that the agency of prohibition seems to be created by, or derives from, the masculine side of things.

The other agency, begun in latency and continued in early adolescence, is a figure put together from disparate fragments of "who I want to be." It's an imaginary companion, and the one that stays with us longest. It can be male or female in tone, but there's something lofty about this being. It's a Lofty Companion. With its help, you begin to feel you're not like those others: "I am made for better things."

William Stafford, in his great poem "Thinking for Berky," describes that longing in a high school girl:

In the late night listening from bed
I have joined the ambulance or the patrol
screaming toward some drama, the kind of end
that Berky must have some day, if she isn't dead.

The wildest of all, her father and mother cruel,
farming out there beyond the old stone quarry

where high-school lovers parked their lurching cars,
Berky learned to love in that dark school.

Early her face was turned away from home
toward any hardworking place; but still her soul,
with terrible things to do, was alive, looking out
for the rescue that—surely, some day—would have to come.

Windiest nights, Berky, I have thought for you,
and no matter how lucky I've been I've touched wood.
There are things not solved in our town though tomorrow came:
There are things time passing can never make come true.

We live in an occupied country, misunderstood;
justice will take us millions of intricate moves.
Sirens will hunt down Berky, you survivors in your beds
listening through the night, so far and good.

Creating a Lofty Companion, which is your life's work for about ten years, tends to isolate you from others, because you need to listen, to him or her or it, but the creation also brings you closer to great people alive now whom you hear of, an artist, an inventor, a musician, also the great people who are dead, and whom only you understand. This agency of aspiration is more adept than we are, and will be our entry into success, authenticity, and achievement. I made my Lofty Companion from a careful choice among my actual qualities, plus qualities I pulled out of the air, with much denial and wish fulfillment as glue. The Lofty Companion wants a tensionless state and so is given to daydreaming, and "out of the family" experiences. It holds itself aloof from vulgar folly, and whispers, "You can do it all alone." One can tell it is a dangerous companion. The psychologists often call this the ego-ideal, but that's boring, and the name misses the companionship it provides. This being is like a friend, *is* a friend. It travels with us. It was my mother who liked poetry, and it's often the feminine that has such a deep passion for beauty and what is fine. The Lofty Companion, then, and the imaginative work around it, is considered, rightly, I think, as spring-ing from the feminine side of the psyche.

When latency is over, at about ten years old, the boy and girl will have two constructed figures or companions inside, if all goes well. One, wisely or unwisely, will apply standards, notify you what the current standards of goodness or success are, tell you what not to do, and in general lower your self-esteem for the sake of standards. The other, the agency of aspiration, works to lift you out of the moral, intellectual, and feeling shortages that your family has always lived with, and helps you become one of the better ones, or wiser ones, or deeper ones, or nobler ones. It is a companion and friend—a little high toned, but faithful. Not all children are lucky enough to find the materials in the house to create the Lofty Companion.

SOMEWHERE AROUND AGE TEN, THE TRAIN OF ADOLESCENCE stops at the local station, and we get on. The train of adolescence follows quite different tracks when it is carrying boys as opposed to girls, but it goes at high speed in both cases. The train starts when hormonal orders come in, and any fool can tell that something is happening. Steam escapes at several spots by the wheels, there are jolts and stops; the time on the siding is over. When boys are about eleven, everything becomes sexual, or rather, they can't tell what is and what isn't. Fearing a dog or shaking a hand can bring on an erection, as can simply picking up the chalk at the blackboard. All language becomes smutty, first in relation to "bottoms" and a little later to genital matters. Dostoyevsky speaks of it:

> There are "certain" words and conversations unhappily impossible to eradicate in schools. . . . Boys, pure in mind and heart, are fond of talking . . . of images of which even soldiers would sometimes hesi-tate to speak. . . . There is no moral depravity . . . but there is the appearance of it, and it is often looked upon among them as some-thing refined, subtle, daring and worthy of imitation.

The boy's sexual attraction to the mother, so familiar from the years three to five, returns abruptly, and new irritations arise with the father.

The boy's fear that he may have traces of femininity in his body returns. Perhaps he isn't masculine enough, perhaps he could still become a girl. Now he wants to mock girls, belittle all females, run around in gangs of boys only. He is irritated with his father, who seems stupid, but the boy needs his father now, who has apparently endured the company of females successfully. He wants to ask his father how he did it. Some boys will idealize the father again, imagine him as powerful and dominant (an idealization they will later have to unravel slowly and painfully).

After several years of coarse, smutty obsessions, such as Dostoyevsky remembers, all of a sudden the boy feels a tender attraction to another person, perhaps one of the same gender he has been mocking for so long. He will be attracted tenderly, if he is gay, to a young man; if he is straight, to a girl. Perhaps he has seen the girl before, but now when she lifts a hand to brush back her hair, she seems mysterious beyond words. He needs courage to go over and talk to her, and sometimes he has it and sometimes not. Sometimes he thinks of his father, because the fascination he feels with the feminine makes his defenses against softness start to collapse, and he can't figure out what to do. Moreover, he feels self-assured and commanding at one moment, and clumsy, ugly, and stupid at the next, someone who has no right to be on earth. A coach may say to him, "I got girls who can dribble a ball better than you."

He sometimes inhabits two feeling states simultaneously: mourning and being in love. His mourning is for his lost mother: it is deep, wordless, the grief of an exile. At another moment, he is at home on the earth for the first time. Trees and their leaves are astonishing; children move like walking jewels; the face he loves has a beauty so deep that he knows it is divine in some way no one else understands; he understands classical music; he experiences exalted emotional states.

He tests his "I" now to see how strong it is: he may decide to stay up for three nights, or to drink only water for a week. Thinking becomes a joy; he invents great systems that put in place all civilizations since the beginning of time; he invents a new theory every day.

This activity becomes more complicated because his superego is attacking him every day; and his Lofty Companion reminds him to think about perfection. The Lofty Companion loves perfection. He has given up on his parents; he still wants society to be perfect: so he becomes a rebel. He'll be a rebel for a while. And yet he feels life hasn't begun. Sherwood Anderson said he felt at this age as if he were walking on a fairgrounds the night before the fair starts.

Two hazards lie ahead: One is that he will plunge on into life too far or too quickly, and end up as a coarse person, cheating on everyone, unfathered, unmothered, insatiable, addicted, in jail. The other is that he will retreat into isolation and make his life perfect with a computer. He will still be excited, but now he will have fallen out of the community and will be alone. He doesn't know about feelings. He thinks excitement is the door to feeling, but all he gets is more excited. He's an adolescent.

Adolescence has been, for fortunate boys, an amazing experience. Some cultures consider adolescence a state of its own, only slightly transitional, like the butterfly state, a world of its own, with its own air, fire, earth, and water.

As adolescence ends—if there is no effective initiation or mentorship—a sad thing happens. The fire of thinking, the flaring up of creativity, the bonfires of tenderness, all begin to go out. It's as if the Army Corps of Engineers channels wild rivers into concrete banks. This happens to many boys, perhaps most. They become consolidated. They take what is around them—the pulp-cutting job, the few local opinions, the drinking culture, the "Vocational School"—and they consolidate. They feel they have to decide who they are right now. They have no time to feel the traumas; and now that numbing of pain takes over; that numbing often becomes the essence of male life, much more the essence than domination or power over others. They adopt their dad's way of "holding it in." They store anger in their bodies, but worse, as John Lee has said over and over, the men do not learn how to express the anger in a healthy, eloquent, or fruitful way. They experience anger but don't know what to do with it. There is a continuum that runs from experiencing anger passively to expressing it verbally to trying to expel anger from the body by hitting. A man may go, John Lee says, from experiencing anger to expelling anger in two seconds, skipping over verbal expression completely, and the result for some men will be domestic violence, hitting wives and children.

Most men will not be violent. They will live in this state of expressionless consolidation all their lives, without violence, but without spontaneity or creativity either. The numbing of anger and grief will be the primary task of their psyches.

The man who remains creative will make art for the rest of his life out of the remnants of infantile and adolescent conflicts. For other men, the end of adolescence means a shutting down of expressiveness and a fading of the fires. That is the way it has been for hundreds of years.

Losses for Sons in the Sibling Society

Like daughters, sons stand to suffer considerable losses in the sibling society. We'll mention here five such areas.

The consequences of fatherlessness could be called the first loss. The loss begins early. For a son with no father at all, it's obvious that no matter how generously his mother raises him, the initial love affair with the father between ages one and a half and three cannot take place. One could say a son loves masculinity first by loving it in his own father; having no father means that one half of his love energy is not activated or developed; and he will never be sure if he likes masculinity or not. With no father in the house, he may love his mother more for a while. He will appear to have won possession of his mother, which is for him not a good outcome.

It's doubtful that an adolescent son without a father could complete his oedipal task, which amounts to wrestling with the father and testing himself against this imposing being. He needs to renounce dependence on his mother as well. The fatherless son may repudiate his mother instead, or merge with her, and then put off the wrestling with an older man until later in his life, meanwhile hating male authority without much knowledge of it. Eighty-five percent of male convicts are fatherless. If a son has appointed himself as his mother's guardian, he may also end up worrying about his "abandoned" mother all the time, rather than living his own life.

The son in the sibling society will also find that his latency period is drastically shortened. We'll call that the second loss. Sexuality, originating in the adult sphere and arriving in the form of X-rated films, suggestive advertising, and pornographic videos and magazines, penetrates more deeply each year into the child's world. It stirs up sexuality before the psyche has been properly prepared. When that happens, the boy becomes a premature adolescent and perhaps later a perpetual adolescent. The ego has not been given time for its brooding and dreaming, nor for its curiosity about the positive, mysterious sides of adult life. Junk culture's shortening of latency damages both the sons and the daughters.

Thirdly, economic relationships in the sibling society tend to be cutthroat. Competitiveness in the corporate world is so intense now that it has been described as "toxic." The result is that genuine mentoring—essential to young men—is disappearing; a young man learns not to trust older men. He's stuck with people in his own age group, many of whom, like him, have neither father nor mentor.

The computer culture, an ineradicable element of sibling life, is producing isolation. We'll call that the fourth loss. The punished son exiled "to his own room" is now replaced by the Internet son. Computers, as we know, lead to a further drying up of conversation with adults; and the son becomes locked away from his own feelings. The ritual teacher Martín Prechtel believes that computer use is damaging young people more deeply than we understand. Young men have often expressed their distance by putting on a hard exterior shell, a kind of mechanical skin; but many young men now, modeling themselves—unconsciously—on computers, tend to be machine-like on the *inside*. They experience input and output. There's a loss of expressiveness and affiliation.

Finally, the sibling society offers very little generosity or support to young men. We'll call that the fifth loss. The words, opinions, and tastes of siblings have a lot of acid in them: "That music is shit, man." More broadly, the ridicule of masculinity that has poured out of comic strips, from Dagwood Bumstead to Homer Simpson, from sitcoms and Letterman monologues, and from university class-rooms, has had a profoundly damaging effect on young men. Gen-der feminists have contributed to this problem, encouraging stereotypes of masculinity that would be totally unacceptable if directed toward any other group. The French writer, Elisabeth Bad-inter, remarks, "The new equation, male equals bad, has given rise to a loss of identity for a whole generation of men."

The "consolidation" or fading of fires characteristic of post-adolescence is worsening for young men, many of whom fall into chronic despair because of economic hopelessness and a sense that the society has thrown them away. Because of bad schools and spiritual poverty, the "agency of aspiration" fails to develop in mil-lions of boys; because of parental neglect, the "agency of prohibi-tion" is twisted. How can young men—or women—in the inner city create a Lofty Companion? They don't see preachers or scientists; they see drug dealers or crackheads. Schools are too disintegrated or distracted to give them news of depth or nobleness; and we know what the newspapers and televisions deliver.

The unprecedented failure of fathering in our time will have ef-fects to the sixth and seventh generations. Many single mothers have had no choice in their family—whether it is fathered or un-fathered. But other women choose—foolishly I think—to have chil-dren and skip over the father part. If raising a child alone in a paternal society was precarious, even with many extended families existing, raising a son alone is doubly precarious in the sibling society. Our society does not offer reliable mentors to help a son establish a link to the adult masculine. The sibling society is without vital religious institutions, so a son cannot easily find a second father in religious work or in the spiritual world. Capitalism has siphoned off male energy so as to allow deeper exploitation of children. If we knew what children are suffering inside, we would beg every man we meet on the street to give up his career and become a father.

CHAPTER EIGHT

Disdain and Contempt for Children
in the Sibling Society

THE SIBLING SOCIETY IS A FUNCTIONING AND SELF-CONSISTENT
structure whose principles have not yet been fully observed or
articulated. We know that the paternal society had an elaborate
and internally consistent form with authoritative father reflected
upward to the strong community leader and beyond him to the
father god up among the stars, which were also arranged in the
hierarchical levels, called "the seven heavens." Children imitated
adults, and were often far too respectful for their own good to
authorities of all kinds. However, they learned in school the adult
ways of talking, writing, and thinking. For some, the home was safe,
and the two-parent balance gave them maximum possibility for
growth; for others, the home was a horror of beatings, humiliation,
and sexual abuse, and school was the only safe place. The teaching
at home and in school encouraged religion, memorization, ethics,
and discipline, but resolutely kept hidden the historical brutalities
of the system.

Our succeeding sibling society, in a relatively brief time, has
taught itself to be internally consistent in a fairly thorough way. The
teaching is that no one is superior to anyone else; high culture is to

be destroyed, and business leaders look sideways to other business leaders. The sibling society prizes a state of half-adulthood, in which repression, discipline, and the Indo-European, Islamic, Hebraic impulse-control system are jettisoned. The parents regress to become more like children, and the children, through abandonment, are forced to become adults too soon, and never quite make it. There's an impulse to set children adrift on their own. The old (in the form of crones, elders, ancestors, grandmothers and grandfathers) are thrown away, and the young (in the form of street children in South America, or latchkey children in the suburbs of this country, or poor children in the inner city) are thrown away.

When I first began to write this book, I found it hard to understand why a society run by adolescents should show so much disregard for children, who are, in the mass, worse off under Bill Clinton than they were under Theodore Roosevelt or Warren Harding. And yet, in an actual family, adolescents do not pay much attention to the little ones or to the very old. Newt Gingrich's inflation has much to do with adolescence. But I think women have recognized that children are in jeopardy; and so there was, and is, a gender gap in the votes for Newt Gingrich's revolution. Men still have their eyes covered.

THE DEEPENING RAGE OF THE UNPARENTED IS BECOMING A MARK of the sibling society. Of course, some children in our society feel well parented, and there is much adequate parenting; but there is also a new rage. A man said to me, "Having made it to the one-parent family, we are now on our way toward the zero-parent family." The actual wages of working-class and middle-class parents have fallen significantly since 1972, so that often both parents work, one parent the day shift, another at night—family meals, talks, reading together, no longer take place.

What the young need—stability, presence, attention, advice, good psychic food, unpolluted stories—is exactly what the sibling society won't give them. As we look at the crumbling schools, the failure to protect students from guns, the cutting of funds for Head Start and breakfasts for poor children, cutting of music and art lessons, the enormous increase in numbers of children in poverty, the poor prenatal care for some, we have to wonder whether there might not be a genuine anger against children in the sibling society.

THE WORK BY BOWLBY, WINNICOTT, AND KOHUT SUPPORTS THE idea that children are basically "warmth-seeking mammals." They attach themselves to whatever object seems to offer warmth and comfort, even if the promise is mostly illusionary, and even if "the object is hostile or frustrating to them." Children "will search for the faintest flickers of light, even if the light illuminates nothing, and even if it carries little warmth." They search—if there is little warmth at home—for light in teachers, random adults, pop singers, acquaintances who may abuse them. Children who must make such choices have, as one observer remarked, "settled for so little from the start that they think a little is a lot."

A dignified adult life, with its heights and depths, protected by wisely kept secrets, once attracted children in such a way that they wanted to become adults. Now they see incoherent emptiness and chaos.

The sibling society does not effectively protect even those children who *are* parented. The media are given full access to childhood privacies. Children are asked to digest things even adults find indigestible; talk shows tell all the secrets before the child has learned to trust life, or accumulate meaning and value. Neil Postman calls such neglect of children "the disappearance of childhood."

MORE AND MORE CHILDREN NOW MANAGE TO SHIFT FROM BEING bit players in the family drama and in national life—which they were in the nineteenth century—to becoming stars. A son or daughter, for example, may act out, and soon the rest of the family is in court, watching that child. The movement from bit player to star is evident during the last decades with the increased presence of children in the Olympics, in fashion, in modeling, and so on. Street children with spiked hair and safety pins through their cheeks are really our current child stars, who have unfolded themselves from their families and become noticeable to all. Younger and younger children are brought onto talk shows; and they are told that their opinions and observations are important to everyone. This singling out of the very young to be celebrities or sources of wisdom is really a form of child abuse.

CHILDREN NEED AN ELABORATED LANGUAGE IN ORDER FOR brain development to occur. One way to achieve an elaborated language is through hours and hours of conversation with adults. Conversation means not only "How was the game?" or "Have you cleaned your room?" but also slow, quiet talk in which the child gets a glimpse into the strange countryside of the grown-up's brain, in which the grown-up says, "I always give money to a beggar, even though I don't want to," or "The test of a culture is a decent provision for the poor," or "The problem with the pirate is that he is lacking in empathy." A poll a few years ago revealed that the average American father talked to his child for about ten minutes a day. We know by contrast that in certain parts of Russia, earlier in the century, the Russian father spent more like two hours engaging in such talk. Russians have a word for "soul-talk," and it wasn't unusual for a grandfather to say to a granddaughter, "Let's go out by the tree and have some soul-talk." We don't even have a word for it.

Mothers in the United States have always taken on the joy and the duty of talking by the hour to children, but that has changed. The average mother talks for a few minutes, and then, understandably tired from her job, sits down in front of the television with the child and lets herself be entertained. Grade-school teachers all over the country report that children in their classes know no Mother Goose rhymes and haven't heard even the major fairy tales, let alone participated in discussions as to why the Dwarves take Snow White in, or why the bear comes each winter to play with the children, or why the parents didn't want to keep Hansel and Gretel, or why

Mommy and Daddy are divorcing.

Good conversation with grown-ups provides what some researchers call a "verbal bath"; the children soak in it, and the elaborated language "arranges their synapses and their intellects." The brain is ravenous, as all parents know, for language stimulation and language fun in early childhood. The brain is fluid and open to change—new branches can appear on the dendrites—early, but the brain becomes less able to enlarge its connections as puberty arrives. Language deprivation can affect the brain as vitamin deprivation affects the body. The language vitamins are taken in from parents or mentors, who talk about everything: their failures, their longings, politics, God, bodies, angers, opinions. Joseph Chilton Pearce remarks, "Nature's imperative is, again, that no intelligence unfolds without a stimulus from a developed form of that intelligence." He called his last book *Evolution's End,* meaning that the evolution of human intelligence has stopped. He offers as an alternative image a naked three-year-old with its thumb in its mouth looking at a television set.

The matter of new words clearly excites the brain; but the range of vocabulary being used on television steadily shrinks. Corporations that pay for commercials don't want anyone watching their programs to feel ignorant, so news anchors find their scripts stocked with very ordinary words and the vocabulary is contracting. Sadly, the range of language at home similarly contracts. "What's for dinner?" "Who's got the remote?" "What do you want from the mall?" Language centers itself around objects. Children from such homes have little help in distinguishing their emotions and finding the right word for the difference between despair and depression, or between irritation and anger, or between sympathy and empathy.

When a wide vocabulary interconnects with an intricate syntax, language people call the result an "elaborated code," which is actually good brain food. Until recently, children had to code-switch when they visited grandparents. "I'm sure you're an avid reader. Do you have a favorite writer in your studies at school?" "Have you been able to make any connections between your reading and your church life?" The child thirty years ago might reply: "I'm afraid that I'm becoming an atheist, because I find it hard to accept—even on my best days—that a god could be so indifferent to suffering" . . . and so on. Now most children don't have to switch codes. It's just "How ya doing, Grandma?" all the way.

LATCHKEY CHILDREN ARE TELEVISION CHILDREN. One out of six primary-age children and two out of five grade-school children arrive home after school to an empty house. Mothers struggle to do everything in this age of absent grandparents, absent uncles and aunts, absent or emotionally absent fathers, collapsed schools, but the realities are not encouraging. As of this writing, the editors of *The Parental Leave Crisis* (Yale University Press, 1988) report that the majority of babies born in the United States are placed in full-time day care within a year, commonly within two or three months, so that their parents can both work.

Middle-class and upper-class mothers are more aware than disadvantaged mothers of the possible dangers of early day care. And yet advantaged women go back to work more quickly after their children are born than do disadvantaged women. The education editor of *The New York Times*, Fred Hechinger, mentions that most day-care providers in New York are foreign-born and have a small vocabulary in English, so the verbal bath necessary to the child's development is simply not happening for children, poor or rich. One observer wrote:

> *You visit some infant care centers, and it is so sad; I went to visit one two doors down from me and they have eight to twenty babies there, all under the age of one. I walked in and there was absolutely nothing—I mean it, no pictures, no toys, nothing. The babies were just sitting there on blankets on this carpeted floor—this is a licensed, recommended infancy center in California. There were three caregivers: two were Spanish-speaking and one was Iranian; none of them spoke English, but all the babies were English-speaking.*

In the old paternal society, fathers automatically put their jobs ahead of talking with children. Mothers are now doing the same. The time that mothers spend in conversation with their children is falling rapidly. *The New York Times* reported in January of '95 that the *average* is down to about ten minutes a day for mothers as well as fathers. And, according to *The New York Times*, mothers at home do not spend significantly more time in conversation with their children than do working mothers.

Brain development not only requires a verbal bath, made of adventurous words, grandmother and grandfather language, religious and philosophical terms, but also requires syntax—elaborate syntax. Elaborate syntax is itself a form of brain food.

Some proponents of spontaneity and flow have urged for decades that lively flow of language is more important than syntax, which they call antiquated. They have a point, but then they excuse the child from learning syntax. The problem lies in regarding complex syntax as an enemy. Syntax teaches the brain to make leaps in the air before it settles down to its main point. For example, if a speaker is feeling three emotions—"I am sad," "I am resentful," "I am angry"—elaborate syntax requires that person to tuck two of the emotions away in subordinate clauses and offer one as the main one. That is very helpful to children who have difficulty distinguishing between simultaneously felt emotions. Complicated syntactical rules in tense or conjugation require a child to become used to the differences between "shall" or "will," or between "what I would do" and "what I would have done," or between "might" and "could." The surprise is that the study of syntax, whether in Swahili or Latin or any other language, encourages the brain at any age to grow.

Some syntactical matters need to be learned early. That was discovered from studies of deaf persons, in which one group learned American Sign Language—which also has firm grammatical rules— early, and another group learned the language later in life. Only those who learned American Sign Language before the age of eleven could master the complete syntax. An observer reports: "After age eleven, it appeared, their brains had lost the ability to master more complex forms of syntax. They made the same types of errors that show up increasingly in the writing of today's schoolchildren." So work on language and syntax cannot wait until high school, or even junior high.

Boredom in our high schools is rising to unheard-of levels. Karl Bissinger visited Proviso West, a high school near Chicago, for which parents and teachers had great hopes when it was founded during the 1960s. He reported for *The New York Times Magazine*:

> *It's the end of another day at Proviso West, and for Dennis Bobbe, a social studies teacher, it's not a moment too soon. He came to the school in 1966 when it was at its apex, filled with those seemingly timeless shows of spirit, the pep rallies, the sock hops, the earnest debates over war and peace. Now, it's nobody's school, all the spirit sucked dry. He finds nothing remarkable about Proviso West at all, except, perhaps, for the pathos. "They're actively resisting learning," he says of his students. "They just don't want to learn. It's not fun. It's too much effort." He pauses, and then takes a turn inward.*
>
> *"Maybe it's me."*
>
> *He knows they're bored to tears. He knows what their ability to analyze or do something in-depth is. He knows what the pop culture effects of television and music are, "the bing-bang-boom," as he calls it.*
>
> *"I can't compete."*
>
> *Yet he wonders what happened to the notion of the American public school as a sacred place, a vital place, a place unlike any other in the world. "What was it that peeled away? What was it that was lost?"*
>
> *It is a gray, late-winter day as he teaches his seventh-period class. He has pulled down a map depicting the boundary changes in Europe during World War I. Over another blackboard hangs a pithy state-*

ment that reads, "Not Preparing! Is Preparing Not to Pass." As Bobbe talks about the war, he tries to engage everyone, including those who have their heads on their desks.

"Who is Herbert Hoover?" he asks.

"The vacuum guy?" asks one student.

"Overall, there were 10 million killed in the military in World War I," says Bobbe.

A girl yawns.

He tells them that Woodrow Wilson had once been the president of Princeton University.

"What do you mean, while he was President?" asks a student.

"No, before," says Bobbe.

He introduces Wilson's points. He introduces some of the post– World War I European leaders: Clemenceau, Lloyd George.

"Boy George?" says a student.

"All right, we'll stop here. Monday, I won't be here. We'll have a movie."

The bell rings and the students shuffle out of class.

Most adults are about one-third of the way into the sibling society. Children are two-thirds of the way in.

Looking at the decline in discipline, inventiveness, persistence, reading abilities, and reasoning abilities of adolescents now compared with adolescents thirty years ago, we must be ready to grasp how much steeper the decline will be thirty years from now. As these children, who mistake Herbert Hoover for the maker of the vacuum cleaner, become directors of movies, critics of literature, curators of museums, and high school teachers, we will see a drop in coherence all across the board.

TELEVISION IS THE THALIDOMIDE OF THE 1990S. IN 1995, AMERI-can children spent about one-third of their awake time watching television. The National Association of Educational Progress reported that only 5 percent of high school graduates could make their way through college-level literature. In a study, Dr. Bernia Callenci of New York University asked fifth graders across a wide scale the time they spend each day outside of school reading: four minutes a day or less for 50 percent of the fifth graders, two minutes a day for 30 percent, and none at all for 10 percent. The same group of children watched 130 minutes of television each day.

A study conducted by the education department at Kent State University found surprising changes in the new teachers' attitudes toward reading in general. Prospective teachers "enter our courses with negative attitudes toward reading in general. . . ." More than one-fourth of potential teachers confessed to a "lifelong discomfort with print." Television has deformed the minds of many students who are now teachers.

A recent comprehensive study, supported by the National Institute of Mental Health and guided by Mihaly Csikszentmihalyi and Robert Kuby, which involved twelve hundred subjects, found that more skill and concentration was needed to eat a meal than to watch television, and the watching left people passive, yet tense, and unable to concentrate.

Television provides a garbage dump of obsessive sexual material inappropriate to the child's age, minute descriptions of brutalities, wars, and tortures all over the world: an avalanche of specialized information that stuns the brain. Even lyrics of songs come too fast for the brain to hear.

Grade-school teachers report that in recent years they have had to repeat instructions over and over, or look each child in the face and give instructions separately, which interrupts class work. We know that the sort of music that children hear much of—that characterized by a heavy beat—is processed mainly by the right brain, which hears the tune as a whole and doesn't see its parts or question it. The brain goes into an alpha state, which rules out active thinking or learning.

Sesame Street is a little better than other television shows, but in its effort to hold the attention of children, it makes constant and abrupt jumps to new scenes. *Sesame Street* producers have violated the natural slowness in which learning takes place. For example, letters such as *M* or *S* leap about, suddenly turn into lions or giraffes who dance, then become airplanes, or snakes, grow huge, or vanish entirely. The speed is too great. The transformations may seem sophisticated to an adult, or charmingly childlike, but the child's mind is left behind; it feels incomprehension and, once more, tunes out the meaning even as it tunes in the entertainment. One observer remarks that the habits of mind necessary to be a good reader are exactly what television does not teach: language, active reflection, persistence, and internal control.

The Story of Two Kittens

In a famous experiment, a pair of twin kittens was taken into a room whose circular walls had prominent black and white vertical stripes; the kittens were kept there during the weeks in which their visual cells were developing.

Each kitten rode in its own basket, which was attached to the end of a long beam revolving on a central point. The legs of one kitten hung down through or below the basket, so its paws could touch the floor. That kitten, when it walked, could make the beam revolve. The other kitten rode in a basket that prevented its paws from touching the floor.

The surprising result was that only the kitten whose paws touched the floor could see vertical stripes; its receptor cells for sight developed normally. The other kitten could not see vertical stripes, in that room then or anywhere else later.

The experiment appears to say that body motion or movements of the motor systems are essentially connected to brain development—certainly to seeing, and possibly to learning.

Seeing "scenes"—that is, stripes—while in a passive position apparently does not help in brain development. Some of the learning difficulties that children are experiencing in school now may be connected to passive television watching. We know that thirty-five hours of television watching a week (very mild for most youngsters) means thirty-five hours not on the playground. We have to consider the possibility that the brains of such children might be physically different from the brains of children who still play outdoors for long periods, especially children who direct their own play. Perhaps the riding-kitten children, metaphorically, can't see ideas, or perhaps they are blind to their own thoughts, which are like black and white stripes on their inner walls.

> *Scores on the National Assessment of Educational Progress have shown particular deficiencies in higher-order reasoning skills, including those necessary for advanced reading comprehension, math, and science. . . . For example, only 44% of high school graduates could compute the change that would be received from $3.00 for two items ordered from a lunch menu. The 1986 report . . . showed such a drastic and "baffling" decline in reading performance of nine- and seventeen-year-olds that the report was delayed for five months while researchers refigured the statistics and reexamined the test items. They still could not explain the decline. NAEP officials had planned to publish a study showing trends in students' reading performance since 1971, but these plans were canceled because no one wanted to believe the results.*

Piaget over the years laid out with immense documentation the stages in children's thinking that lead to "formal operational thinking." Herman Epstein of Brandeis reports a clear decline in the number of children achieving formal operational thinking:

> *In American universities at large, the general faculty complaint has been that the caliber of the student body has been deteriorating year by year. In 1988, 80% of all academic honors and scientific awards in the United States went to foreign born students, a mere fraction of the student population.*

These anecdotes don't prove anything, of course. Perhaps all through history one could gather such anecdotes providing steady evidence that the current crop of students doesn't please teachers.

Some schoolteachers, parents, and sociologists will always come forward and say, "Oh, these new students are just different! Some people can't face anything new; they want everything the same as it was. Perhaps these new children will have utterly new thoughts, and be wonderfully inventive in ways the old fuddy-duddies could never imagine."

But a flood of new thoughts is not what is happening among our young. Instead we have depression, confusion, and teen suicide.

CHILDREN SUFFER TREMENDOUS BLOWS TO THEIR DIGNITY AND self-esteem when they can't read at an appropriate level, when they are unable to formulate their thoughts clearly, even to say what they like or don't like, or want, or yearn for, or desire. They sink into depression, delinquency, and hopelessness more deeply each year, and the increasing inability of sibling society children to create new images adds to their despair. Joseph Chilton Pearce says that the child whose brain has been impaired by too much passive watching cannot find hope, for the simple reason that he or she "cannot imagine an inner scenario to replace the outer one." The outer scenario is violent, corrupt, ugly, and dying; and the child who cannot imagine any new scenario will feel victimized by the environment. This is one source of the victim mentality and victim art that we see all around us.

According to Pearce, although many factors contribute, the school system has collapsed fundamentally because the children that teachers must teach are now "damaged goods." Such a shocking statement needs qualification. He believes that 70 percent of the students are now damaged: "In our schools, only 30% can still learn."

The considerable damage our children have suffered and are still suffering today is the result of many forces at work in the sibling society: chemical pollution, which includes lead poisoning; poor nutrition in the millions of families that do not have enough food; the wasted hours of playtime given to video games, television, and computers; and trauma from violence observed in action movies, neighborhoods, and even our own homes.

The sibling society has already developed, in just a few years, an internal consistency, so that what happens in one part of the United States happens in all parts. The damage to children happens in all states and all townships. We have to have a strong stomach to take in the knowledge of how deep the damage to children is. The danger is that the half-adults will laugh it off. Bill Gates will walk down the road singing, while men and women weep.

Part Three

OUTSIDE
THE FAMILY

CHAPTER NINE

Benjamin Franklin's Pig: Economics and Our Heaviness of Heart

Economics has played an important part in the current heaviness of heart, the widening gap between whites and blacks, the rarity of beauty in the culture, and the fading passion for justice.

Domesticating Money

When the French gave patriarchy its first heavy blow in 1789, many Europeans had high hopes and they longed for more life, more spontaneity, and more creativity. That the old hierarchy, so brutal, repressive, rigid, hypocritical, greedy and dull-headed, could be finally brought down. Some of those hopes were realized. But now, when the patriarchal structure has been effectively demolished in the social world, we discover that the sibling society, which has replaced it, is "dangerous to children and other living things." The swift movement of our first thoroughly sibling Congress to open holes in the safety net, and to close down affirmative action, shows that we should not expect more compassion or fairness from the siblings than we expected from the paternalists. It looks as if the new leaders are not going to defend children, nor wetlands, nor blacks, nor women, nor full-growth forests, nor the Alaska wilderness. Some sibling meanness has interrupted the understanding people had in the 1960s that we are all related.

The sibling society is shaping up as a place where business finds few forces that hold it accountable. Today's Democratic sibling leader, President Clinton, and Republican sibling leader, Newt Gingrich, favor profit over wilderness and favor large business over small business. The passage of NAFTA with President Clinton's support was a strong blow against small business. The defeat of the unions by corporations in recent times and the replacement of working-class intent and austerity by consumerism are trends that probably cannot be reversed. In our current society, acquisitive capitalism has won, more completely than in any other complicated culture on earth.

The spirit of acquisitive capitalism, or "limitless acquisition," as some call it, rose up energetically in Europe during the Middle Ages. In response, humanist thinkers in the Renaissance demanded that capitalists respect community values, and the Catholic theologians of the time demanded that acquisitive people obey the "laws of nature."

When medieval writers used the phrase "laws of nature," they were referring to certain community concerns built into the whole structure of a universe ordered by God, which naturally placed limits on individual self-interest. When a property owner cried, "May I not do what I like with my own?"—which seemed to him a proper question—the medieval religions answered no. The struggle of Church versus capitalism is a complicated one; the Church's hierarchy has been aligned at times with business, but its best thinkers have asked for some control of greed.

The abrupt expansion of capitalism in the seventeenth century (when the Empires began), a capitalism that had been held in or compacted during the eras in which Christian doctrine penetrated all levels of European activity, took everyone by surprise. Adam Smith, John Locke, Thomas Hobbes, all tried to think their way through it. At first they adopted the same principle that Japan later adopted: it is the business of government to support, protect, and encourage business.

In the seventeenth century, Adam Smith, Thomas Hobbes, Bernard Mandeville, and David Hume, speaking for English property owners, gave to the strong "the right to pursue their own self-interest." As R. H. Tawney remarked later, "[it gave] to the weak the hope that they too one day may be strong." Dean Tucker brought in Providence: "National commerce, good morals and good government are but part of one general scheme in the designs of Providence."

Locke, an admirer of property, declared that "the State which interferes with property and business destroys its own title to exist. . . . The great and chief end of men uniting into commonwealths and putting themselves under government is the preservation of their property."

As we know, English business began to proceed on its path, and the State helped. The English State enclosed, that is, abolished, the "commons"—the free pasturage at the center of English villages, which allowed a poor family to get along with their cow, and their idleness. Some of the traits of these garrulous, incompetent villagers blossom in Shakespeare's *A Midsummer Night's Dream* as a band of "rude mechanicals." John Clare wrote:

Enclosure came, and trampled on the grave
Of labour's rights, and left the poor a slave;
And memory's pride, ere want to wealth did bow,
Is both the shadow and the substance now. . . .
For with the poor, scared freedom bade farewell,
And fortune-hunters totter where they fell;
They dreamed of riches in the rebel scheme
And find too truly that they did but dream.

In an astonishing turn, the phrase "law of nature" by the late seventeenth century had reversed its meaning and come to mean natural appetite. The longing to make lots of money was considered as natural as the body's endless need for food. Around this time, Adam Smith, in a burst of poetry, composed a fantastic image—the image of the "invisible hand." It applied to ruthlessness. Should a businessman, acting out of the law of nature, push farmworkers off their land and so force them to work in a factory, or hire grade-school boys to work naked underground for ten hours a day in a coal mine, he will find out when he is sixty that an "invisible hand" has been guiding him, and all these seeming cruelties were in the long view very helpful to society as a whole.

Alexander Pope rhymed this gross idea:

Thus God and Nature formed the general frame,
And bade self-love and social be the same.

Adam Smith's image of the unseen hand is probably a better image than the left wing was producing at the time. This famous invisible hand is probably the same hand that President Bush later saw holding up the thousand points of light.

IN 1904, MAX WEBER SET UP A NEW TOWER from which one could survey the battleground of acquisitive energy versus Christianity. He constructed a brief essay, known in English as "The Protestant Ethic and the Spirit of Capitalism." He argued convincingly that the so-called Protestant revolution had a lot to do with giving permission to Christians to throw themselves wholesale into business.

Max Weber's thesis, which historians have uniformly praised as sound and brilliant, embodies a deep irony. Protestants adopted, in effect, Catholic Church practices to further the very acquisitive capitalism that Catholic theologians had fought for centuries to restrain.

The Methodist sect has its root in a "Method" that John Wesley developed to help some Christian young men become successful businessmen through austere, monkish practices. The young men were to expect little sexual release (such restraint is parallel to the accumulation of capital), and to set out their day in time units—so much time for exercise, so much time for Bible reading, so much time for planning the next business move, and so on. They were to be frugal and develop ethical will. Becoming a businessman was a "calling." Becoming wealthy as a result of this method was considered a sign that you were one of the elect. Puritan businessmen, in brief, directed toward the accumulation of wealth the ascetic lives that Catholic monks had developed through many earlier centuries directed toward the divine.

Weber's essay set everyone's hat on backward, and all sorts of details became clear, such as the possibility that our Puritan ancestors came to Plymouth Rock to do business without being pestered by the Catholics. Of course, we know that many Puritans were profoundly dedicated to an examination of conscience, and that is to their credit. But for some, becoming wealthy was a sign that God had chosen you to be one of the elect, so wealth quieted the conscience somewhat. In our time, this monkish asceticism has been twisted into a business frame, altered into the fourteen-hour days that young lawyers and stockbrokers in New York have to give their employers if they want to be promoted, or even stay in the firm.

BENJAMIN FRANKLIN WAS OUR FIRST HONORARY SIBLING. It is interesting that his father bound him, with his permission, as an apprentice to a printer in Boston. The typical apprentice's slow climb, under the tutelage of an elder, from apprentice to journeyman to master, was a characteristic initiation ritual in the hierarchical society. A certain number of years of mutual service was agreed on in the bonding contract. Franklin stayed awhile with his elder but tired of it and later, like a modern person, broke his agreement with his father and his contract, and moved to Philadelphia. So, one could say, he became a sibling at one stroke; and he lived after that as a good Protestant businessman of the newer sort, whose daily psalms contained lines such as "A penny saved is a penny earned," "Early to bed, early to rise, makes a man healthy, wealthy, and wise," and so on. He taught the Method, but without much mention of

God, and without any mention of demons. As for animals, they became metaphors for the way money can give birth to money. Franklin provided in his autobiography this piece of advice to the young:

> *Remember, that money is of the prolific, generating nature. Money can beget money, and its offspring can beget more, and so on. Five shillings turned is six, turned again it is seven and threepence, and so on, till it becomes a hundred pounds. The more there is of it, the more it produces every turning, so that the profits rise quicker and quicker. He that kills a breeding-sow, destroys all her offspring to the thousandth generation. He that murders a crown, destroys all that it might have produced, even scores of pounds.*

By "crown" he meant a large coin. Not to help a crown to reproduce is to "murder" it. We've never known anyone who had such empathy for infertile money.

Once you can feel sorry for money, you may feel your heated sympathy for the poor cooling a little. Even your sympathy for schoolchildren may cool. It was only a few years ago, in Reagan's administration, that ketchup was reclassified as a vegetable in an attempt to meet standards for children's lunches. Ronald Reagan was a sort of Grand Central Station for the trains of disaster.

The workers and the American political Left for a while set up oppositional structures to help restrain unlimited capitalism. Beginning in the late nineteenth century, a vigorous, passionate union movement grew, deepening itself all through the 1920s and 1930s, supporting newspapers, medical help, concerts, lectures, writers. It was a true counterculture movement. The poet Thomas McGrath lived through it all with the Wobblies, and noted that the brotherhood began to fall apart with the impact of overtime during World War II:

> *At Paddy-the-Pig's then stand and drink the payday cup . . . .*
>   *"Slan leat!" says Packy,*
>   *Peers out*

Of his internal Siberia (that's brightened by the eyes of wolves
Only). "Down all the bosses! After the war we'll get them!"

Ay. But the war got us first. Got the working class
By its own fat ass. . .

When consumer culture arrived in full force during the 1950s, union
members were taken in like everyone else; the moves they made to
the suburbs broke up city communities. McGrath implies that greed
was a part of it. Meanwhile business forces brought in machines,
including robots on assembly lines that replaced workers, who now
lost their desirability, and the whole effort for justice for workers was
over.

A Curious Tale

ONCE UPON A TIME THERE WAS A COUNTRY, FAR NORTH AND
far south of here, where farmers found a new domestic creature,
superior to sheep, pigs, or chickens. It happened just after money had
been reclassified as an animal. One day it was a thought; the next
day it was real, and had horns and an udder.

The breeders soon found that the new animal needed much air and
water; and some of the poor had to be moved to the inner cities and
others to the suburbs, to make room. Although it was regret-
table that people had to lose their old homes and their security,
nothing could be more important, the Senate and the House said, for
the future of the nation than this new money cow. What they needed
was one great money bull for the development of the line.

A perfect money bull was finally discovered; his name was Bottom.
For a while, everyone was satisfied with Bottom, and many gifts were
brought to him. Boys wore their caps backward as an honor to
Bottom. He finally learned to speak, and his words and his sperm
were sent all over the known world.

When Bottom began to demand sacrifices, some people became
uneasy. But Congress agreed to his demands. Hundreds of people

lined up to be sacrificed to him. This line of people about to die was called Bottom's line.

THE LINE DRAWN AT THE BOTTOM OF THE SPREADSHEET IS IMPOR-tant, as we all know. The sentence "Let's get out of this airy stuff and look at the bottom line" ends with one small phrase, and yet a whole civilization can disappear through that small hole. The family can't afford a violin, so there are no violinists; building costs run higher than expected, so beauty disappears from our cities; taxpayers vote down a bond increase, so someone's children don't have a place to sit in class. Joseph Campbell remarked that a medieval traveler approaching Chartres or Strasbourg could deduce that the human soul is the most valued thing there; but when we approach New York from New Jersey, we see the buildings of Wall Street and know what is the main thing.

In 1960 the average pay for chief executives at the largest American corporations, after taxes, was twelve times greater than the average wage for factory workers. By 1990 it was seventy times greater. The husband and wife work all day, sometimes at two jobs, in an anxious workplace, and when they get home they are depleted and have nothing to give the children, who feel unwanted. They ask themselves: "Who is in charge here?"

William Greider writes:

Many orthodox economists routinely assume that the American wage decline must continue for at least another generation. The subject came up occasionally during interviews I conducted with various economists at Wall Street brokerages in the mid-1980s and the Wall Street economists, without exception, predicted further erosion for the next twenty to twenty-five years. Unfortunate but inevitable, they said. The trend is driven, they explained, by the deep and ineluctable process in which worldwide wage patterns are moving toward equilibrium—a "harmonization" of labor costs among nations, just as some officials wish to "harmonize" the environmental laws.

Benjamin Franklin's inheritors have pulled the ladder of economic success up, so that the lower rung is out of reach. People in the ghettos, and people in working-class and middle-class neighborhoods, can wave their hands around in the air above their heads, and their fingers will never touch the lower rung of the ladder. The ladder is lowered only for relatives of the transnationals, and a few others.

The closing down of affirmative action means that the ladder is being lifted farther out of reach for black people. The trick of the media is to keep the attention away from those who are pulling the ladder up, and to let the camera zoom in on the people fighting each other to touch a rung.

Reagan, a hero to many, gave so much money through the deficit to his rich pals that little is left for prevention programs, job training, and things that people really need. The confusing contradictory currents in the sibling society are vividly seen in the irony that Ronald Reagan, a poor father by all accounts, utterly unable to genuinely stand for any important "traditional values," managed to represent limitless acquisition, disguised as family. His sibling nature lay in his horizontal emotional range, without a trace of transcendentalism or depth, his emphasis on easily conveyed feeling, rather than depth of feeling, as well as his envy of the rich, which eventually led him to become their puppet.

B OB HERBERT AND OTHER COMMENTATORS WROTE RECENTLY that they were amazed that downsizing, so massive, had evoked so few riots or protests. In the suburbs and small towns, parents are subtly modeling for their children noncombative speech—which the CNN anchors have already modeled for them.

Many college teachers tell me stories of the strange silence in their classes; and the silence has an economic origin. They are in college in order to get a job. The literature of social protest—Dreiser, Steinbeck—produces no resonating passions for justice. William Stafford says in a poem that there is "a shrug that lets the fragile sequence break." Teachers notice that shrug when they discuss the matter of justice. College students are silent because the sequence is breaking. Some corporate executives are far more interested in the available crop of teenage Philippine computer-chip workers than in unemployed teenagers in this country.

Many columnists recently have detailed the rapid decline in citizen participation, in fraternal orders, church sodalities, precinct caucuses, parent-teacher associations, and so on. The heat for public welfare is cooling.

SOME OF THE FEELING OF ABANDONMENT GOES BACK TO THE economic fact that the transnational corporations are abandoning the United States. A vice president of Colgate-Palmolive observed: "The United States does not have an automatic call on our resources. There is no mindset that puts this country first."

But we must not imagine that his mind-set involves compassion for the workers of the world.

Multinational executives work to enhance the company, not the country. The president of NCR Corporation told The New York Times: *"I was asked the other day about United States competitiveness and I replied that I don't think about it at all."*

The market in which the new elites operate is now international in scope. Their fortunes are tied to enterprises that operate across national boundaries. They are more concerned with the smooth functioning of the system as a whole than with any of its parts. Their loyalties—if the term is not itself anachronistic in this context—are international rather than regional, national, or local. They have more in common with their counterparts in Brussels or Hong Kong than with the masses of Americans not yet plugged into the network of global communications.

The psychological and intuitive words of Alexander Mitscherlich, who remarked about the young siblings in Germany and the United States that they "are aware of millions of siblings like them all over the globe," strangely parallel the economic situation of corporation directors who feel they have more in common with their counter-parts in Brussels or Hong Kong than with their high school or college classmates not yet plugged into any job.

We know that robber barons have long been a staple element in American life. Andrew Carnegie, to mention only one, felt a loyalty to the nation, and, as we know, provided thousands of libraries across the United States to large towns and small. The transnational "Carnegies" feel no such loyalty, and this curious lack of loyalty is a genuine sibling characteristic.

The transnational executives don't feel responsibility either, to any country—Mexico, for example—currently being "developed." On the contrary, if wages rise in Mexico, thousands of factories will move elsewhere. During the last thirty years an industrial force made of more than thirteen hundred plants has grown all along the Mexican border, encouraged by low wages and freedom from any social obligations such as health care or prevention of environmental pollution.

There are more than 240 maquila *plants in Juarez (second most after Tijuana), employing one hundred thousand people. Most of the workers are very young—teenagers—and the majority are girls.*

The girls typically find their kidneys affected by the pollution within two years, or their eyesight fading, and are immediately replaced by other young girls.

Indeed, the maquiladora *industry boasts of this attraction in the glossy publication it distributes to prospective companies. In 1981, the industry association reported, the labor cost for a* maquila *worker was $1.12 an hour. By the end of 1989, the real cost had fallen to 56 cents an hour.*

Mexico herself will be abandoned when cheaper labor turns up elsewhere. Free trade actually means that the transnational corporations have won their battle to make working people all over the globe interchangeable.

It is no surprise to anyone to say that business has effectively become our government, and now rules American life on all levels. The long battle that Catholic thinkers, Humanist scholars, and ordinary people instituted against expansive capitalism has been won, and the newly quiet battlefield is called the sibling society.

CHAPTER TEN

Teaching Our Children That Nothing Works

THE ORDINARY MENTAL ENVIRONMENT FOR MILLIONS OF SIB-
ling men and women now is a sort of generalized ingratitude. There
are college students who have never met a single human being who
takes Edmund Spenser or William Wordsworth or Nathaniel Haw-
thorne seriously. Maintaining that our literary ancestors are corrupt
has become a sibling fad.

The Marxist doctrine that private property is the source of evil
proved to be the entering wedge. The inescapable implication of that
doctrine is that our ancestors were either stupid or collaborators.

I FIRST ENCOUNTERED THE SIBLING CULTURE OF INGRATITUDE
when I was a student in college in 1947. Teachers damaged my self-
esteem by reminding me, quite accurately, that I knew nothing. But
on the other hand I was glad to hear that, as a modern, I was superior
to all my ancestors (and yours). Later in a book called *Poems for the
Ascension of J. P. Morgan*, I wrote these lines:

Accountants hover over the earth like helicopters,
Dropping bits of paper engraved with Hegel's name.

159

Badgers carry the papers on their fur
To their den, where the entire family dies in the night.

That's the sort of thing you get when you mix surrealism and ingratitude. The poem says that accountants are somehow connected to Hegel, who, as an ancestor, was the wrong sort of person. The mistakes he made aren't exactly clear; the assumption is that if he lived a hundred years ago, he was very likely wrong, so there is no need to be specific. Mentioning Hegel's name is enough. The badgers are good earthy types, free of any contamination by erring technocrats, so that just a little whiff of the wrong European will kill the whole family, while leaving no incriminating evidence. I like this sort of fantasy, and I still enjoy the lines, but I can't recommend them as philosophical history.

There is a difference between a clean fight with a dead thinker—a fight in which one names his or her main ideas, quotes sentences, offers thought-out arguments, and elaborates the criticisms as bravely as the original offerings were elaborated—and the ungrateful way, which for the most part I took in the poem.

A few devoted New York writers in the 1930s, such as Irving Howe and Lionel Trilling, who imagined themselves as underdogs and heroic battlers, took up the new Marxist ideas to see how the work of writers they had always loved looked in the light of those ideas. They wanted to take readers, through elegant language, into a knowledge that would bring them to tears; they wanted to take readers into the passion in Dostoyevsky and the beauty of E. M. Forster's fiction. Their love of literary ancestors has been swept away by deconstructionists and new historicists who wax enthusiastic about the grant funds for the next language-murdering conference.

It's POSSIBLE THAT AMERICAN CULTURE NOW EXHIBITS MANY qualities we associate with a typical colonialist society. We know now from twentieth-century psychology, if from no other source, that, given the nature of human life, people and nations cannot practice destruction of tribal cultures without having it come back on them.

When colonialist administrators take over a tribal society, their first task is to prove to the indigenous people that nothing in their culture works. It is important also to prove that tribal ways, such as consensus, do not work, and the old ways of talking with the gods, the ways the shamans practice, do not work.

Ships, gunpowder, and armor overpowered the African tribes, and then Westerners, to secure the power, dismantled the elder system. The missionaries who followed the invaders informed the tribes that their gods, carried by their elders, were inadequate, illusionary, or devilish. In America from seventeenth-century New England, when the Puritan leaders began their attack on the Abenaki, the Mohawk, the Algonquin, and the Iroquois, right up through the nineteenth, when the federal government destroyed the Sioux, Comanches, and Cherokees, the most subtle work was to dismantle the elder system. Sometimes it took the form of signing treaties with false chiefs or simply by murdering well-known elders such as Sitting Bull and Crazy Horse. Tribes were ordered to give up their drums, their sun dances, their sweat lodges, and other rituals, that is, to dismantle all their vertical arrangements. Children were forcibly taken to "Indian schools," alcohol was introduced to the tribes, peoples were removed from one reservation to another. Andrew Jackson in more than one way was a leveler. We destroyed the elder system of the blacks at the root by deliberately breaking up families at slave auctions.

We can say that our destruction of the tribal systems, their elderhood and religions, has now come back on us. We now see an entire generation of students living in an impoverished landscape. The elders are without power, and the Christian religion is no longer vigorous. The young, black or white, tend to be rationalists and skeptics, and have nothing to live up to; the mutual dependence of generations breaks down. As in Somalia now, or China in the nineteenth century, there is much drug addiction and a general feeling of hopelessness. The white population, who would seem to be, technically, the masters of their own culture, sense that they are not in control. We could say that the American personality has always been porous, and so easily penetrated by the very ideas we have developed to pry apart other cultures. The increasing ignorance about history, geography, philosophical matters, foreign languages, moral issues, Shakespeare, the Bible, or Greek literature resembles the impoverished world of colonized people. The students' diminished interior landscape, upon which only pop culture shacks have been erected, corresponds with the blasted cultural landscape of the adults. Where the mental countryside of the adults once included well-built old houses and even gardens and those squares where people talked, now adults live in the ruins. The adults have had their ability to admire deeply damaged.

We can say that Deconstruction is a form of technology, like gunpowder and the tank. It is used against our own students.

No matter whether we as readers belong to the Left or Right, no matter whether we as thinkers rejoice in the fall of communism or grieve that certain great socialist ideas were never really tried, no matter whether we are happy or sad about the Red Guard, we have to grieve that we have left contemporary students with their power of admiration basically in ruins. If Generation X is passive or uninventive, it is because their ability to admire has been taken away.

As we have already implied, the role of colonialist administrators has been taken over by the left. It is an amazing turnabout, one full of irony. They teach that European kings were major criminals who dressed well, that the feudalism of the Middle Ages was a transparent failure, that the Renaissance amounted to a triumph of false consciousness, that the Magna Carta solved nothing, that the English royalists were decadent hedonists, that the Puritan governments were brutal, that Saint Teresa was probably sexually disturbed, that the New England town meetings were masks for oppression, that the entrepreneur system set up after the Civil War by industrialists such as J. P. Morgan and Andrew Carnegie produced nothing valuable, that Beethoven wrote imperialist music, that Mencken was a secret fascist, that Roosevelt encouraged Pearl Harbor, that President Kennedy's Peace Corps did not work, that Freud supported child abuse, and that almost every one of his ideas was wrong.

The cultural Left does not mention that, given the brutal chaos of fourteenth-century Europe, feudalism was an ingenious effort to prevent further descent into human disintegration; nor that the Renaissance amounted to a combined effort by Jewish, Christian, and Muslim thinkers to form a common religion; that the Puritan governments began the movement toward private conscience that saved the United States from Spanish fascistic obedience; that Saint Teresa, with all her daring, visited realms that no Marxist could even imagine; that the New England meetings showed an ability to remain in conflict for hours or years and still hold respect; that some Beethoven sonatas have the quality of wild grass; that Mencken was one of the great defenders of Jews in Philadelphia; that Franklin and Eleanor Roosevelt chose working people over their own aristocratic class; and that Freud is the most courageous and disturbing thinker since Galileo.

Our society has been damaged not only by acquisitive capitalism, but also by an idiotic distrust of all ideas, religions, and literature handed down to us by elders and ancestors. Many siblings are convinced that they have received nothing of value from anyone. The older truth is that every man or woman is indebted to all other persons, living or dead, and is indebted as well to animals, plants, and the gods.

MOST SIBLINGS BELIEVE THAT NO TRUTH CAN BE SPOKEN FROM the center; that is a typical attitude of a colonized people. Some words spoken from the center, now and in the past, deserve to be mocked, and rejected. But some truths spoken from the edges are false as well.

If colonialist administrators begin by attacking the vertical thought of the tribe they have conquered, and dismantling the elder system, they end by dismantling everything in sight. That's where we are. We are the first culture in history that has "colonized" itself. The inner dome of heaven has fallen. As for the gods, they are, as Michael Meade remarks, in the garbage. To say we have no center that we love is the same thing as saying that we have colonized ourselves. What we need to study, then, is how a colonized culture heals itself.

CHAPTER ELEVEN

Looking at Women's and Men's Movements from Inside the Sibling House

The Several Women's Movements

Even that marvelous man Richard Maurice Bucke, when he wrote *Cosmic Consciousness,* which mentions many possessors of cosmic consciousness who had preceded Whitman, does not include a single woman. His book was published in 1889. Frederick Douglass, who was born a slave in Maryland and who was present at the Seneca Falls Convention in 1848, wrote: "Many who have at last made the discovery that negroes have some rights as well as other members of the human family, have yet to be convinced that women are entitled to any."

In 1853, Sojourner Truth, another former slave, was in New York to attend a Women's Rights Convention at the Broadway Tabernacle. Her remarks from the platform were so delicious that they deserve another hearing:

Now, women do not ask half of a kingdom, but their rights, and they don't get 'em. When she comes to demand 'em, don't you hear how sons hiss their mothers like snakes, because they ask for their rights; and how can they ask for anything less? The king ordered Haman to be hung on the gallows which he prepared to hang others; but I do not want any man to be killed, but I am sorry to see them so short-minded. But we'll have our rights; see if we don't; and you can't stop us from them; see if you can. You may hiss as much as you like, but it is comin'. Women don't get half as much rights as they ought to; we want more, and we will have it. Jesus says: "What I say to one, I say to all—watch!" I'm a-watchin'. God says: "Honor your father and your mother." Sons and daughters ought to behave themselves before their mothers, but they do not. I can see them a-laughin', and pointin' at their mothers up here on the stage. They hiss when an aged woman comes forth. If they'd been brought up proper they'd have known better than hissin' like snakes and geese. I'm 'round watchin' these things, and I wanted to come up and say these few things to you, and I'm glad of the hearin' you give me. I wanted to tell you a mite about Women's Rights, and so I came out and said so. I am sittin' among you to watch; and every once and awhile I will come out and tell you what time of night it is.

IT IS NOT OUR TASK HERE TO DISCUSS THE RANGE OF THE women's struggle for rights, which has a long and valorous history. Because so much has been written about the women's movement, I won't go into as much detail as in the men's movement, which is relatively new. We want to look at the various women's movements in the United States now—and later, the various men's movements—from the point of view of the sibling society we experience all around us.

In the last thirty years or so, women have been giving other women permission to express their anger consciously. Women's anger is long-standing; it didn't begin flowing yesterday. And yet during the hundreds of years in which Western women were economically dependent on their husbands, anger had to be expressed primarily unconsciously through bodily diseases, hysteria, depression, and early death. The act of speaking anger could put a woman out on the street.

In the 1960s, women joined in "consciousness-raising" sessions that were partly for raising anger; participants were to go home and speak to husbands with energetic fire, pertinent personal facts, and appropriate concepts such as patriarchy, oppression, and privilege. For many, it was a new experience; there were some astonished husbands, for they had been swimming in transparent privilege for so long that they were not aware of the medium.

Anger is a powerful fuel, and the anger that carried many women—some for better, some for worse—out of marriage also carried other women into passionate complaints in essays, novels, and poems. Some working women took this emotion into offices, where they fought for equal treatment and the end of sexual harassment, and they took it into the law courts, where they advocated hundreds of new laws in the area of affirmative action, divorce arrangements, punishment of male abusers, custody decisions, rules for bank loans, and so on.

Men's work in the 1990s, by contrast, began with the permission to express grief and shame consciously, which men have traditionally expressed unconsciously, through alcohol, violence, fundamentalism, and numbness.

Anger vitalizes people; it also temporarily narrows the range of vision. Anger burns through certain husks of apathy like white-hot fire through steel; it does not encourage grief, nor the examination of one's own shadow.

As WE LOOK INTO THE FAR PAST OF THE RACE, IT SEEMS LIKELY that some of the emotions that we now direct to other people were directed at God. Among these emotions was anger. I don't mean that women were not angry at men in the past, or at women. But both men and women saved some of their anger for God, because of the scarcity that oppresses people in some parts of the planet. There was too much snow and ice; you could freeze to death waiting for a seal to rise, and too few seals did come to the ice holes. In the Southern Hemisphere, water was often the problem, or you had to run in the heat for miles after a kangaroo and you forgot exactly where to stop to find a succulent root. Wheat withered in August; floods came down from the mountains and drowned everyone; the cod you caught in the summer rotted in a few days. Men and women were forced into specialization of labor just to keep their clan of fifty people alive, half of them sick all the time; women died in childbirth, no one got enough vitamins; people were old at thirty. The list of deprivations is endless; and the specialized gender roles, adopted out of fear and need, caused deformations in the personalities of both men and women.

So, along with the devotion to God or to the earth, there was some anger. One of the oldest female divinities in India is called Kali, which means "Terror-Joy." It is said that if one realizes how much terror there is on this planet, Kali will be present in an instant.

The habit of holding the goddess or the god responsible for disasters is an old way of thinking. A lot of gratitude as well as anger went to the divinities, or to whatever agency arranged this system.

When cities developed, and it appeared that nature could be tamed, both anger and gratitude turned more toward the human. Something changed; the health of cities depended on training wheat or barley to grow in huge fields alone, whether it wanted to or not. And a class of warriors had to be developed to defend the grain fields. Still, to be a slave to the fields was hard work. The society was no longer a democratic society as it had been in hunter-gatherer times. The development of cities required field work and military defense; it seems likely that the anger of both men and women became directed at the structure of patriarchy, which would include the priestly classes, the warrior classes, and those charged with enforcing work. The dominator group drew anger, and the anger continued unabated for several thousand years. Not only women's but also men's anger flowed toward the patriarchal structure. Euripides sees the dominator mood clearly, Shakespeare in his best plays describes the abuse accurately. Women poets such as Margaret of

Navarre speak of it, as well as Kafka, Kierkegaard, and Swift. The anger against patriarchal structures is a just anger; its structure has damaged both women and men. The women's movement has in general been a vigorous and essential wave of energy, which has brought about deep changes, long overdue, in the relations between men and women. Patriarchal certainty is no longer so firmly implanted in the brain of every man, and patriarchal structures have dissolved in many fields, allowing women to move forward and take a place in the world.

But not all the changes that women have wanted have taken place. Justice is not complete, and some anger has been redirected a third time, this time away from priests, warriors, and foremen to men themselves.

When the two vertical angers become directed sideways, so to speak, then all the arrangements we have made in society seem wrong, as if they had been invented only for the purpose of oppressing women. Engels urged "the abolition of the monogamous family." Charlotte Perkins Gilman, in her book *The Home* (1903), urges a number of changes in patriarchal society, but the essential one is "to break up that relic of the patriarchal age—the family as an economic unit." Some agree with Gilman that the family is an evil institution, and some couldn't be more opposed to that idea. But such arguments have been overtaken by events.

Looking Back from the Sibling House

WE ARE ALL HUMAN BEINGS NOW, STANDING IN THE RUBBLE OF A destroyed literate society, looking at the ruins of education, family, and child protection. Technology has destroyed interrelations in the human community that have taken centuries to develop. The breaking of human beings' connection to land has harmed everyone. We are drowning in uncontrollable floods of information. We are living among dispirited and agonized teenagers who can't find any hope. Genuine work is disappearing, and we are becoming aware of a persistent infantilizing of men and women, a process already far advanced.

The sibling society has arrived. Attitudes that seemed brave thirty years ago are blinkered now, and positions that seemed on target twenty years ago now miss the mark.

The effort to bring some equality back into relations between men and women has been long overdue, bravely fought, and partially successful. A French feminist recently said:

All the same, it was not until the twentieth century that equality between the sexes became a real item on the agenda. Two decades have been sufficient to put an end to the system of representations that for several thousand years allowed men to wield power over women: patriarchy. In so doing, we have not only achieved the conditions in which sexual equality has become a possibility, we have also challenged the archaic model of the complementarity of the sexes, and dealt ourselves new cards of identity.

If I now mention some of the areas in which the women's movement, as we know it, has increased some of the less desirable sides of the new society, I don't want that to imply that the women's movement has been wrong or counterproductive or a mistake. My daughters would not be the fiery and accomplished women they are without it. We need more women in every field: among them teachers of literature, because of women's marvelous grasp of complicated thought and feeling; and above all, we need women's voices in government and international relations, where men are getting caught in the cracks of their brains.

There has been an increase in neglect of the young, which was not intended by those people who urged women to go out into the larger world. Day-care centers are not universally provided, nor are many of the day-care arrangements healthy for children. Often in this culture neither parent wants to stay home to raise the child. In a reversal of the African adage, we can't even afford one parent. In child care, we are looking at a disaster situation.

This country's slow sinking into desirousness, consumer greed, and the loss of what one might call executive control over the lower brains cannot be attributed to women or to the women's movement. *Ms.* magazine has fought consistently against consumer advertising and in fact has lived five years now without it. Women, having found themselves the objects of consumer greed, are not as enthusiastic as men are about giving capitalism what it wants.

Some of the old Charlotte Perkins Gilman anger against the family was a mistake. Sociologists, trying to help, pointed out that when the father was present in the house, there was a lot of anger in him and against him. They didn't grasp, however, that when there is no father in the house, there will be even more anger.

We rejoice to see anger go off at stage right and then are surprised to see anger arriving at stage left.

NO ONE AT THE TIME OF EARLY FEMINIST PROGRESS could possibly have known how fast the old or nuclear family system would collapse with nothing much to replace it; how complete the abandonment of children would become. What seemed eternal—the father and mother house—was only a house of cards.

The spokeswomen for "leaving the house" feminism bear some responsibility for telling a woman that she could follow her career for years and still have a child, and for telling a mother that she could be a supermom and do it all. Moreover, raising children alone has not proved to be a great source of freedom for women. They still hold in their hearts the responsibility for what happens to children—as many distanced men do not—and women's doing it alone has simply increased the lamentable distance in many men. It is the job of men to help in closing that distance in other men, but the men's work has affected only a few men so far.

Some older women, still very much a part of the feminist movement, no longer blame men in the way that was fashionable in the 1960s and 1970s, and some parts of the women's movement have never blamed men. At the same time, the habit the women's movement has had of locating all forms of toxic authority in the patriarchal structure and then confusing it with men has increased the general hatred of authority that is so damaging to the younger generation. Many women meant to attack only the unjust authority of men, but adolescents find the emotion of authority-hating catchy, and many of them reject maternal authority as fiercely as they do paternal authority, even extending the hatred of authority to grade-school teachers and bus drivers.

Blaming is not new. Mothers have felt blamed for centuries, and parents in general feel blamed unjustly by teenagers. But the virulent new kind of blaming that we see today is sanctioned by thousands, if not millions, of well-educated people and has become a standard part of all intellectual debate in the last forty years.

Then there is the question of the superego and its perfectionism. The superego of women, as we know, is just as perfectionist as the superego of men, and tends to concentrate more on physical appearance. Marion Woodman titled one of her books *Addiction to Perfection* and found that most women she saw in therapy hated their body for one reason or another. The women's movement has tried to free women from this obsession that all female bodies should be slim and young, and they've done wonderful work in this regard, although their work has affected only a few. At the same time, perfectionism hovers around the spokeswomen in other ways. Men in general are not good enough, fathers are not thoughtful enough, sons are not pacific enough, men don't express their feelings enough: there's a lot of "not enough." But some harsh criticisms are softening; many women realize that the problems we face are too enormous to be solved by one gender alone.

The Various Men's Movements

Some people still find the term "men's movement" confounding. Others say, "The whole of Western literature is a men's movement. Why do we need another?"

In talking of men's movements, I'm going to leave out the Masons, the Scottish Rite, and the Shriners. They are basically spiritual study groups influenced by Muslim culture, but they have never affected the great majority of men.

The western frontier has had a powerful effect on men in the United States. As the western frontier opened up, an increasing number of American men were drawn out of their houses in more than one way. Jane Tompkins of Duke University, in her witty book *West of Everything,* describes how women began to fill that empty space with devotional exercises, ethical ideas, passions, and religious sentiments congenial to them. For example, many women during the mid-nineteenth century sponsored prayer meetings in the house, and mothers offered each other and their children the virtues of forgiveness, compassion, sensitivity, and empathy; they opposed provocative actions, revenge, and all forms of violence. Jane Tompkins says that the men waited about fifty years to respond, and when they did, their response took the form of the Western novel and the Western movie. She sums up the attitude of the Western writers:

> *American men are taking their manhood back from the Christian women who have been holding it in thrall. Mercy and religion as preached by women and the clergy have stood in manhood's way too long, and now men are finally rebelling. . . .*

So we will maintain that the attitudes embodied in the Western movies and novels amount to a sort of mind-set with which the recent men's movements have all had to deal.

What do westerns stand for? Instead of the expressiveness of language, the playfulness of language, the contradictory motions that flow upward in language whether or not one intends them, they stand for silence. Men look at the hills for a couple of hours without talking, and then they look at their horse for an hour, and summarize it all by saying, "See ya, bud." Instead of the inward struggles of conscience, the hours on one's knees asking forgiveness, and the examination of the inner life, westerns provide suffering and blizzards. It's well known that any man would prefer to walk thirty miles upwind in a blizzard than talk for ten minutes about his relation to a woman or to God. Friendship with men was recommended rather than life with a woman. Gary Cooper is famous for drawing the tender affections of a young schoolteacher from the East toward him: he may save her cattle or her life, but at the end of the movie he will tip his hat to her, kiss his horse, and ride off toward the hard, silent hills. The important action in a western takes place in a canyon, not in the kitchen or the living room. Western men throw out the idea of forgiveness; and retaliation through violence comes to the center. A woman will say of some duel that is planned, "Please don't do it, Jake!" He says, "I'm sorry, Margaret. I don't have any choice. I gotta do it." When someone dies, Western men enjoy not being able to remember the Christian liturgy. Men in westerns stand around the grave, saying things like "Well, he was real good with horses." Finally, the westerns emphasize total victory or the stoic endurance of defeat, but notably short-circuit grief.

Western novels show a genuine love of landscape and solitude, and yet the recommended behaviors make a unified field. The ideas have a lot of consistency and spring out of a desire to (partly) refuse what women want. The movement produced books with titles like *Riders of the Purple Sage* instead of *A Room of One's Own*. We remember President Reagan's fondness for Louis L'Amour. We could say that Ronald Reagan was a late-coming Phyllis Schlafly for this group, although true to the western type, he spoke very little and it was mostly jokes. President Reagan was probably reading westerns when he invaded Grenada and sent illegal arms to the Contras. President Bush could also be said to have been "west of everything" during the Gulf War.

THE FEMINIST MEN'S MOVEMENT IS THE EARLIEST CONSISTENT men's movement. Some of its earliest theorists were Marc Fiegen-Fasteau in *The Male Machine* (1974) and Warren Farrell in *The Liberated Man* (1975). In 1981, Joseph Pleck wrote *The Myth of Masculinity*. In 1987 Harry Brod published *The Making of Masculinities*. More recent leaders of the feminist men's movement have been Michael Kimmel in *Changing Men: New Directions and Research on Men and Masculinity*, Jeff Hearn's *The Gender of Oppression*, and John Stoltenberg, who carried the feminist theory all the way in his book *Refusing to Be a Man*. If he can find in himself a thought he considers masculine, then he is determined not to think it. This movement, as its leaders say clearly, takes its cue from feminism, and the polarity from which it takes its cue is not women's values but "traditional masculinity." They put forward the view that traditional masculinity authenticates itself through oppressing women. Masculinity to them is essentially toxic, like a poison.

Traits traditionally imagined as masculine, such as competitiveness, wildness, and aggression, spring, they believe, from culture, not genetic inheritance. Since masculinity is made, it can be remade. They want a new man, and they want him now.

Most feminist men hate the concept of "deep masculinity." The feminist writer Tim Beneke says: "There is no such thing as deep masculinity, because there is no such thing as masculinity." Whatever comes out of the masculine soul is, in their view, wrong by essence.

Male feminists call for determined battles against all forms of the male power structure, and most forms of male authority. The movement deserves respect for its battle against sexist language, against the hardening of men in the military, and against male violence in the home and in the world at large. Some feminist pieces include "What Every Woman Should Know About Men" by Alan Alda; "Men and Muscles" by Barry Glassner; "The Dirty Play of Little Boys" by Gary Alan Fine; and "Prisoners of Manliness" by Joseph Pleck. The movement makes strong alliances with the gay community, and its speakers frequently lecture in women's studies departments. When feminist spokeswomen talk of the men's movement they would like to see, it's usually this one. Gloria Steinem praises particularly the extremist work of John Stoltenberg.

The feminist men's movement is widely accepted in universities. The language that feminist men use is basically sociological; and they are accustomed to phrases such as "hegemonic, phallocentric literature." Male feminism is "horizontal" in the sense that it regards all mythology and religion as hopelessly polluted by masculine wrongness. Not all male feminists agree with each other; there is more variety than would appear in this brief summation.

Some are related to the Maoists in their demand that "man" change immediately, and to the Marxists in their addiction to specialized and indigestible language. Most want nothing to do with God, but, being sociologists, they don't have much good to say about nature, either. Michael Kimmel complains that many feminist men are perfectionistic and full of judgment. Their strong side is that they want men to take responsibility for their privileges. They oppose all forms of war and empire, they understand how deeply contemporary man has been distorted and damaged by industry and patriarchy, and they are fierce fighters.

A MORE RECENT MEN'S MOVEMENT WE'LL DISCUSS WAS ORIGInally named the Mythopoetic movement, although I think a more accurate title is the Expressive Men's Movement. So far it has not had much influence on the culture as a whole, and what it longs for most, initiation of young men into spiritual life and the mentoring of young men by older men, seems to be precisely what the culture is most unwilling to give.

It tries to bring men out of their macho silence. Its teachers emphasize ritual, although not only Christian ritual; it cares for elegant and expressive language in poetry or storytelling; it works for initiation of young men and the introduction of an elder system; it asks for grief.

In contrast to the feminist men's movement, most of its teachers believe that masculinity has a genetic base in the cells of the body and is not only learned. Certain qualities called masculine are learned, but not all. Certain experiences men have had in tensions with their fathers, in hunting or raising animals, in times of solitude in nature, have been inscribed so deeply that one cannot entirely wash the letters out of the stone. Through story, men can recognize spiritual energy or warrior energy or lover energy, and men then have a choice of how to live that energy. The movement is based in small men's groups. The teachers—among them the mythologist Michael Meade, the theologian Robert Moore, the tracker John Stokes, the therapist John Lee, the psychologist James Hillman—often disagree with each other. No central point of view has been found, and is basically a form of adult education outside the bounds of the university. Two of its teachers, Malidoma Somé from West Africa and Martín Prechtel from Guatemala, are initiated men, and work toward achieving some sort of initiation practices for young men and women that will not be harmful and will help fill the gap left by fatherlessness and a collapsing culture.

The movement began primarily with white men, but recently, particularly in conferences organized by Michael Meade, it has been able to achieve week-long conferences in which half of the men are black and Hispanic, many from youth gangs. Harris Breiman and Bob Roberts work extensively with men in prisons and with newly released convicts. Some of the younger men have learned to be better fathers and to work. The movement has many faults.

TWO NEW MEN'S MOVEMENTS HAVE ARRIVED MORE RECENTLY. Both have thousands of men in them. One calls itself the Promise Keepers. Founded by a former coach for the University of Colorado football team, the movement's meetings take place in football stadiums where many men tend to feel at home. Emotion is allowed for men in sports stadiums, even though the emotion tends not to be very personal or inner; moreover, the presence of as many as sixty thousand men makes them feel safe. I think the emphasis they put on men keeping promises to their wives—that they will remain in the marriage—and to their children—that they will come back to the house as concerned fathers and remain there through the long course of childhood—is admirable. It is exactly the kind of promise that many men need and want to make. The movement also pays attention to the tremendous spiritual energy that men have, which they often don't feel is appropriate in small prayer meetings or in more conventional churches. These men are not, like Gary Cooper, looking for a sort of natural god in the canyon; they are not afraid of religious language, and they recognize that much of the healthy and steadfast energy of men is not being used. It is being wasted; and one way to make men conscious of the amount of healthy energy they have is to bring sixty thousand of them together. They also put a lot of emphasis on healing between the black community and the white community. There is great wisdom in that. They ask men to become part of small men's groups, so that others are there to remind the individual man to keep his discipline and his promises. We'll return to discussion of the Promise Keepers shortly.

Other men's movements include the men's rights movement; the gay men's movement, which some see as a part of the feminist men's movement and others feel to be separate; and the New Warriors, who provide, as their name suggests, training in developing assertiveness and centering. The many groups of black men who have been meeting, some under church auspices for years, joined thousands of new men for the Million Man March in Washington, D.C., organized by Louis Farrakhan. This movement, emphasizing responsibility and fatherhood, has tremendous possibilities.

Looking Back from the Sibling House

I think one can fairly say that the macho attitudes embodied in western movies have contributed to the disappearance of fathers. The lone rogue male is presented as the norm; and the rebellion against Christianity has contributed to the horizontal mood of sibling culture. There is a disrespect for social authority deep inside the western. A man with a good eye takes authority into his own hands.

Feminist men have a powerful hatred of hierarchy and authority, which fits well with sibling attitudes. Like the political Left, they teach that none of our structures work, because they are all poisoned. They are opposed to the nuclear family for the same reason; like many siblings, they locate corrupt authority in the blood insistences of the father. Having decided that fathers and grandfathers have been poisoned by sexism, they find themselves only able to rely on each other. In one way, feminist men, as a group, are a small model of the sibling society; in another sense, their passion sets them apart.

The expressive men's movement, one could say, is not expressive enough. Its stories are tuned primarily to the Anglo-Saxon world, and only in the last three or four years has it succeeded in attracting men from the black and Hispanic communities, who are in many ways more expressive than white men. The expressive men's movement tries to make shame among men conscious, just as one wing of the women's movement has tried to make women's anger conscious. In many families, shame has been carried down the male line from father to son for generations, and is usually treated with alcohol. There is a breaking of the line of unconscious shame in this generation. At the same time, anger brings one more quickly into political battles than shame does. The expressive men's movement has been slow in asking for political change and developing enough clarity so that the program they stand for can be apprehended even by the media.

The Promise Keepers seem to suggest that men can throw out all the work that women have done in the last thirty years. The recommended conversation with a Promise Keeper's wife is this: "Honey, I'm going to take the leadership of the family back now. I'm not asking you about this, I'm telling you." For some women that will be satisfying; for others it will be intolerable. And the relaxed tone of the suggested conversation implies that men are completely out of touch with what women have achieved. The Promise Keepers are trying to reverse some sibling society tendencies, including fatherlessness, neglect of the young, and the hatred of authority and codes; and they are attempting to help the "I" regain some control over the two lower brains. But they pay very little attention to the dark side of any missionary movement.

People do have a shadow, and the Promise Keepers show no evidence of dealing with it practically. Jimmy Swaggart paid no attention to his shadow, and it returned to haunt him later. If sixty thousand men pay no attention to their shadows, what happens?

The leaders are clearly literalists. Apparently, the only stories accepted are those from the Bible, and they are not told to help people think but as carriers of doctrine. So such work doesn't help men to overcome the literalism that appears all the time in the sibling society, nor to overcome the literalness learned in law school or business school. Literal thinking tends to make an enemy out of anyone who thinks differently, so their descent into fundamentalist attacks on so-called pagans and homosexuals may be a single-minded attempt to cure the worsening social climate.

THE VARIOUS MEN'S AND WOMEN'S MOVEMENTS ARE VERY recent, and we mustn't expect too much of them. In the absence of fathers, and in the chaos of the sibling mentality, these places of intensity are precious, both for men and for women.

One essential matter that neither the women's movement nor the men's have addressed vigorously enough is the socialization of young males in the absence of fathers and mentors. This is the basic problem the whole sibling society faces. When Mary Wollstonecraft published her *Vindication of Women's Rights* in 1792, young males in the west were in general still socialized. They went mad in war, and some brutality was always present domestically, but most men labored steadfastly and soberly to support parents, wives, children, and the general culture. When the Seneca Convention was called in 1848, young men in America were for the most part still socialized, some by force, some by literate values, some by community pressure, some by habit, some by necessity, some, among black men, by cruelty and their need to survive among clever enemies. A hundred years later, in 1950, some steadfastness among young men still held. "In the year 1950, in all of America, only 170 persons under the age of 15 were arrested for what the FBI calls serious crimes, i.e., murder, forcible rape, robbery, and aggravated assault. . . . In the same year, 94,784 persons 15 years and older were arrested for serious crimes. In 1950, adults (defined here as those over and including 15 years of age) committed serious crimes at a rate 215 times that of child crimes. . . . Between 1950 and 1979, the rate of serious crimes committed by children increased 11,000%." And we know that most crimes committed by adult men are committed by men ages 13–24.

The fundamental problem in the continuation of a decent life everywhere in the world is this question of the socialization of young males. In Kenya, the government five years ago ordered male initiation practices in the villages ended, insisting that all young boys go to school instead. Two years later, a group of young men in

Kenya, in an unprecedented event attacked a dormitory and raped a number of young women. In New Guinea, where initiation of young men is ending, there are for the first time reports of gangs of young men, up to a hundred in a group, roving the countryside.

It is not women's job to socialize young males. That is the job of the older men, or from another point of view, it's the job of the entire culture. The feminist movement has unfortunately not supported the attempts made so far to reinstitute initiation of young men. Early efforts in that direction have received wholesale attacks from gender feminist spokeswomen; and yet all the advances made for women can be undone in several strokes by unsocialized young males. It's important for women to agree that there is a place for all-male high schools for young men. It's important for them to support the mentoring system. It's important for women to think of the genders working together. Some women oppose initiation for young men because they mistakenly think it is always brutal, or it takes away resources that should be given to young women. Even though women have continued to succeed better in civilizing their daughters than men have in civilizing their sons, nevertheless we know that girls' souls are also dying. Girls are joining gangs; a certain hardness and brutality is appearing; girls are also in prison now for shootings of total strangers. Millions of young women are taking drugs, and their primary pressure to enter drugs and violence comes from unsocialized males.

Part Four

CULTURE

CHAPTER TWELVE

Exultation in the Midst of Flatness

THE PAINTINGS IN THE DORDOGNE CAVES ARE RELIABLY dated at 26,000 B.C.; and they show intricately remembered images of deer, running bison, mammoths who are wounded, in elaborate detail.

The Dordogne caves also show a scene that is now famous, with thousands of words written about it. The scene is a thin man with a bird head and an erection (near a wounded mammoth) apparently falling (backward) into ecstasy. His bird head does not appear to be a mask. The artist has created a new image: a bird-headed man falling with an erection backward into ecstasy. No such marvelous being actually exists. We can say that one job of the midbrain is to produce such images, which helps us to be free from the repetitive world.

THERE IS A STORY OUT OF AFRICA ABOUT READING THAT OFFERS some new information. Teachers were training men and women, about thirty-five years of age, to read for the first time. The teachers eventually learned to warn them: "When you are practicing reading in your room, put a blanket over your shoulders." It turned out that the effort involved in reading was so large that it could drop the body temperature two or three degrees and so could bring on a cold or a sore throat. Most of us, having learned to read at a time of inexhaustible energy, have forgotten how difficult it was.

Apparently when the visual cortex takes in the word *bridge*, for example, it refers it to the forebrain, which in turn refers it to the midbrain, which creates the image of a bridge in the "mind's eye" and sends it back. So reading means a journey from the visual cortex to the forebrain and a microsecond later to the midbrain, and then the image leaps back. Such travel through the brain, with "arsenic lobsters," as Lorca says, "falling on your head," is the joy of reading.

A profound athletic energy is evoked when we read "The three Billy-Goats Gruff stood under the dark bridge, waiting." We see the bridge first, then the darkness under the bridge, and then the three Billy-Goats Gruff, waiting in the darkness. It is as if a great horse leaps across the space between neocortex and midbrain, then leaps back, with its rider, six times in that single sentence in order to carry the darkness under the bridge, the bridge itself, the goats, and their horns and their gruffness over to the "mind's eye."

Television short-circuits all that work, that exercise, that play, that joy, by providing the image. The neocortex does not need to bring out its great leaping horse. The television set delivers the image directly to the midbrain. Neil Postman, in *Amusing Ourselves to Death*, has written cogently about the damage to brain labor caused by this short-circuiting. Joseph Chilton Pearce believes that heavy watching of television means the end of the evolution that the brain has experienced so far:

> The average child in the United States sees six thousand hours of television by their fifth year. . . . Television floods the infant-child brain with images at the very time his or her brain is supposed to learn to make images from within. . . . Failing to develop imagery means having no imagination.

Both painting and poetry in our time are beginning to suffer from lack of images. Some painters find themselves unable to create images in the way Chagall or Van Gogh did; they have to cannibalize Botticelli or convert advertising images to art. The damage that television has caused to the brain's image-making ability is one reason for some of the flatness in fiction, poetry, and art in recent decades.

We know that artists, at least since the time of the Dordogne caves, have been able to leap if asked, providing visual images and even creating images never seen in this world. Georg Trakl, a poet born before television, says in "Mourning":

The dark eagles, sleep and death,
Rustle all night around my head:
The golden statue of man
Is swallowed by the icy comber
Of eternity. On the frightening reef
The purple remains go to pieces,
And the dark voice mourns
Over the sea.

Lorca says:

There is a wire stretched from the Sphinx to the safety deposit box
that passes through the heart of all poor children.

I once saw a television program trying to report on the attempts of a company in the South to reinstitute segregated bathrooms. To hear of such a regressive project brings up a flood of thoughts, but the camera couldn't suggest the thoughts; it needed to show an object. We were shown two white wash basins, then a toilet; first we saw the toilet from the front, then we looked directly down into it; but since the report wasn't finished, we saw the wash basins once more, then the toilet, then the interior of the toilet—three times. One felt a little like one feels when reading some contemporary poetry, like a deranged bird in a cage, pecking at the floor.

Some art and poetry imitate television of that sort now, showing objects over and over but no new images. The mood is flat, passive, and depressed. It is a contrast to the happiness of genuine creation, which offers something between joy and exultation, as in these lines by Emily Dickinson:

Exultation is the going
Of an inland soul to sea,
Past the houses—past the headlands—
Into deep Eternity—

MANY AFRICAN POETS TAKE GREAT PRIDE IN BEING HUMAN. ONE
poem says:

Do not seek too much fame,
but do not seek obscurity.
Be proud.
But do not remind the world of your deeds.
Excel when you must,
but do not excel the world.
Many heroes are not yet born,
many have already died.
To be alive to hear this song is a victory.

The paintings of Vermeer exhibit this pride, and Chagall as well, but
it is not a sibling feeling. In sibling art, its hero tends to be replaced
by dead horses, or a video installation. Few contemporary novelists
can imagine a hero, and the characters in Bret Easton Ellis, Douglas
Coupland, and Tama Janowitz novels are just ordinary folks. David
Hewitt remarked in *Esquire*, "Mine is a generation perfectly willing
to admit its contemptible qualities." There is evidence that on some
level we are sick of seeing human beings, and even sick of being
human beings. Pablo Neruda expressed that feeling perhaps for the
first time in 1933:

It so happens I am sick of being a man.
It so happens that I walk into tailor shops and movie houses
dried up, waterproof, like a swan made of felt
steering my way in a water of wombs and ashes.

The smell of barbershops makes me break into hoarse sobs.
The only thing I want is to lie still like stones or wool.

The only thing I want is to see no more stores, no gardens,
no more goods, no spectacles, no elevators.

Neruda was by ancestry Basque. We can say playfully that the European body that once found Pascal's love of God and Montaigne's
deep friendliness for humanity in its cells now feels a disgust for
human beings. Our disgust, Neruda implies, is neither right nor
wrong but simply there; and the dog's nose found it. How different
it is from Pope's "The proper study of mankind is man." Neruda lays
out one sniff after the other, one sniff per line. What could have
happened in the interval between Pope and Neruda? Ortega raises
the question in *Revolt of the Masses*:

> *The fact is this: from the time European history begins in the VIth*
> *century up to the year 1800—that is, through the course of twelve*
> *centuries—Europe does not succeed in reaching a total population*
> *greater than 180 million inhabitants. Now, from 1800 to 1914—little*
> *more than a century—the population of Europe mounts 180 to 460*
> *millions! I take it that the contrast between these figures leaves no*
> *doubt as to the prolific qualities of the last century. In three genera-*
> *tions it produces a gigantic mass of humanity which, launched like a*
> *torrent over the historic area, has inundated it. This fact, I repeat,*
> *should suffice to make us realize the triumph of the masses and all*
> *that is implied and announced by it. Furthermore, it should be added*
> *as the most concrete item to that rising of the level of existence which*
> *I have already indicated.*

Neruda, too, senses that the disgust has to do with the increasing
numbers of people:

> *It so happens that I am sick of my feet and my nails*
> *and my hair and my shadow.*
> *It so happens I am sick of being a man.*

Sixty years have passed since that poem was written, and now
millions of people feel that disgust. The Impressionists' love for the
human face and body is gone. Despite our obsession with malls, we

all want "no more goods, no spectacles, no elevators," and, one could also say, "no people."

And there's nothing we can do about it. The siblings in Czechoslovakia and China are just as greedy as those in Maryland. More malls are being built everyday. What does one do after finding out that one is sick of being human? We understand how easy it would be for the speaker in the poem to feel that nothing can be done, nothing works, that we have screwed up everything so deeply that everything is garbage, the feeling that "I will never recover from what has been done to me." This response is characteristic of sibling art and poetry.

But Neruda is a reader. Moreover, he feels behind him all the fierce energy of the French surrealists, the satiric intensity of Quevedo and Goya, the grounded laughter of Villon, and the delicate sensibility of Lorca. Neruda says:

> *Still it would be marvelous*
> *to terrify a law clerk with a cut lily,*
> *or kill a nun with a blow on the ear.*
> *It would be great*
> *to go through the streets with a green knife*
> *letting out yells until I died of the frost.*

Great literature asks us to keep our defiance and our laughter. Our vigor cannot be sustained by giving in to the victim emotions—self-pity, passivity, blaming, claims for exemption, perpetual requests for a grant on the grounds that I am worse off than my next-door neighbor. We can see that Neruda is risking some inaccuracy here. It's wrong to categorize all law clerks as people who would be terri-fied by a cut lily—some wouldn't be—but so what? Let's repeat what he says:

> *Still it would be marvelous*
> *to terrify a law clerk with a cut lily,*
> *or kill a nun with a blow on the ear.*

It would be great
to go through the streets with a green knife
letting out yells until I died of the frost.

I don't want to go on being a root in the dark,
insecure, stretched out, shivering with sleep,
going on down, into the moist guts of the earth,
taking in and thinking, eating every day.

I don't want so much misery.
I don't want to go on as a root and a tomb,
alone under the ground, a warehouse with corpses,
half frozen, dying of grief.

This grief is utterly modern, and it can't be described without words like *guts* and *warehouse*. But in the face of our contemporary misery, we need the exultation of great images:

That's why Monday, when it sees me coming
with my convict face, blazes up like gasoline,
and it howls on its way like a wounded wheel,
and leaves tracks full of warm blood leading toward the night.

And it pushes me into certain corners, into some moist houses,
into hospitals where the bones fly out the window,
into shoeshops that smell like vinegar,
and certain streets hideous as cracks in the skin.

Human beings have hate in their natures without knowing why. It's a part of their dog nature, their unheroic sloppiness, their inability to distinguish their mother from a Czechoslovakian general or their father from a stick of wood. Neruda admits that he not only hates certain people but hates the doors behind which they live:

There are sulphur-colored birds, and hideous intestines
hanging over the doors of houses that I hate,

and there are false teeth forgotten in a coffeepot,
there are mirrors
that ought to have wept from shame and terror,
there are umbrellas everywhere, and venoms, and umbilical cords.

Neruda's rebuke of certain mirrors because they don't feel enough shame and terror is lovely. He surprises us when, after saying "umbrellas," he moves not to "parasols" but to "venoms" and then to "umbilical cords." He and T. S. Eliot, one of his old ideological enemies, were brother geniuses in sensing the disgust that is a part of our daily life now. Neruda knows that the people really suffering in this slide are those in cramped apartments who hang their wash from a line. Parents who feel disgust in their own parenthood are everywhere. Pablo Neruda smells all this as if he were a dog. Still keeping his defiant and spirited Goya-like intensity, he lets compassion come through for those human beings who cannot live on the heights, for whom Monday doesn't get excited at all when it sees them coming. He ends the poem with these lines:

I stroll along serenely, with my eyes, my shoes,
my rage, forgetting everything,
I walk by, going through office buildings and orthopedic shops,
and courtyards with washing hanging from the line:
underwear, towels and shirts from which slow
dirty tears are falling.

His poem is great because, without turning aside for a second, he expresses our aversion in this time of overpopulation and our repugnance at the shallowness of our culture. And Neruda can express this loathing in art because he feels the exultation of creating new images, as Goya and Rembrandt did. And like Emily Dickinson, he knows that great art rises out of grief over our own life, or someone else's.

In this new sibling society built on the ruins of the society of readers, few grieve. If we could grieve—over Iphigenia, who died for the sake of the winds; over the wisdom gone because of Internet highways, and the damage to children's brains because of television; over grandparents lost through inattention and parents lost because of our great disappointment—then we could, by this descent, find a way out of the flatness of our current culture.

CHAPTER THIRTEEN

The Difficulty of Understanding Mythology in the Sibling Culture

The Coming Flood

William Butler Yeats, who with Lady Gregory reenergized ancient Irish mythology, and who received the Nobel Prize in literature in 1936, invented the character "Noah's sister," who "didn't learn how to read symbols" and so drowned in the Flood. The name Noah means, mythologically, someone who, when the flood of materialism pours in, is able to stay alive through those symbols that connect us to the world of light. Rembrandt is a Noah; Georgia O'Keeffe is another. The "Ark," we might say, then, is the ability to live a symbolic life, that is, to read symbols and experience them, so that ship of meaning—whose architectural plans are stored in all our memory systems—can save us as materialism floods in. Of course, we take the animals and plants on board with us—a ship of meaning without them would be merely academic. Our interior wolf and her mate roam the ship, and the oldest of living mammals, the elephant, and his mate, and so on, and below deck are all the birds of spirit. And the real wolf with his claws and teeth comes along, too.

The story of Noah's sister is a warning story fitted to American life now. From clouds on the horizon consumer goods roll in like fog or

194

rain; people have little "interiority," as the Europeans say; instead we experience daily the rising flood of communication devices. Lively students hit an iceberg disguised as the public school, and French rafts cannot save them anymore. Because information pours in from all sides, we have little attention left for symbols.

The average age of the advertising executives in say, McCann-Erickson, is now thirty-four or so. As in television, movies, the music business, advertising is run by the young for the young and almost no older mentors are left. The deepening and heightening of the psyche that was the distinctive virtue of older men and women is not a part of the sibling-driven corporation. The increasingly hurried and harried college education that comes before business means that many men and women graduate without ever having any experience of the "other worlds," or of deeper meanings.

Current academic fashions like deconstruction mean taking the Ark apart, and being short on nails when it's time to put it together again. Or we might decide to keep the plans for the other world on a computer disk and experience an unfortunate power failure.

The New York art world capitulated to sibling flatness thirty years ago. Hieronymus Bosch's hopeful men and women carrying huge strawberries turn into a solid wall of red. The two wild geese flying alone to the other world don't arrive.

THE SIBLING SOCIETY DRINKS, ONE MIGHT SAY, A CONCENTRATED literalism that America has longed to drink ever since the Boston Tea Party. That is why the religious right-wingers fit in as never before. For them the Ark is made of wood; it landed on Ararat, only once, and archaeologists from a Baptist college will find the wreck one day. The Seven Days in which the world was created are not metaphorical, and the little snails and pterodactyl bones that suggest evolution over millions of years were planted in sedimentary layers by leftist geologists. The Divine incarnated only once. The Bible makes all this clear in black and white. Religious right-wingers don't realize that their literalism is the spiritual twin to the sibling shallowness and hedonism that they rail against. The flood of cheap pearl necklaces, fake fur coats, and exercise machines, all made from unloved matter, make a kind of Golem robot who walks through our minds; and his metallic sister is precisely the rigid body that the right wing carries into Republican conventions. The determined and successful effort that the religious right is making to control school materials means that the inability to think metaphorically will increase. Eventually those who try to interpret the Virgin Birth mythologically or metaphorically will be fired from their positions, and the teachers will all drown in the Flood.

William Stafford, a Christian writer and one of the most playful poets of the twentieth century, wrote this little warning called "First Grade":

In the play Amy didn't want to be
anybody; so she managed the curtain.
Sharon wanted to be Amy. But Sam
wouldn't let anybody be anybody else—
he said it was wrong. "All right," Steve said,
"I'll be me, but I don't like it."
So Amy was Amy, and we didn't have the play.
And Sharon cried.

THE WORD *SYMBOL* HAS RISEN OUT OF THE GREEK WORD *SYM-bolon*, which means one-half of an object deliberately broken in two. Ancient Greece was full of tricksters, robbers, and con men, and so a man who wanted to pass a true message to a friend eighty miles away had a problem. He couldn't go himself, and how can you trust the go-between? The message might have been: "Send your oldest child to me for schooling and a visit," or "I need to borrow two thousand dollars; send it with this man." The solution was to use a symbolon. He broke a gold ring in two and gave half to his friend before he left. Or he took a small pottery shard, or a deer bone, and broke it in two. If the messenger brought the other half, and they fit together, the messenger was the right person. The half of the shard that he kept—as well as the part he gave to his friend—was a symbolon.

A symbol in our time is no longer a physical thing. Half of the symbols, one could say, belong to our physical world, with its wombs, haystacks, yardsticks, flowers, volcanoes, porcupines, tax collectors, and body dirt; and the other half belong to the world that the spirits inhabit, from which they occasionally wave to us, or peek at us naked, or knock us off a horse with a shot of lightning, or feed us visions of themselves. Sometimes during Greek and later Roman times a man or woman would awaken in the middle of the night and see Athena or Minerva standing at the foot of the bed, her helmet on, her whole body luminous, the shield and all its carvings clear. She wasn't a symbolon; she was a rather pushy energy that had crossed over, perhaps to give a message, perhaps just to increase your grandiosity.

Tibetan monks speak matter-of-factly of visitations from their mythological people, who wear skull necklaces and jade boots, carry swords in all four hands, perhaps have a tongue with a shiny surface in which you can see yourself. They wear whatever style of clothes is current in their territory of the mythological layer. These beings can come to us, over bridges variously described as rainbows, or arches made of tears, riding on horses made from the breath of cats. Those bridges would break under us.

We are dense, because our bodies are actually made of matter, of gravity-attracting materials, water and zinc and lead and calcium and all those things that end up as ashes in the urn. To gain qualified entrance to the spiritual world, then, we need a soul-thing, or symbol, half of which is dense and worldly and yet fits perfectly into the other half of the ring that is invisible and has the consistency of cat's breath.

In art, the wild gander is a symbolon. Our half of it is a sculpture of a gander exactly as ganders appear in our muddy-pond world; and the other half is the shaman-horse, "hamsas and paramahamsas" ("the wild gander and the unbelievably wild gander"), that the shaman's soul becomes as it flies "there." If you see a Buddhist painting of the wild gander, and you can't "read" it, then you have to stay down here with the domestic geese. It was a dark day for the wild swans when the Protestants under pressure of the Enlightenment or the Endarkenment threw out the Virgin Mary from churches. She was and is a symbolon—on our side she is a young woman who is heavily bearing like a grape arbor; she has trouble sleeping and is bloated with water; but on "their" side, this half of the carved bone is a magnificent spirit-sun-moon divine being, from whom luminous rays shoot out in an oval pattern all around her. Women giving birth in caves saw her making the whole cave full of light. If you touch her, you will die; but the light from her flows into a baby still in the womb as a soul, and one glimpse of her produces the radiant smile on the new mother's face. Sometimes during labor, the mother, invigorated by pain, goes out ten thousand miles into the atmosphere to meet her. Perhaps it isn't so much that men want to have babies; they want to do *that*.

And they can, to some extent, if they hold the symbolon firmly in their left hand, throw away this life with their right hand, and let the symbolon carry them over that river where the bridges are made of the jade eyes of the stars. Rumi says in Coleman Barks' translation:

"I would love to kiss you."
"The price of kissing is your life."

Now my loving is running toward my life shouting,
"What a bargain, let's buy it!"

The mother of a newborn has already accepted the deal; and so some mothers want to see an image of this symbolon, this Virgin Mary or Spirited Mother, every day of their lives.

It was a sad day for my town in Minnesota when Luther threw the Virgin Mary out of the churches. We had to grow without her anywhere on the white walls, in the candle flames or floating on the blue ceiling. A Rilke poem is a symbolon; so is a Mirabai poem. If you can't read those symbols, then you're in grave danger of falling off the raft and being pulled down with the Titanic, to live at the bottom of the ocean with the icebergs of public education drifting over your head.

TO READ A SYMBOL MEANS TO WALK ALONG IT UNTIL YOU CROSS into a world where events other than those on earth happen.

Children don't need a symbolon to get to the imagination's world. They go in a fraction of a second. Children are playing at being characters in "Snow White." The mother calls, "Come to dinner!" The daughter says, "I can't! I'm asleep now." A small boy pretends he is a chimney sweep. When someone approaches, he says, "Don't touch me! You'll get dirty!" Or "Mother, a bug came to visit me. He wanted to shake hands with me and put out his little paw."

Joseph Campbell loves stories about children's readiness to live in imagination. Campbell and his wife lived in a Greenwich Village apartment; and Joseph, arriving one day, found no place to park. After circling the block awhile, he saw a space open. As he began to back in, a child standing on the sidewalk said indignantly, "You can't park here. I'm a fire hydrant." Campbell drove away and found another place.

The great Russian children's writer Kornei Chukovsky describes in *From Two to Five* his adventures when he tried to read imaginative stories to children in a Crimean sanitorium in 1929. He read *Baron von Munchausen*, and the sick children sat up and laughed and shouted, "Go on! Go on!" until a woman "with red spots of anger all over her face" ran up and snatched the book out of his hand. "She looked at it as if it were a frog," and carried it out by the ends of her fingers. Then a young man in a uniform appeared and gave him a lecture, saying that everyone knows that books for Soviet children must not be fantasies and fairy tales, which are ridiculous false-hoods; they must be only about realistic facts, about diesel engines and concrete stress. The Soviets did their damnedest to prevent any child or grown-up from crossing the bridge to the other world.

We have many people like that in the United States; however, we are dealing not with lack of intelligence but with a real hatred of symbols and the "other world."

Such people insist on the lower physical half of the carved reindeer bone only. They achieve more success with adults than with children in their plan to keep everyone from going to the mythological world, because adults need longer time, need help, need permission, need symbolons.

Lᴇᴛ's ᴛᴀᴋᴇ ᴀɴ ᴇxᴀᴍᴘʟᴇ ᴏꜰ ᴀ sʏᴍʙᴏʟᴏɴ ᴇᴍʙᴇᴅᴅᴇᴅ ɪɴ ᴀ sᴛᴏʀʏ and see if we can walk on it. The story is "Hans My Hedgehog," from the stories that the Grimm Brothers collected. It begins with a man regretting the fact that he has no children. When neighbors in a bar mock him maliciously for not having produced a child, the man replies, "I'll have a child, by God, even if he's a hedgehog!" Some months later his wife gave birth to a boy who was human down to the waist and a hedgehog below the waist.

We can understand that his mother would have difficulty breast-feeding him. The father didn't like the boy from the start. This father built a little bed for him behind the stove, and the boy ate and slept there.

In the physical or literal world we now have a child whom the family doesn't want, and each of us has experienced enough of that so that we know what that half of the reindeer bone feels like. We know what it feels like not to be wanted, and to "live behind the stove." The instant that we take in that picture, a Hedgehog Boy appears in the other world. If we associate with both boys, we are now living in two worlds at once. Whatever the storyteller says about the Hedgehog Boy's adventures, we shout, "Go on!" and we relate it immediately to the pain of the nonhedgehog child we once were.

When the Hedgehog Boy is twelve, he says to his father, "If you give me a rooster to ride on, and shoe the rooster's feet with iron shoes as if it were a horse, and give me a bunch of pigs and a bagpipe, I'll get out of your sight forever." The father says, "That's a good deal." In our world, the disregarded boy, if he's not going to die emotionally or physically of depression, needs a grandiose thing like a rooster to ride on; and the pigs can stand for the life instinct, eating, rooting, reproducing, slopping around in the mud, which he's liable to lose track of in his depression or self-disgust. We can worry about the shoeing of the rooster later. So on this earth we have a depressed boy who has somehow found the right to ask his father for what he wants; but in the other world really colorful events are going on. The Hedgehog Boy tells the rooster to fly about two-thirds of the way up a tall tree, and he sits up there on the rooster playing his bagpipes while the pigs happily eat and fornicate in their piggy way on the forest floor. On this earth, the boy is feeling tremendous grief and trying to hide it by being cheerful, but in the other world the Hedgehog Boy is openly playing the bagpipes, giving out the saddest of all musical sounds.

The hardest thing to understand, if we're not used to such living-in-two-places-at-once thinking, is that the Hedgehog Boy playing his bagpipes in the other world may be able to help the boy in this world, who isn't doing well.

THE TWO PARALLEL STREAMS—LITERAL LIFE AND MYTHOLOGI-cal life—resemble the contrast between ordinary life and ritual life. Ritual creates a second flow of events—and we can enter that stream or not, as we wish. The idea of ritual is strange to our ears; it says that if something is healed in the other world, something is healed in this world also. Christ spoke of that precisely when he said, "What is loosed in heaven is loosed on earth."

We can say, then, that what the mythological visioning has in common with ritual practice is that we have *two chances* to do something. For now we'll say that doing something in the mythological world means that we don't have to do it here. For example, when Hansel and Gretel put the witch in the oven in the other world, it means that we don't have to put an old woman in the oven here. When Shiva cuts off Ganesha's head in the other world, violently, it means that the violence does not have to occur in this world.

The Bolsheviks did not want anyone to go to the mythological or imaginative world at all. That parallels our own American cherry-tree hatred of elaborate universes, multiple interpretations, truths that both can and cannot be.

Thoreau in *Walden* mentions that, in India, Kabir's poems are understood to have four levels of meaning:

> *"They pretend," as I hear, "that the verses of Kabir have four different senses; illusion, spirit, intellect, and the exoteric doctrine of the Vedas"; but in this part of the world it is considered a ground for complaint if a man's writings admit of more than one interpretation. While England endeavors to cure the potato-rot, will not any endeavor to cure the brain-rot, which prevails so much more widely and fatally?*

Taking the mythological world seriously, or simply going to the mythological world, means having two chances to do the one thing we want to do. It also means paying for that chance the way a pianist pays for the ability to feel Bach in every cell of the body—through practice. In mythological travel, the traveler has to do all the work.

For example, if your father wanted you to live behind the big stove so he didn't have to look at you, and your mother found it unpleasant to be near you and held you out away from her body, then you grew up deprived, unprotected, and abandoned. That's the way it is in this world. "Society" gave you a deprived childhood, and that will never change. But you have to know that in the mythological world, a mad-looking Hedgehog Boy is perched about two-thirds of the way up your spine; he's sitting on a long-beaked, red-wattled rooster, with long silver and gold tailfeathers hanging down, playing great music in the Van Morrison mood, and watching the big-teated sows below feeding the piglets and grunting.

If you don't try to see that boy or don't do the work—which

includes laughing—to experience that scene with the rooster, then you will probably be flat. Recognizing that the Hedgehog Boy is riding with his bagpipe on the rooster doesn't imply that you will protect your parents from the knowledge of the damage they did to you. On the contrary, it says that one day you may ride back into their farm with a lot of squealing pigs.

The goat-riding in our earlier Norwegian story is happening in the mythological world, reached along the upper half of the carved reindeer bone. On the earth, there is a Norwegian girl walking around in a room, learning to serve tea.

That girl needs to understand, and experience in her body, that during her birth a wild girl was born in the other world, and an ordinary girl here, one absolutely wild and the other obedient and tame. The two are utterly loyal to each other. Because each is loyal to the other, the ritual can take place, and both change.

Unfortunately, English teachers in American universities increasingly deconstruct symbols rather than read them. That is a great loss. One half of the universe is omitted. Male and female students see themselves sitting behind the stove, and that's all they see. They imagine themselves as victims, because the rooster and the bagpipes have not been taken seriously, nor the other world in which the bagpipes are playing. Studying symbols doesn't mean that one automatically wants to, or can, transcend evil or suffering. In Stafford's poem, Sam "wouldn't let anybody be anybody else." The result is that we don't have the play.

Adventures in Mythological Writing

By the time I was fifty or so, I had published nine books of poetry and three books of prose, but they were all written for the community that understands metaphor.

Having written for that community, I threw *Iron John* out the way one launches a canoe on the ocean. I hadn't realized how many misunderstandings are possible in a single book when one speaks in myth form. Because the word *iron* was in the title, some people did free association around that word and assumed I was in favor of pumping iron. Metaphorically, the Wild Man, we are told, has hair the color of rusty iron; that is a sort of witticism, testifying to the centuries the Wild Man has been kept out of sight under the water. When brought to the castle, he is imprisoned in an iron cage. The traditional image for imprisonment of men is iron, just as the traditional image for imprisonment of women is glass. The Wild Man doesn't use iron; he is imprisoned by it.

Most reviewers followed obediently the flat, literal, or sociological mode, in which there is only one world—this one. So people believed that by a Wild Man I meant bikers, and that John really rides a Harley-Davidson. The word *wilding* made some say that Iron John was a rapist and belonged to the patriarchal ruling circles along with the then President Bush and the CEO of Boeing Aircraft. Actually, the Wild Man is a god, most likely Dionysus. He is the least macho of all gods, being a god of grief and the nervous system, partly female and partly male, and the overwhelming favorite of Greek women in classical times. He is noticeably not a part of the group of twelve official gods and goddesses that ruled Greek public life. He is always a rebel, speaking from the feeling point of view, and, as Euripides makes clear in *The Bacchae*, a deadly enemy of male domination and male reason. All that was missed by the literal minded critics.

One women's magazine published a long article accusing me of starting the Gulf War. The drawing commissioned for that issue showed me as a warplane diving on a desert, along with General Schwarzkopf and President Bush. It turned out that the author, who lived in Paris, noticed in the *International Herald Tribune* that *Iron John* was at the top of the best-seller list on the day the Gulf War began. She put two and two together and wrote the piece.

People trained in literal thinking live in a culture of scarcity, so that if a writer writes tenderly of men, he obviously hates women. That interpretation astounded me as well. Mythology doesn't deal in either/or, but both/and.

Susan Faludi could stand as a representative of the kind of writer who knows only adversarial thinking. Her book is an early example of sibling reportage, with its character assassination. If men gather to grieve over the lives of the Vietnam dead, it must be a backlash against women. Similarly, if Betty Friedan begins to notice the denigration of motherhood and praises motherhood, that, too, must be a backlash phenomenon.

I understand that alert women—when they take in the centuries of mistreatment, physical violence from disturbed men, condescension from Italian popes and Alexander Pope, deliberate destruction of Eleusis after two thousand years of soul work there, and the slow pace of change in behavior—may feel jumpy, and some are so afraid that they can't read a story or a book dispassionately enough to see where it fits. Some writers were right in saying that many important matters were left out of *Iron John*. I wrote the book not as the bible of a men's movement but as an amplification of a fairy story and the discussion necessarily depends on what is in the story. There are lots of stories, and each is partial in a different way. Some critics noted that homophobia, domestic violence, the flight of fathers, and the dangers of separatist conferences were given scant attention, and those are just criticisms.

Likely Misunderstandings of the Ganesha Story

The Ganesha story is very difficult, mythologically, for people who tend to think sociologically, or literally, in either a fundamentalist or a scientific way. First of all, the son, Ganesha, is made out of nothing, out of some skin flakes, or some lotion soaked into a bedsheet. This way of making a son is close to the Virgin Birth; but lots of people don't believe in that, either. Moreover, some Christians of goodwill may allow it for Joseph and Mary, but not for Shiva and Parvati.

The issue in any myth is what belongs to the mythological world and what belongs to our doggy world. The issue of two worlds doesn't turn up so much in the Oedipus story, because the later Greeks treated Oedipus and his wife as if they were *people*. But the

Greeks were, by the so-called classical time, in the business of confusing people and gods, letting the two groups get too far entangled, and urging, one could say, democracy onto the gods, or trying to lift—as the Romans later did in a gross manner—men with full digestive systems up into the divine by government decree. That Oedipus is actually a god is hinted at toward the end, when he is welcomed by the Earth Mother back into the divine world.

The Hindus have never changed gods into people; and the Ganesha story wants us to keep gods and people distinct. Shiva is a god; he does ascetic work alone for ten years sometimes, and that's the way it is. He is not meant as a model for an earthly father. Parvati is a goddess, divine in every cell; and her son, Ganesha, is divine as well from the first moment. Later, when he receives the elephant head, he becomes divine in a specific way, as the kind of god who helps human beings when they try to accomplish something on this earth. He stops being generally divine and becomes a specific god.

Gods do as they do, and it's not up to us to imitate them. Again, that Shiva cuts off Ganesha's head doesn't mean that any father should cut off the head of his son.

Shiva's coldness may make one think that he is too remote, like a businessman. Personality matters are good to think about, but the story has no opinion on them one way or the other. Similarly, that the Great Mother, for example, sometimes becomes a lion and eats up the living doesn't mean that a woman should eat anyone around her. On the contrary, because the Great Mother herself takes all living beings back into the grave, all we have to concern ourselves with on our doggy earth is that our parents and spouses will be able to live as long as they can.

We must do our own deeds out of impulses in our own world, for our own reasons, thinking them out with the limited brains we have. We must hold to our center and not let the gods pull us too far out of our center, just as we mustn't try to pull the gods too far out of their center, in asking them for special favors, such as finding us a new apartment, or even perhaps saving someone's life. It's a delicate matter.

Perhaps some men will object to the story, saying, "I don't like this, that the woman in the story is so important, and it all centers around her bedroom. I want to be back out in the rocks of northern Greece, where the men hit each other with sticks, and no one goes on about sacred females and their rooms."

Others will say that if Shiva had stayed home, he would have known who his son was, and so the encounter by the door would not have had to take place. But there aren't any ifs in a mythological story. The father doesn't recognize his son because he doesn't.

Similarly, the Giant who lives on top of the beanstalk is not a secret image of the corporations, distorted by Freudian censorship; he is a divine being who is doing his work, which is to eat fatherless boys; and his so-called wife or daughter is a goddess doing her work, which is to protect certain kinds of fatherless humans. The Giant dies when he comes down from his plane to ours because that's what gods do when they come down to our world.

It may be difficult for some mothers to hear the Ganesha story without being shamed, imagining that it says they should be celibate. Similarly, some men may feel shamed by Shiva's loutish behavior. Some women may say, "Shiva gets away clean, and just does his meditations," etc.; men may say, "Parvati should not have made the boy her guardian. That was wrong." The answer is that young men guard their mother's bedroom door because that's what they do. It's as natural as it is for a seabird to fly. To see what happens without blame is the gift of a mythological story.

CHAPTER FOURTEEN

What Is Vertical Thought?

That is no country for old men. The young
In one another's arms, birds in the trees,
—Those dying generations—at their song,
The salmon-falls, the mackerel-crowded seas,
Fish, flesh, or fowl, commend all summer long
Whatever is begotten, born, and dies.
Caught in that sensual music all neglect
Monuments of unageing intellect.

Yeats presents these complaints as if he had thought of them only when he was old. Yeats was sixty-two in 1927 when he wrote about the abundant sexuality of young men and young women ("the young in one another's arms"), the abundance of the fish tribes ("the mackerel-crowded seas"), and the obsession in Irish society with "whatever is begotten, born, and dies." He was growing old himself, but actually the contrast between sexuality and the ageless had been a prime element of his thought since he was very young.

Yeats's longing is not that all "sensual music" would disappear, for he loved sexual energy and wrote of it magnificently. He worries instead about what is forgotten in the headlong pursuit of sexuality.

> *Caught in that sensual music, all neglect*
> *Monuments of unageing intellect.*

We know from his essays that the word *intellect* here does not mean practical intellect, that is, the reasoning power of the scientist or the engineer. It means the spiritual intellect, out of which Mohammad wrote the Koran, Hildegard of Bingen wrote her poems, Saint Augustine wrote his *Confessions*—that spiritual intellect that Plato and Plotinus loved so much. What the spiritual intellect creates does not die. Poems created by the spiritual intelligence, such as Dante's *Divine Comedy*, are as alive now as they were in the year they were written. Ibn Arabi, Gerard Manley Hopkins, Emily Dickinson, Margaret of Navarre, all welcomed the spiritual intelligence.

When Yeats was seventy-three, a few months before his death, he heard a voice that said, "Lie down and die." He replied:

> *That were to shirk*
> *The spiritual intellect's great work*
> *And shirk it in vain. There is no release*
> *In a bodkin or disease,*
> *Nor can there be a work so great*
> *As that which cleans man's dirty slate.*
> *While man can still his body keep*
> *Wine or love drug him to sleep,*
> *Waking he thanks the Lord that he*
> *Has body and its stupidity,*
> *But body gone he sleeps no more*
> *And till his intellect grows sure*
> *That all's arranged in one clear view*
> *Pursues the thoughts that I pursue,*
> *Then stands in judgment on his soul,*
> *And, all work done, dismisses all*

Out of intellect and sight
And sinks at last into the night.

Yeats is not making a great contrast between sensuality and the spiritual intellect, as between day and night. He talks of what is easily forgotten in Western culture. Spiritual intelligence needs to be the base on which sensuality and all else rests. But fish, flesh, or fowl

. . . commend all summer long
Whatever is begotten, born, and dies.

In the summer, we could say, no one cares about the afterlife. The Romanian writer Ciorin remarked wittily, "Now that no one believes in the afterlife, everyone writes." Many human activities, writing among them, can be thought of as an attempt to create an immortality without the help of the immortals. Most Egyptians, as far as we know, by contrast, lived in simple wooden huts, but built enormous, permanent mansions for the gods. We build such mansions for brokers.

Buddhists have a term for the obsession with copulating, having children, raising children, passing property on to them, getting sick, and dying. They call it being on "the meat-wheel." The meat-wheel goes around century after century; millions are born and die. Then a spirit, perhaps Buddha, comes along who wants to get off the meat-wheel. This is felt by ordinary people as a revolutionary idea, and it inspires hundreds of years of intense "vertical" devotion in Asia. A thousand monks in Ceylon or Tibet live in a single monastery, all anxious to leave the meat-wheel.

The sibling society is almost the pure antithesis of a Tibetan monastery. We have drunk beer so long that we have virtually forgotten the taste of real wine. Rumi and Hafez refer over and over to wine, which carries the flavor of the longing for God, the taste of the vertical, which is the afterflavor of ecstasy:

How blessed is the man who like Hafez
Has tasted in his heart the wine made before Adam.

To become a genuine artist in our society is more and more difficult because fewer and fewer people "have tasted in their heart the wine made before Adam." Even if an artist creates a spiritual work, the readers are so flat, the art critics are so horizontal, that its "wine" is not recognized.

THE NATIVE AMERICAN VIEW THAT WHENEVER ONE MAKES A decision, one should think of its effect down to the seventh generation, is a vertical thought. The opposite of that would be a decision based on "short-term" profits, which often means refusing to invest in the plant or in the people who work in the plant. In vertical thought there is no distinction between men and women; one becomes an elder when one learns to think vertically.

Another instance of vertical thought is the idea that a "spiritual twin" was born with you. At birth the two of you separated, and perhaps you might not see your spiritual twin again in this life, although you would always long for her or him. In such a culture, the candles at the birthday party are lit for the twin, not for you. There is a hint of that in Russian birthday celebrations, in which a person shares a name-day with a saint; so one's birthdate is also a celebration for that saint. In American birthday parties, the little boy or girl thinks the cake and the candle are for them; there is no hint of any other being, to whom one might be grateful.

Vertical poetry and art like to imagine the patterns of water flowing under the earth, dragons exploding out of earth waters and rising into the clouds. Vertical thought likes to imagine the vast distances between the stars. Giacomo Leopardi, as he sat alone on an Italian hillside at dusk, said:

This hermit's hill has always been dear to me,
Also this hedgerow, which keeps me hidden
Partially from the gaze of the wide horizon.
Sitting here and looking, I fashion with my mind
The spaces beyond the earth that have no end,

And those silences that are not human at all,
And the deepest of all quiet; for a little while
My heart feels no fear. Then as I hear wind
Freshen through the leaves, I go farther
And compare this sound to that ever-
Lasting silence; and I remember eternity
And all the long dead seasons, and this present season
Alive with her voices. And so my thoughts
Find themselves, in that immensity, shipwrecked;
And sweet to me is the drowning in that sea.

Drowning and descent are not so much feared by the vertical gazers. Antonio Machado said:

Mankind owns four things
That are no good at sea;
Rudder, anchor, oars,
And the fear of going down.

Hadewijch of Antwerp says:

I do not complain of suffering for Love,
It is right that I should always obey her,
For I know her only as she is in herself,
Whether she commands in storm or in stillness.
This is a marvel beyond my understanding,
Which fills my whole heart
And makes me stray in a wild desert.

The higher the spirit goes, the more deeply the soul sinks down into the waters of melancholy and tragedy. And going down into those waters is a sweet thing. Rumi says:

The captain walks on the planks of fearful things that might
  happen;
He walks on the decking of marvelous things that might happen.

*When both decking and planks are gone, nothing remains but the
drowning.*

Christo art projects, detective stories, Disneylands, Madonna-like
singers, Muzak, disco music, Hollywood movies, and that water
running under the bridges of Madison County carry a certain single-
minded optimism that fits with the excitement of aimless murder
and aimless art, making a sideways view that leaves out all drowning. The influence of popular art is so great that many human beings
now live their whole lives without meeting vertical attention in any
embodiment that makes it feel real.

Vertical attention implies the ability, or at least the longing, to
look downward; or the ability to look upward, at the stars, at the
energies beyond the stars, at angels. One problem with the sibling
society is that, in its intense desire to get away from hierarchy, it
unintentionally avoids all vertical longing.

We could say that vertical longing has to do with feeling, and
hierarchy with power. The Catholic Church took over, or adapted
the power hierarchies of, the Roman Empire, and that has conflated
the two—longing and hierarchy—ever since. It has confused everything.

The European monasteries of the Middle Ages, particularly the
Franciscan, with their gardening and vows of poverty, did try to
separate longing and hierarchy. The bishops and the Franciscans
themselves violated these principles. The Church said then and still
can say to a priest, "If you leave our hierarchy, you are forbidden to
receive the communion that will save your soul." In other words,
"No salvation outside the walls of the church." (*Extra ecclesiam nulla
salus*.)

The Hebrew rabbinical tradition tries to separate vertical longing
and hierarchy by declaring that a rabbi is not a person with a
"calling," he is not imagined as a holy man or one chosen by God.
He is merely a scholar of the Torah. That arrangement faces at least
the distinction between holiness and service. Certain forms of Bud-

dhism go even farther, and say, "If you meet the Buddha on the road, kill him."

The European and Christian identification of vertical longing and hierarchy has proved to be a severe drawback in the long run, and for many Westerners the normal human longing for the vertical has been compromised. Many Marxists that I knew in the 1960s thought it was their duty never to look upward with religion or downward with psychology. We know that the Chinese Red Guard, with their lateral thinking, destroyed about one-third of the vast cultural inheritance of China in three years. Most of the paintings, buildings, sculpture, and ceramic work they destroyed had been inspired by a love of elegant upward-looking, by attempts to balance energies in the heavens, by praise of the heavenly winds, by admiration of the water dragons below the ground, and by the deities of sun and moon.

The longing that impels the vertical gaze appears to be identical in its intensity whether in men or in women. Saint Teresa and Saint John of the Cross are great travelers, and neither arrives first.

Margaret of Navarre says:

If someone insults you,
Go on, with light heart;
If they all do it, pay
No heed to what they say.
  There's no new art
  In talk of that kind.
Wind will blow it all away.

If someone praises Devotion
Implying of course it's OK,
But says of course the works
Of the Law are much greater,
  It's weird dogma,
  Pass by, don't bother.
Wind will blow it all away.

And if they next, to make
You less open to God,
Say (to flatter you)
That you are truly great:
      Turn your back
      To talk of that sort.
Wind will blow it all away.

And if the world itself
Should come, money, castles,
Great sweets in its hand, just say,
"I have enough today."
      For worldly things
      Return whence they came.
Wind will blow it all away.

And if people name a place
(Not God's) where all sorrow
Will be settled, all be saved,
They have an evil aim.
      Be strong, say no
      To these odd people.
Wind will blow it all away.

When a woman looks up, her gaze may fall on a god or a goddess. Mirabai says, speaking of Krishna:

My friend, I went to the market and bought the dark-faced one.
You claim by night, I say by day.
Actually I was beating a drum all the time I was buying him.
You say I said too much; I say too little.
Actually I put him on a scale before I bought him.
What I paid was my social body, my town body, my family body, and
   all my inherited jewels.
Mirabai says: The Holy One is my husband now.
Be with me when I lie down; you promised me this in an earlier life.

In the following poem the Muslim poet Lalla's gaze fell on the moon. Once more, the mood is that of a lover. Coleman Barks' translation says:

The soul, like the moon,
is new, and always new again.

And I have seen the ocean
continuously creating.

Since I scoured my mind
and my body, I too, Lalla,
am new, each moment new.

My teacher told me one thing,
Live in the soul.

When that was so,
I began to go naked,
and dance.

Men's vertical attention is of long standing as well. The twentieth-century Spanish poet Juan Ramón Jiménez says:

I am not I.
          I am this one
Walking beside me whom I do not see,
Whom at times I manage to visit,
And whom at other times I forget;
The one who remains silent when I talk,
The one who forgives, sweet, when I hate,
The one who takes a walk where I am not,
The one who will remain standing when I die.

Men love to describe ascensions; sometimes they lay out the ascent in stages, as Loyola did in his *Exercises*. The image is a stair. Here is Saint John of the Cross going up that stair:

In the night that was dark,
Made fiery by the furies of love

—Oh blesséd moment!—
I left without being noticed,
All the doors of my house closed for the night.

Secure and in the dark,
On the secret staircase, stealth
—Oh blesséd moment!—
And darkness protected me,
All the doors of my house closed for the night.

In the delicious night,
In privacy, where no one saw me,
Nor did I see one thing,
I had no light or guide
But the fire that burned inside my chest.

That fire showed me
The way more clearly than the blaze of noon
To where, waiting for me,
Was the One I knew so well,
In that place where no one ever is.

Oh night, sweet guider,
Oh night more marvelous than dawn!
Oh night which joins
The lover and the beloved
So that the lover and beloved change bodies!

In my chest full of flowers,
Flowering wholly and only for Him,
There He remained sleeping;
I cared for Him there,
And the fan of the high cedars cooled Him.

The wind played with
His hair, and that wind from the high
Towers struck me on the neck
With its sober hand;
Sight, taste, touch, hearing stopped.

I stood still; I forgot who I was,
My face leaning against Him,
Everything stopped, abandoned me,
My being was gone, forgotten
Among the white lilies.

CHAPTER FIFTEEN

The Snake That Wants to Eat All Its Brides: A Swedish Story

WHAT HAPPENS TO PEOPLE WHO GET THROWN OUT OF THE window? That is the subject of the next story, which comes from Sweden, and is usually referred to as the Lind Wurm story, Lind being the region and the Wurm being a creature midway between snake and dragon.

During World War I, the greed of empire builders, the jealousy among nations, came back on the Europeans in central Europe; it wasn't unusual to offer forty thousand young men a day to the machine guns. Robert Graves' book was called *Goodbye to All That*. The elders had not done their work—they had not protected the young men.

We could say that French and English old men threw thousands of young men *out the window*; German elders threw young German men out the window during the same period. When the young German men reappeared in different bodies twenty years later in 1936, the German nation, by embarking on warfare on the eastern and western fronts, threw young men out the window again; when the U.S. entered the war, thousands of American men were thrown out the window from 1941 to 1946. When these young men reappeared twenty years later with different bodies at the time of the Vietnam War, the old men threw their bodies out the window again.

Many of the extravagant characteristics of the sibling society showed up in the 1960s, for example the reliance on drugs; many activities were done in genuine fear, even terror, of the elders' culture. The new "consciousness" was not in the world to support the old culture, but to wipe it out and replace it. Jerry Garcia said that at Altamont in December 1969, the place smelled of sulfur. He said, "The light was weird and demonic."

The psychedelics promised, and temporarily at least delivered, a mythological or cosmic world, of which the elders knew nothing. Many Sixties youth felt that they had gone on far ahead of their parents. Elders were symbolically killed in the very taking of acid, done without any grasp of what that might mean. Native Americans felt horror that white people would take peyote with no elders present, no one to clear the air or protect the souls from invasions by those spirits who do not wish us well.

The killing of elders in Cambodia clearly had to do with the settling of old scores, with Marxist slogans, and with psychosis; the killing of elders in Somalia, by contrast, rose out of the destruction of the elder system when both Russia and America flooded the culture with guns, trying to line the young up on the capitalist or communist side.

We have to recognize that Bosnia, Rwanda, Somalia, and Cambodia are now sibling societies. In Cambodia, the elders, teachers, priests, journalists, and artists were killed with intent. To do that requires a lot of rage. That rage rose out of young people and resulted in the deaths of millions of fathers, mothers, uncles, and teachers; those still living are left with a second rage over the murders.

Our sibling society came into existence by different means, but there is a comparable elimination of elders, accompanied by increasing anger on the part of youth.

This story, of the Lind Wurm, points to the source of the anger we feel all around us, and makes clear how difficult it will be to end the destruction caused by the anger.

The story begins with a situation much favored in fairy stories: the King and Queen are looking forward to a child.

The birthing moment arrived. The midwife was seated at the foot of the bed, and the first thing that came out of the mother was, to her immense surprise, a tiny snake. There happened to be an open window near her seat, and without saying a word to the Queen, she took the tiny snake and threw it out the window. A few minutes later, a boy child came out, perfectly formed. The midwife and the Queen were glad. The father came in to see his new son. There was much celebration, and that was that.

For a while, nothing unusual happens. The boy grows up the way princes do: he sleeps in a soft bed, he rides horses, he chases geese around, he stands in front of mirrors.

When he is sixteen or so, his father arranges a marriage for him with a princess in a neighboring kingdom. One morning then the prince sets out in a suitor's carriage, driving two handsome horses, down the road to meet his bride for the first time. About five miles from the castle, there is a crossroads.

As the Prince arrived at the crossroads, he saw an enormous snake, a kind of dragon, rearing up in the center of the road and roaring so that the horses became frightened. The Prince said, "Move out of the way! I'm going through." The Wurm, in a loud and terrible voice, cried, "A bride for me before a bride for you! *I am the older son.* A bride for me before a bride for you."

What could he do? The Prince turned the horses around and drove home. He then went to see his father and told him of the event. "He claims he is my older brother. Do I have an older brother?" The King said he never heard of such a thing. The Prince went to his mother. He said to her, "Dear mother, I have a serious question I must ask you. Am I the firstborn child, or do I have an older brother?" She replied, "I don't know anything about it."

The next morning, he started with his horses and carriage down the road again. At the same crossroads, the same immense dragon, roaring with anger, reared up in the road and cried: "A bride for me before a bride for you! *I marry first.* A bride for me before a bride for you."

The Prince turned around and drove home for a second time. The Queen remembered the midwife. It turned out she was still alive, living in a little house in the woods. The Prince found his way there. "May I ask you: Do you recall the day my mother gave birth to me?" "Oh, I do." "Was there a child born before me?" "It's true that you were not the firstborn. It wasn't exactly a child. It was a tiny snake. I thought your mother had enough to do as it was. I tossed it out the window into the grass. That's all that happened. I don't know any more."

The King realizes that his son can never be married until he finds a bride for the Wurm. The King sent word out that a bride was required for a King's son. A young woman was chosen out of the numerous applicants, and a date was set for the wedding.

You must know that in this country, an evening ceremony was held for the bride and groom at night, and the final wedding took place the next morning. The bride arrived at the castle, her parents, her friends, many flowers, many cakes had been baked. When the evening came, the bride stepped to the altar, and the Wurm, who had been taken into the castle, appeared from his chamber, came in with his immense length, faced the bride, wrapped his tail seven times, chum! chum! chum! around her body, and claimed her as his own.

The Wurm and his bride were escorted to the bridal chamber. No one in the castle slept much that night. When they knocked at the door the next morning, and went in, only the snake was in the room.

A month later, the Prince climbed in his carriage and drove fast along the road away from the castle. But at that same crossroads he found the Wurm rearing up, even larger. It cried out: "A bride for me before a bride for you! *The ceremony did not happen.* A bride for me before a bride for you."

Several months later, the same sequence of events happened again. This bride came from a kingdom a little farther away. Once more she stood at the altar full of expectations. Once more the Wurm entered

the chapel, stood next to her, wound his tail—chum! chum! chum!—
seven times around her body, and claimed her as his own. The maids
and attendants who came to the bridal chamber in the morning
found only the Wurm in the room.

Whenever the Prince tried to leave the castle, the Wurm was on the
road, his longing for a true marriage still unsatisfied. "A bride for me
before a bride for you!"

Ten more brides entered the castle and were eaten by the Wurm,
who still remained unsatisfied, and declared that no real marriage
had taken place.

A woodcutter and his daughter lived in the woods a long way
from the castle. The woodcutter had once worked at the castle, and
knew all. One morning his daughter said to her father, "Father, I've
decided that I will be the next bride." The father couldn't believe his
ears. "Don't worry about me, dear father," she said. "I know what
to do."

A wise old woman lived in the woods whom the young girl had met
on one of her walks. She went to this old woman and said to her,
"What shall I do?" The old woman told her to postpone the wedding
for eight months, and during that time to make seven wedding shirts,
each of them elaborately embroidered. The crone said that the bride,
when she arrived at the castle, was to ask for a bucket of lye, two
brushes with stiff bristles, and a pail of fresh milk. Then the old
woman told her what to do with them.

When the thirteenth bride arrived at the castle, she was cheerful
and composed. She requested a bucket of lye, the two stiff brushes,
and the milk; and they were provided. When evening came, she stood
near the altar. The Wurm came in in his usual way, slipped quickly to
the side of his new bride, wrapped his tail seven times around her
body, chum!, chum!, chum!, and claimed her as his own.

The bride and the Wurm were escorted to the bridal chamber. The
Wurm reared up in the room. He was terrible to look at, with his fierce
eyes and his savage body. When all was quiet, the Wurm spoke to his
bride, and in a rough, gravelly voice said, "Take off your wedding

shirt." The bride did not move. She replied to him, "I will take off my shirt if you will take off one of your skins." The Wurm was silent and then said: "No one ever asked me to do that before."

The Wurm reached up and took hold of some skin over his head and began to pull. Groans and howls intensified as the skin came down off the shoulders and chest. The process took a long time.

When the Wurm had finished, and was still standing, swaying, the bride removed one of her wedding shirts. The Wurm, seeing she was still clothed, said to her, "Take off your wedding shirt!" She replied as before. "I will take off another of my wedding shirts if you take off another of your skins." He replied, "No one has ever asked me to do that before."

After he had taken off the seventh of his skins, he lay on the floor exhausted, and he no longer had any shape at all; he was a mass of white flesh with no skin.

The bride then dipped her stiff bristled brush into the bucket of lye, and began scrubbing his flesh. She scrubbed his body so long that she wore out both her two brushes with their wire bristles, wearing them down to the nubs, and used up all the lye.

When that was done, she took the fresh milk and poured it over his body.

The Wurm then stood up as a man, and a handsome, well-proportioned man. A week or two later the true wedding ceremony took place. No one had seen a wedding so marvellous for many years. I was there too, and I received the best food and drank the best liquor for three days; but where did it go? Now I'm walking around pulling cold air through my teeth like everyone else.

The story says that it is not good to ignore the spiked hair, and the safety pins through the cheeks. We have to turn the Volvo around, go home, and ask our parents if they know anything about this.

The story says that if one throws a being out the window, it grows up, but the being who grows up in the wild, in the wilderness, in the waste places, becomes a different being than the one who grows up "inside the castle," valued, admired, noticed, taught, encouraged, and corrected. Richard Wilbur once wrote a fine poem about a snow-man who stands looking into the windows of a lit, warm house.

> *Seeing the snowman standing all alone*
> *In the dusk and cold is more than he can bear.*
> *The small boy weeps to hear the wind prepare*
> *A night of gnashings and enormous moan.*
> *His tearful sight can hardly reach to where*
> *The pale-faced figure with bitumen eyes*
> *Returns him such a god-forsaken stare*
> *As outcast Adam gave to Paradise.*

When we look at the sibling society, its absences, its flatness, its numbness, we realize that people have been thrown out the window—women, Marines, black people, Hispanic people, and children. The story says that the being thrown out will return and prevent us from "marrying."

The way the story arranges the details is good, so that the mother and father can both truthfully say they didn't know anything about it.

This image of the boy-infant who is born in snake form, and then thrown out the window, only to return later in some terrifying shape, is valuable for our subject, because it gives an image for the anger and rage we feel all around us. Many people still hope that improved communication will bring us closer to each other, and in the midst of new inventions and new paradigms, we will have peace; we will have equality and pacific emotions, the calm state the French originally named "reason." But reason is itself a kind of sleep, and as Goya said, "The sleep of reason produces monsters."

A friend living in Europe, who visits New York every two years or so, remarked that each time he returns, the anger on the streets is deeper; and American faces are more and more angry.

The Lind Wurm story says that giving the rage a chance to express itself does not solve the problem. And yet the rage is a fact. We know that from the drive-by killings, if from nothing else.

Simply allowing children to watch television as many hours as they watch is to throw them out the window. Garbage is what we throw out the window. Metaphorically, the place where we throw them is not far away, just "over there."

Because of "downsizing," parental neglect, and bad schools, almost every member of Generation X, or the Day-Care Generation, feels thrown out the window. Inner-city children of all races have been thrown out into a wasteland.

When a men's conference invites young gang members, it becomes clear that much integrity and a fierce longing, for creativeness and for fathers, lie beneath the dangerous surface. Orland Bishop, who works with gang members in Los Angeles, says, "When you're dealing with a person who is doing violence, you're dealing with someone whose electricity is already channeled into the muscles. . . . Try to find a youth to work with. You'll be working with what has not been used. . . . Their capacity for feeling is equal to their capacity for violence." Most people don't want to hang a picture of their enemy in their house. But that's "what we have to do." Doing such work, as Michael Meade and Orland Bishop have found out, is dangerous. And to get the skins off takes a long time.

The Hostile Being Inside

We can also interpret this story personally, as it relates not to society but to our own soul. How old are we before we realize that someone inside us doesn't wish us well?

That one sometimes turns up in dreams; he shoots at us, or chases us down an alley. A friend turns out at the last minute to be a Saboteur. The Saboteur intervenes at crucial moments in our life to ensure a wrong turn, a bad decision, the road that leads to an icy bridge. The Saboteur foments rebellions and plots a takeover. A suicide means that he or she wins. Naive people know nothing of the One Inside Who Doesn't Wish You Well, and think that their enemies are all in the outside world.

It's clear from our story that the Hostile Interior Being doesn't want us to "marry." The luckier we are, the harder the hostile interior person works. Malidoma Somé remarked that a person who is cursed always goes to the house of a person who is blessed to make war.

The hostile being wants to destroy relationships, and his visit lurks behind much male violence against women. Women may find a hostile being inside, who is not male but female. The hostile interior woman works as well to break up relationships. The story says that if we wish to be truly married—to a human being or to God—we have to convince the Wurm-man or the Wurm-woman inside to pull off his or her skins. It can't be done by force, but has to be a deal.

This part of our life involves the relationship between the good brother and the hostile brother, or between the good sister and the hostile sister. We have left the parent-child story world, and we are back now in the Cain and Abel, Jacob and Esau story world. The sibling society, having chosen the brother-brother road and the sister-sister road (over the parent-child road), has opened itself to the painful process described in "The Lind Wurm."

Epilogue

I BEGAN THIS BOOK IN A RATHER LIGHTHEARTED TONE. I ENJOYED at the start the delicious contradictions we see all around us. At a convention for sixteen-year-olds who had gone through drug recovery, a T-shirt read, "Do you feel like we do?" I remembered a pre-sibling T-shirt: "Do you think like me? If so, I'm changing my mind."

Everyone seems to feel that it's good to call strangers by their first name. When we call to get our checking-account balance, we hear a chilling series of impersonal orders, such as "Press one. Now press six. Press the pound key. Press in the Social Security number"; then an intimate voice says, "Robert, what can I do for you?" I say, "Mister Bly, to you."

The first names make sense in a sibling way. The speaker doesn't want to imply by using your last name that your family is different from hers or his. To omit the last name is to say, "Your ancestors are totally unimportant to us. You are a highly individualized individual floating in a bright ocean of individuals, and we just love your particular essence." We are so deeply on a first-name basis that a total stranger can call you into a consultation room and tell you on a first-name basis that you are about to die.

But as I began to realize the extent and implications of the sibling society, my lightheartedness went away, and some weight, as of economics, settled in. The fading of the father as a provider in American culture seemed a significant event to me, and I had assumed that anger against the patriarchal family, some of it justified, was the primary cause. But work on this book has convinced me that other forces have taken part. Those devoted to the bottom line have effectively interposed themselves between the father and the family. Part of the effort has been to get at the children more easily. The more the parents' dignity and strength are damaged, the more open children are to persuasion.

All of us who have been angry at the fathers rejoiced at first when the fathers lost authority, but the picture becomes more somber when we realize that the forces that destroyed the father will not be satisfied, and are moving toward the mother. Mothers are discounted everywhere. When mothers and fathers are both dismembered, we will have a society of orphans, or, more exactly, a culture of adolescent orphans.

I was surprised, as I began writing the book, that a culture run by adolescents, or by adults in an adolescent mood, would treat children so badly. But in fact adolescents living in an actual family do not pay much attention to the ones "above" them, nor the little ones beneath them. That is particularly true if the adolescents *feel* like orphans.

I was startled one day walking on Madison near Eighty-fifth Street, when I saw a poster that asked this question:

What is 24 stories tall, carries the most sophisticated armament on earth, and is run by a crew of 21-year-olds?

The answer was "an aircraft carrier," the poster being an advertisement for a program on the Discovery channel. The "most sophisticated armament on earth" means the ability to devastate entire countries—and this is to be run by a crew of twenty-one-year-olds? There is a lie involved, spoken to flatter young men and women: a lie that resides in the ambiguity of the word "run." The ad people want to have twenty-one-year-olds running the carrier; and the twenty-one-year-olds believe they can and should run it. We understand that they don't "run" a carrier, but why is this word made inexact? The confusion of who should run the carrier is a confusion deep in the sibling society. Freshman members of Congress believe they can and should run the government.

One day I discovered that the Swedish poet Harry Martinson could describe all the confusion of the sibling society in eight lines. He imagines a place that is eternally flat; he connects its flatness with Euclid and mathematics.

> *When Euclid started out to measure Hades,*
> *he found it had neither depth nor height.*
> *Demons flatter than stingrays*
> *swept above the plains of death. . . .*
>
> *There were only waves, no hills, no chasms or valleys.*
> *Only lines, parallel happenings, angles lying prone.*
> *Demons shot along like elliptical plates;*
> *they covered an endless field in Hades as though with moving*
> *   dragonscales.*

(Those moving dragonscales are especially fine.) He suggests that burial mounds in such a world get flattened by "forgetfulness," and that the damned in such a hell are

> *victims of flat evil,*
> *with no comfort from a high place*
> *or support from a low place*

This sounded familiar, and made me think that *we*, as the population of the United States, may be that very place where there are no hills, no chasms, no valleys. Then I had to ask myself what part of me is flat. I thought of my own fatherhood, which was often flat in the sense of making few steep demands on my children. Cultures with depth have firm codes. One can feel the codes in old movies; promises must be kept, pleasure comes after relationship, you talk in a polite way to grandparents, there is something more important than money, and so on. Parents of my generation taught our children the codes of responsibility, restraint, and renunciation, but also we taught them how to evade the codes. Stepping through the codes was a secret game among parents in the 1970s, a little payback for being a parent. That would be all right—at least humanly normal—if the code were strong. But widely varying codes from dozens of attractive cultures flood our receptors. If we want to evade a certain element in our code, the renunciation of selfishness or thievery, for example, we can always find another code—the codes by which the Hindu gods live, for example—in which the forbidden is allowed. Some of us spend our whole lives looking, successfully, for holes in the codes. When our parents teach us how to do that at the dinner table, we find those lessons very appealing. We could say that flatness lies in saying yes to everything.

In a sense, we say yes in this culture to everything but adult human beings. To human beings we often say no. Neruda remarks that "it so happens I am sick of being a man," by which he means a human being. The increasing dislike of human beings by human beings concentrates itself in the current neglect of children. Perhaps this is the first time in human history that children, en masse, have picked up the idea that they are not wanted, not needed. A child will cost its parents $400,000. "If I'm going to cost my parents $400,000 and I'm no good to them, then what am I? Nothing." Reading the figures on the neglect of children, the teenage wastelands that exist along the strips, the children who find difficulty in learning because of too much television and too little food or constant trauma in the house and the street took away the last lightheartedness I felt.

Most of us feel grief and fear at the newest developments, but we also know that what is happening is simply a part of the leveling process that has been going on since the time of the French Revolution. The United States was born in that excitable moment of early leveling; the stars looked down on us then, and leveling became a part of our astrological sign forever. Kierkegaard says, "No single individual . . . will be able to arrest the abstract process of leveling, because the negative power of leveling is stronger than any individual. No group or association can arrest that abstract power, simply because an association is itself in the service of the leveling process."

He calls the leveling process a sort of spontaneous combustion of the human race. He probably wants us to see a pile of rags in the corner of a warehouse that suddenly bursts into flame. People aren't exactly people anymore, but more like a pile of rags about to ignite. The fire will burn your clothes if you get too close. Many people are too busy burning to worry about the good of the community.

THERE HAS TO BE SOME GOOD IN ANYTHING THAT HAPPENS IN such a massive way. If we find ourselves in the closing stages of a leveling process that has been going on for two centuries, what good can possibly come of it? We know that some old structures of the family are now altering. For instance, the patriarchal society inevitably and invariably put the husband on top economically, personally, socially, politically, sexually, and legally. The marriage building now has to be remodeled, given new retaining walls, footings, and piers, and the inside redesigned. A genuine equilibrium and, on the personal level, a genuine equality will have to be established between husband and wife. And we know that many husbands and wives are doing exactly that.

THE TROUBLE IS THAT THE HORIZONTAL GAZE, SO DEEPLY A PART of sibling arrangements, amounts to making mirrors out of the people we see around us. In a sibling society we want other people to be like us; we pay attention to the ways we resemble other people. They then reflect back our own image. Our image of course is compromised somewhat by the other person's nature, but we still tend in a mirroring culture to see ourselves rather than the other. By mirroring, I don't mean responding or resonating to the other person; on the contrary, a mirror is by nature static, and it gives back a generalized, not exact, image. Seeing our inexact image over and over finally floods our receptors, and we don't know who we are. In antiquity, by contrast, a Caesar or a Queen Boadicea stood out, their distinctiveness was clear, and we could decide whether we wanted to go their way or another way.

Now no one is allowed to get that big. Seeing images of oneself in our chosen group, whether our group be Hispanics or poets or doctors, one doesn't decide to go anywhere. One can't take any passionate steps, nor feel admiration for Beethoven or Mother Teresa or Freud or one's own marital partner, because—by being hobbled, cut off from the horizon by the hundreds of mirrors on all sides—we have nowhere to rest but in envy. The look associated with gratitude—upward—breaks our contact with the mirrors.

As for husband and wife, if they accept the "resemblance model" (the idea that men and women should be like each other as far as possible), they will find themselves facing a mirror that is disguised as a partner or husband or wife or lover. Then, stunned by seeing only herself, the woman will lose all passion and inwardness, and will not know what she wants, and can only envy manhood or masculine freedom; and the man, seeing only himself, will lose all passion and inwardness, and will not know what he wants, and can only envy motherhood, women's freedom, or genuine laughter. Each feels a Euclidean emptiness. The recovery of inwardness could free each of us, if not the culture, from the compulsion to see ourselves in others.

Finally, in the new situation, where the wife can leave the marriage and support herself, and the husband is not religiously or legally bound to remain in the marriage, much latitude is possible. But isolation is likely. Each partner at any moment has the power to withdraw. That power to withdraw, as observers have noted, is the price of the current liberty. We could say that the only power men and women have over each other now is the power of indifference. Indifference is an old power, but it is being used now to solve problems in marriage, and indifference becomes a poison that destroys children.

W E CAN BE SURE THAT WHEN POWER HIERARCHIES, IN PLACE FOR thousands of years, have been dismantled, some part of that leveling must be a gift. Some of us, however, have become alarmed at the destruction of culture that follows such a dismantling. The pleasure that adolescents take in destroying the serious work of their predecessors is a kind of novel pleasure to them, but that will soon wear out. I hope it will wear out before the culture is entirely destroyed. In any case, clearly the end of hierarchies means that our responsibilities, individually, increase. Each of us has to take the responsibility for the continuation of discipline and fineness that was once the responsibility of the people "up there." We have to choose. If we want a leveled society, we cannot expect those "up there" to support us, because there isn't any "up there."

Each of us living is a bona fide member of the sibling society, which is in fact a mass society. But each of us, individually, refuses to acknowledge that we are a part of any mass or group, because we have a little detachment machine inside, which allows us to be ironical and critical whenever we find ourselves at a lecture or a huge concert or a large sports event. This little tape recorder tells us that we don't belong to any mass, that each of us is truly individual. But we remember how many Germans thought they were individual at the same time that they enjoyed the mass rallies. The little detachment machine is dangerous. William Stafford said:

If you don't know the kind of person I am
and I don't know the kind of person you are
a pattern that others made may prevail in the world
and following the wrong god home we may miss our star.

For there is many a small betrayal in the mind,
a shrug that lets the fragile sequence break

sending with shouts the horrible errors of childhood
storming out to play through the broken dyke.

And as elephants parade holding each elephant's tail,
but if one wanders the circus won't find the park,
I call it cruel and maybe the root of all cruelty
to know what occurs but not recognize the fact.

And so I appeal to a voice, to something shadowy,
a remote important region in all who talk:
though we could fool each other, we should consider—
lest the parade of our mutual life get lost in the dark.

For it is important that awake people be awake,
or a breaking line may discourage them back to sleep;
the signals we give—yes or no, or maybe—
should be clear: the darkness around us is deep.

Part of the darkness lies in the fact that, because of the detachment machine, the signals we give—yes or no or maybe—are not clear. But if we own a television set, we are a registered member of a mass society. There is a danger that we will acquiesce to the next generation without honoring its members.

The people we need to understand are the young siblings—the thousands of young siblings we see around us. Many of them are remarkable and seem to have a kind of emotional knowledge that is far older than they are. Some have sharper intuitions into human motives and people's relationships with each other than any of us had at that age. Some who expect to die early—as many do—see with a brilliant clarity into the dramas taking place all around them. A large number of young siblings, not burdened by the expectations associated with war and empire, see our little island as the shipwrecked do. Ortega y Gasset said:

The [person] with the clear head is the [person] who frees himself from all fantastic "ideas" and looks life in the face. . . . Instinctively,

as do the shipwrecked, he looks round for something to which to cling,
and that tragic, ruthless glance, absolutely sincere, because it is a
question of his salvation, will cause him to bring order into the chaos
of his life. These are the only genuine ideas: the ideas of the ship-
wrecked. All the rest is rhetoric, posturing, farce. . . .

What is asked of adults now is that they stop going *forward*, to
retirement, to Costa Rica, to fortune, and turn to face the young
siblings and the adolescents. One can imagine a field with the adolescents on one side of a line drawn on the earth and adults on the
other side looking into their eyes. The adult in our time is asked to
reach his or her hand across the line and pull the youth into adulthood. That means of course that the adults will have to decide what
genuine adulthood is. If the adults do not turn and walk up to this
line and help pull the adolescents over, the adolescents will stay
exactly where they are for another twenty or thirty years. If we don't
turn to face the young ones, their detachment machines, which are
louder and more persistent than ours, will say, "I am not a part of
this family," and they will kill any real relationship with their parents. The parents have to know that.

During the paternal society, there were representatives of the
adult community: highly respected grade and high school teachers,
strong personalities of novels and epics, admired presidents and
senators, Eleanor Roosevelts and Madame Curies, priests untouched
by scandal, older men and women in each community, both visible
and capable of renunciation, who drew young people over the line
by their very example. But envy and the habit of ingratitude have
ended all that.

The hope lies in the longing we have to be adults. If we take an
interest in younger ones by helping them find a mentor, by bringing
them along to conferences or other adult activities, by giving attention to young ones not in our family at all, then our own feeling of
being adult will be augmented, and adulthood might again appear
to be a desirable state for many young ones.

In the sibling society, because of the enormous power of the leveling process, few adults, as we have mentioned, remain publicly visible as models. Because they are invisible, the very idea of the adult has fallen into confusion. As ordinary adults, we have to ask ourselves, in a way that people two hundred years ago did not, what an adult is. I have to ask myself what I have found out in my intermittent, poem-ridden attempts to become an adult. Someone who has succeeded better than I could name more qualities of the adult than I will, but I will offer a few.

I would say that an adult is a person not governed by what we have called pre-oedipal wishes, the demands for immediate pleasure, comfort, and excitement. Moreover, an adult is able to organize the random emotions and events of his or her life into a memory, a rough meaning, a story.

It is an adult perception to understand that the world belongs primarily to the dead, and we only rent it from them for a little while. They created it, they wrote its literature and its songs, and they are deeply invested in how children are treated, because the children are the ones who will keep it going. The idea that each of us has the right to change everything is a deep insult to them.

The true adult is the one who has been able to preserve his or her intensities, including those intensities proper to his or her generation and creativity, so that he or she has something with which to meet the intensities of the adolescent. We could say that an adult becomes an elder when he or she not only preserves those intensities but adds more.

An adult is a person who, in the words of Ansari, goes out into the world "and gathers jewels of feeling for others." Finally, the adult quality that has been hardest for me, as a greedy person, to understand is renunciation. The older I get, the more beautiful the word *renunciation* seems to me. We need to re-create the adult and to honor the elder. The hope lies in our longing to be adults, and the longing for the young ones, if they know what an honorable adulthood is, to become adults as well. It's as if all this has to be newly invented, and the adults then have to imagine as well what an elder is, what the elder's responsibilities are, what it takes for an adult to become a genuine elder. In this problem, the example of the Native American community will be of great help.

Here is one final story—a Norwegian story. A man walking through the forest and in danger of dying from cold sees at last a house with smoke rising from the chimney. He sees a thirty-year-old man chopping wood and says to him, "Pardon me, but I am a traveler who has been walking all day. Would it be possible for me to stay overnight in your house?" The man says, "It's all right with me, but I am not the father of the house. You'll have to ask my father." He sees a seventy-year-old man standing just inside the door and says, "Pardon me, but I am a traveler and have been walking all day. Would it be possible to stay overnight in your house?" The old man says, "It's all right with me, but I am not the father of this house. You'll have to ask my father, who is sitting at the table." He says to this man, who looks about a hundred years old, "Pardon me, but I am a traveler who has been walking all day. Would it be possible for me to stay overnight in your house?" The hundred-year-old says, "It's all right with me, but I am not the father of this house. You'll have to ask my father." And he gestures toward the fireplace. He sees a very old old man sitting in a chair near the fire. He walks over to him and says, "I am a traveler, and I have been walking all day. Would it be possible for me to stay overnight in your house?" In a hoarse voice this old old man says, "It's all right with me, but I am not the father of the house. You'll have to ask my father." The traveler glances at the boxed-in bed, and he sees a very, very old man who seems no more than four feet tall, lying in the bed. He raises his voice and says to him, "Pardon me, I am a traveler, and I have been walking all day. Would it be possible for me to stay overnight in your house?" The little man in the bed says in a weak voice, "It's all right with me, but I am not the father of this house. You'll have to ask my father." Suddenly the traveler sees a cradle standing at the foot of the bed. In it lies a very, very little man, hardly the size of a baby, lying curled in the cradle. The traveler says, "Pardon me, but I am a traveler. I have been walking all day. Would it be possible for me to stay at your house tonight?" In a voice so faint it can hardly be heard, the man in the cradle says, "It's all right with me, but I am not the father of this house. You'll have to ask my father." As the traveler lifts his eyes, he sees an old hunting horn hanging on the wall, made from a sheep's horn, curved like the new moon. He stands and walks over to it, and there he sees a tiny old man no more than six inches long with his head on a tiny pillow and a tiny wisp of white hair. The traveler says, "Pardon me, I am a traveler, and I have been walking all day. Would it be possible for me to stay overnight in your house?" He puts his ear down close to the hunting horn, and the oldest old man says, "Yes."

We know there is a Seventh Mother of the House, who is also very small. Perhaps she is far inside the womb, or sitting in the innermost cell of our body, and she gives us permission to live, to be born, to have joy. Her contribution is life. The contribution of the Seventh Father is a house. Together they grant permission from the universe for civilization.

Notes

"Mass society, with its demand for work without responsibility": Alexander Mitscherlich, *Society Without the Father*, trans. Eric Mosbacher (London: Tavistock Publications, 1969), p. 269. The entire passage reads: "Mass society, with its demand for work without responsibility, creates a gigantic army of rival, envious siblings. Their chief conflict is characterized, not by oedipal rivalry, struggling with the father for the privileges of liberty and power, but by sibling envy directed at neighbors and competitors who have more than they."

Alexander Mitscherlich was born in Germany in 1908. During his twenties, he participated in the left-wing anti-Nazi movement and in 1932 displayed in a bookstore window a pamphlet called *Adolf Hitler—Germany's Doom*. He spent six months in the Nuremberg prison, and had to report to the gestapo twice a day for the remainder of the war.

After the war, German medical societies chose him to head the German Medical Commission to the American Military Tribunal dealing with medical war crimes at Nuremberg. During this period, Mitscherlich went through rigorous psychoanalytic training and became a key figure in the reestablishment of German psychoanalysis. He published *Society Without the Father* in Germany in 1963. Four years later he and his wife, the analyst Margarete Mitscherlich, wrote *The Inability to Mourn*, in which the two authors concentrate on the German citizen's "forgetfulness" of the Nazi era. Mitscherlich later became a professor at the University of Frankfurt and the director of the Sigmund Freud Institute there. *Society Without the Father* was published in English translation by Tavistock Publications in 1969 and reprinted in a paperback edition by HarperCollins in 1993.

"a gigantic army of rival siblings": Kierkegaard considered the present age to be one of thought, brooding, and considering, rather than action: "This reflective tension ultimately constitutes itself into a principle, and just as in a passionate age *enthusiasm* is the unifying principle, so in an age which is very reflective and passionless *envy* is the negative unifying principle." Soren Kierkegaard, *The Present Age*, trans. Alexander Dru (New York: Harper and Row, 1962).

"My students usually come with ego boundaries": Robert Sapolsky, "Ego Boundaries, or the Fit of My Father's Shirt," *Discover* 16, no. 11, November 1995, p. 67.

"There is little in the sibling society to prevent a slide into primitivism." The part fantasy plays in sibling society is comparable to the part repression played in the paternal society. Two sorts of fantasy have been increasing in recent years: one involves a return to one's childhood, that is a sliding back, the other a return to the childhood of the race. The latter appears from areas of the soul long thought to have be superseded.

One archaic fantasy concerns the ritual killing of a scapegoat, which sometimes is a human being. *The Journal of Psychohistory* tries to keep track of such archaic fantasies as they drift upward into political cartoons, obsessive writing, and violent acts. One example is the fantasy that a woman with power is a witch. It rises from a very old level of the brain, but Hillary Clinton knows how present it can be in our time. Another archaic fantasy is that there is an evil person or evil group somewhere and in order for us to return to normal, that group or person must be wiped out. A leader of the Montana militia, several weeks before the bombing in Oklahoma City, said to a reporter, "There cannot be a cleansing without the shedding of blood." (*The New York Times,* April 25, 1995.) The paternal society, with its premium on nationhood, gave permission for us to imagine Russia as the "Evil Empire," and the cost of that fantasy has been the economic wealth of the United States. Our new sibling society is an inward collapsing structure, so the hateful group has become the U.S. government; and loosely organized, anti-government hate groups are springing up. On the ultimate sibling medium, the Internet, which has no filters, fantasy feeds fantasies in an exaggeratedly horizontal fashion.

Another old fantasy which seems to be gathering force is the fantasy that sacrificing children, making them scapegoats, will somehow bring the golden days back. One's words falter as soon as the tongue has expressed such an idea. But the rise of child prostitution, Satanic sacrifice of infants, Congressional assault on support for children, the abandonment of children to television, a cruelty almost Aztec in its thoroughness, suggests that, despite all our rationality, a deep-lying and archaic belief is taking hold: namely, that if we sacrifice our children, we may become healthy and sound again. W. B. Yeats said:

We had fed the heart on fantasies,
The heart's grown brutal from the fare....

The Journal of Psychohistory can be contacted at 140 Riverside Drive, Suite 14H, New York, NY, 10024.

"Drastic change [has produced] this social primitivism": Eric Hoffer, "A Time of Juveniles," *Harper's*, June 1965, pp. 17–24.

"The society of half-adults": There are some good sides to the siblings too. For many young people, the birds, whales, and animals are siblings also. The wren, the dolphin, the whale, the falcon in its threatened nest, the owl among the maddened loggers, and the mink standing in the snow are important siblings, and tend to be naturally ecological.

Some siblings are willing to accept the idea that the earth's resources are limited, and many are passionate recyclers. Siblings used to wearing identical T-shirts and shoes, are not much bothered by the question of borders. Also, the sources of male power are no longer so hidden; the secret price that each gender pays for occupying its predetermined role is much clearer than it used to be in the days when Humphrey Bogart and Lauren Bacall fit so simply into their social assignments. Finally, some siblings, having felt abandoned by their own parents, are determined to be good parents to their children.

"It is hard in a sibling society to decide what is real": Once the sibling society is well in place, the citizens may find great difficulty in maintaining distinct viewpoints or rebellious trains of thought. As William Greider points out in *Who Will Tell the People: The Betrayal of American Democracy*, we no longer find major American newspapers or their reporters who set themselves to defend the workers or the poor against the rich and powerful. *The New York Times* and the *Washington Post* stand with the rich and powerful. Reporters like Bob Woodward seemingly cannot maintain their anti-establishment point of view for more than a decade.

In the old father-organized society, the citizens simply looked up at the men at the top of the high stairs and opposed them with an outrage that was partly fueled by anger at one's own father and his power. But when the father does not present himself, or appears as a pitiful object, and the mother alone, and with great sacrifice, has to hold the power, then how does the citizen fuel his or her political anger? How can the oedipal anger be accurately focused? It's possible that our whole Western tradition of fiery outrage will fade. We notice that political cross-dressers like Reagan basically escape all serious censure.

"Kierkegaard once, in trying to predict": Soren Kierkegaard, *The Present Age*, trans. Alexander Dru (New York: Harper and Row, 1962), pp. 37–38.

"Nonevents are now a regular national feature": For many siblings, the art that is most acceptable or legitimate is art that can be consumed by large numbers of siblings all over the globe *at the same time*. The night a few years ago when hundreds of musicians and singers got together on television and sang "We Are the World" to millions of other siblings was a model sibling event. Whether the art is good or bad doesn't matter; the important thing is how many people experience it.

"In the past twenty years, the American press has undergone": Adam Gopnick, "Read All About It," *New Yorker*, December 12, 1994, p. 86. He also remarks, "A media that in its upper, more self-conscious reaches . . . once dealt in quiet signals now sounds loud and acts mean.

Pure, unmodulated belligerence and hostility has become, as Michael Arlen noted, a favorite American form of entertainment. The *McLaughlin Group* is a form of ritualized aggression, as are the conversations of Pat Buchanan and Michael Kinsley. The aggression often seems to be fueled by envy, an emotion that joins together journalists and ordinary citizens. The habit of envy keeps people from feeling gratitude, and the media encourages voters to remain in that adolescent place, in relation to the responsibilities of citizenship.

"The superego or Interior Judge has altered his requirements": Harry and Yala Lowenfeld, in their article "Our Permissive Society and the Superego," published in the *Psychoanalytic Quarterly* (39) 1970 pages 590–607, noticed that "in large parts of the population there is little discipline. . . . The aggressive drives meet with weak control. Television . . . stimulates and satisfies sadistic fantasies; at the same time it blunts responsiveness to one's sadistic impulses." As early as 1954, Annie Reich discussed this implacable judge in her essay "Early Identifications as Archaic Elements in the Super-ego," *Journal of the American Psychoanalytic Associates*, **2**, 1954, pages 218–38. Alexander Mitscherlich, in *Society Without the Father*, p. 160, found that many young German men in the 1960s, particularly the fatherless ones, were dealing with an Interior Judge who wanted them to die.

"The Interior Judge's changed requirements": We notice, at least in the United States, that fantasies that began as affectional fantasies, full of idealisms or foolish sorts of sentiments, those endearing fantasies that we notice in the Myrna Loy movies and the Clark Gable movies, gradually shifted over the years to be replaced by destructive fantasies. So *Casablanca* is replaced by James Bond, *Gone with the Wind* is replaced by *Fatal Attraction*, *Little House on the Prairie* is replaced by action movies and *Kids*. The Beatles are replaced by the Stones and finally by Nine Inch Nails. The fantasies of the transcendental separatists in Concord are replaced by the fantasies of the separatists militia groups in Montana or Oklahoma.

"The superego presents itself under the guise of demands": Giles Li-povetsky, quoted in Elisabeth Badinter, *The Unopposite Sex: The End of the Gender Battle* (New York: Harper and Row, 1989), p. 194.

"Most adults have been slow to grasp": The work of the psychologist Heinz Kohut throws light on the tyrannical judge. Kohut was trained in Vienna in classic Freudian theory, which posits that people become neurotic when and if their sexual drive or aggressive drive does not find satisfaction. When

Kohut began to do psychoanalysis in the United States, he discovered that such theoretical concepts did not fit his American patients. Some Americans he saw seemed to have no drives at all. The psychoanalyst Robert Moore remarks: "Some of my clients fall asleep telling their own stories."

Kohut began to center his thought and work around the concept of grandiosity. The word grandiosity is used negatively in the phrase "infantile grandiosity." A child in such a state is called "the King in the high chair"; but there is a true grandiosity, or a genuine grandness, that is a part of our health. We were Queens and Kings in the womb. It is not wrong for parents to praise their infants, and care for them when they call, and tell them how beautiful they are. But what if we live in a culture in which praise is disappearing? What if the parents no longer praise their children, because they don't have time to notice them, because both parents are working? What if the children look at television every day and see how worthless human life is? Some parents adopt the fundamentalist mind-set, which has always maintained that children are sinful. It's not unusual for children to hear phrases such as these over and over: "Who do you think you are?" "You're too big for your britches." We can hear an effort toward grandiosity in the sentence: "I don't have to clean my room," and in the desire to have Nikes and grandiose amplified music. If we agree that youth culture encourages an inappropriate grandiosity at times, we can suppose a force encouraging deflation is already at work, which we would call the "grandiosity killer."

CHAPTER ONE
THE WOODSTOCK MOMENT

"When Elvis Presley let his pelvis move to the music": Michael Ventura, personal communication; see Ventura's *Shadow Dancing in the USA* (New York: Jeremy Tarcher, 1984), pp. 42–51, 151–157.

"The Indo-European, Islamic, Hebraic impulse-control system": Jules Henry, *Culture Against Man* (New York: Random House, 1963), p. 20. The passage reads, "The second modern commandment, 'Thou shalt consume,' is the natural complement of the first—'Create more desire.' Together they lead the attack on the key bastion of the Indo-European, Islamic and Hebrew traditions—the impulse control system—for the desire for a million things cannot be created without stimulating a craving for everything. This is the second phase of the psychic revolution of our time—*unhinging the old impulse controls*. The final phase will be the restoration of balance at a new level of integration."

"By 1969, it felt as if human beings": The 1960s people received a loosening of controls. We can also say that they were forced by circumstances to become adult morally and ethically earlier than most previous generations. Having to give up old idealisms, such as "America is always right," required an end to comfortable collective regression. Certain clarities, honesties, and moral insights developed by the 1960s generation marked a high point in the life of popular culture; and that is one reason the Reagan-Bush generation pulled away from those insights so quickly.

"What the children talk about most": Jules Henry, *Culture Against Man*, p. 138. "What permits impulse release is 'good' and anything that blocks it is 'bad.' . . . What we see so much in America, then, is that the psychoanalytic metaphor according to which the child introjects the parent (copies the parent, tries to come up to parental expectations) is stood on its head, and the parent copies the child."

"a certain asceticism for the young" is abandoned. That mothers have to give up as much of their freedom to pregnancy and birth and child rearing and get so little back, that fathers give up so much of their emotional life in order to support wife and children and get so little back—those complaints have been getting louder. And now grown-ups and youths have other complaints: that playing the violin is hard, that people get tired of each other, that God is so far away, that we get sick, that we get old, that we will die, that no one cares for us enough to die for us, that we have to travel through our adult life with our parents looking the other way. We could say that siblings have a hard time accepting such hard choices and such limits which come along with having a body on this particular planet.

"When the Englishman Geoffrey Gorer": Geoffrey Gorer, *The American People, A Study in National Character* (New York: W. W. Norton, 1948).

"Deprived in his work life of personality aspirations": Jules Henry, *Culture Against Man*, p. 132.

"audience that now attends a grunge music concert": Fantasy in the past was usually associated with overleaping obstacles, transcending death, heroically defeating whatever represents death, in short, with the sort of optimistic themes that Disney liked. Now death is not transcended; it is as if while a person is having the fantasy, death attaches itself *to* the person, and that is what the fantasy is about.

   We might call many rap lyrics death energy in aggressive form. But thousands of teenagers have death energy in passive form as well; children, alone in their room, who devote themselves to fantasy, are being captured by death energy, which they usually cannot effectively fight. Other adolescents actively court death. Imagination contrasts with fantasy, in that imagination often brings health to the psyche.

CHAPTER TWO
JACK, THE BEANSTALK, AND THE GIANT WITH A LARGE APPETITE

"In the days of King Alfred, there lived a poor woman": Iona and Peter Opie, *The Classic Fairy Tales* (New York: Oxford University Press, 1974). The passages quoted are from pp. 214–220.

"In the Grimm Brothers story called 'The Raven'": "The Raven," in *Grimms' Tales for Young and Old: The Complete Stories*, trans. Ralph Manheim (New York: Anchor Press / Doubleday, 1977), pp. 326–330.

"My own consciousness is possessed by the eruption": George Steiner, *In Bluebeard's Castle: or Some Notes Towards a Redefinition of Culture* (London: Faber and Faber Limited, 1971), p. 10.

"We can take the Giant to stand for our archaic, brutal underpinning.": Serious loss of culture is taking place. The numbers of men and women living without inwardness, imagined to be huge in the Middle Ages numbers that were supposed to have lessened during the Enlightenment of the eighteenth and nineteenth centuries, have now increased once more so as to include almost every city and suburb one can see from an airplane. Robert Lowell remarked, "A savage servility slides by on grease." Mitscherlich remarks that primitive behavior turning up in the so-called civilized person is noticeable also in "regressions at group level, all the way from primitivization of ideas in disciplined bodies down to the formation of gangs and the increasing narrowing of horizons to selfish group interests." In 1991 Bush could harness vast aggressive energies in a patently unreal war, and the sibling media, including PBS and CNN and Congress, offered no brakes. Video and movie producers put no curb on the desires to see bodies blown apart or women tortured and raped; the level of literary culture declines; fewer and fewer people can find the energy to stand up for old disciplines in language, syntax, dance, figurative art. We know that the instinctual desire for pleasure among addicts becomes terroristic, and the social desire for "rightness" among ordinary citizens can become terroristic as well.

"Brain researchers have established": For the tripartite brain, one can read Paul MacLean's *A Triune Concept of the Brain and Behavior*, ed. D. Campbell and T. J. Boag (Toronto: University of Toronto Press, 1973) and his several other books. Arthur Koestler discusses the tripartite brain in his *The Ghost in the Machine*, and Charles Fair relates the lower brains to the id in *The Dying Self*. My book *Leaping Poetry* (Boston: Beacon Press, 1975) relates Paul MacLean's characterizations of the brains to the quick changes of mood and content we experience in French and Spanish surrealist poetry.

"This is the phylogenetically oldest part of the brain": Arthur Koestler, *The Ghost in the Machine* (New York: Macmillan, 1968), p. 278.

"when the psychiatrist bids the patient to lie on the couch": Paul MacLean, "Man and His Animal Brains," *Modern Medicine*, March 2, 1964, pp. 95–106.

"The reptilian brain and the greater part of the old": Paul MacLean, "Man and His Animal Brains."

"investigations of the last twenty years have shown": Paul MacLean, "Man and His Animal Brains."

"Colin Turnbull, in his *The Mountain People*, describes what happened": Colin Turnbull, *The Mountain People* (New York: Simon and Schuster, 1972).

"His calves and feet turn in reverse position": Michael Meade, *Men and the Water of Life* (New York: HarperCollins, 1993), p. 264.

"By degrees, Jack recovered himself sufficiently": Iona and Peter Opie, *The Classic Fairy Tales*, p. 220.

"The commanding *nafs* is that which has not passed," Dr. Javad Nurbakhsh, *The Psychology of Sufism* (London: Khaniqahi-Nimatullahi Publications, 1992). The passages that follow are quoted from pp. 11–29.

"Listen to this, and hear the mystery inside": Rumi, *The Essential Rumi*, trans. Coleman Barks (New York: HarperCollins, 1995), p. 220.

"The animal soul has given birth to all fetishes": Rumi, *The Soul Is Here for Its Own Joy*, trans. Robert Bly, (Hopewell, N.J.: Ecco Press, 1995), p. 55.

"Considered in the light of Freudian psychology": Paul MacLean, quoted in Arthur Koestler, *The Ghost in the Machine*, p. 287. Gurdjieff, the twentieth-century teacher from the Caucasus, summarized the relations between the human components this way. Two horses, that is, powers, are pulling a carriage. On top of the carriage, a driver is sitting; and his job is to communicate to the horses through the reins. The driver, however, doesn't know the destination. Only the Master, the one hidden inside the walls of the carriage, knows where we are going. Sometimes he shouts a message up to the driver, but the driver doesn't always hear. This chaotic scene has been going on for centuries.

But recently, the horses have learned not to obey the driver. They ignore instructions from the driver, and increasingly do what they want. The Master inside the coach doesn't like the arrangement very well either, because every trip is endless, and the driver is increasingly deaf. If the horses feel they want to turn right, they do so. If they get hungry for grass, they pull the carriage into the ditch, where it turns over. See *Views from the Real World: Early Talks of Gurdjieff;* New York. E. P. Dutton, 1975, pp. 143–147.

"At the farther end of the gallery there was a winding staircase": Iona and Peter Opie, *The Classic Fairy Tales*, pp. 220–221.

"The loudest sound in northern Europe at the end": See Henrik Ibsen, *A Doll's House*, final scene.

"When the West opened up": Alexis de Tocqueville noticed in the 1830s that the father's authority was already much weakened by that time: "Paternal authority, if not destroyed, is at least impaired." (*Democracy in America*, Schocken Books, p. 229) Carl Degler, in his book *At Odds: Women and the Family in America from the Revolution to the Present* (New York, 1980), notes that manuals on child rearing in the 1830s began to be addressed to mothers, and he reports on the increasing absence of the father from the house during that time.

David Blankenhorn, in *Fatherless America: Confronting Our Most Urgent Social Problem* (New York: Basic Books, 1995), remarks: "Within the home, fathers have been losing authority; within the wider society, fatherhood has been losing esteem. Many influential people in today's public debate argue that, when all is said and done, fathers are simply not important."

"The transition from the father to the mother": Susan Juster and Maris Vinoskis, quoted in David Blankenhorn, *Fatherless America* p. 237.

"Having these parent tracks laid out": Marion Woodman, personal communication.

"Are people feeling guilty nowadays?": Owen Barfield, *History, Guilt, and Habit* (Middletown, Conn.: Wesleyan University Press, 1979), pp. 55–57.

"Feelings of guilt tend to turn rather easily": Owen Barfield, *History, Guilt, and Habit*, p. 58.

Ruth Sidel, "But Where Are the Men?", in *Men's Lives*, ed. Michael S. Kimmel and Michael A. Meissner (New York: Macmillan, 1989), p. 537.

"From 1980 to 1993, the Fortune 500 companies": Andrew Kimbrell, *The Masculine Mystique* (New York: Ballantine Books, 1995), p. 114.

"The unskilled black man has little chance of obtaining": Elliot Liebow, quoted in Ruth Sidel, "But Where Are the Men?", p. 536.

"Unemployment among Native Americans": Ruth Sidel, "But Where Are the Men?", p. 537.

"Patriarchal industrial production system": Andrew Kimbrell, *The Masculine Mystique* p. 39.

"Fathers are vanishing legally as well as physically": David Blankenhorn, *Fatherless America*, p. 10.

"Why not have a child of one's own?": Katha Pollitt, "Bothered and Bewildered," *New York Times*, July 22, 1993, p. 23.

"Daniel Patrick Moynihan, in his famous article of 1965": "The Negro Family: The Case for National Action," (Washington, D.C., the Office of Policy Planning, and Research, U.S. Department of Labor; reprinted by Greenwood Press, Westport, Conn., 1981). At first glance we assumed that the missing social father has been replaced by a massive, many-breasted state mother. But it's more accurate to say that when the father is gone, everyone becomes a sibling. The spirit of sibling rivalry as Mitscherlich says, soon "turns into envy and 'begging behavior' resembling that of nestlings on the approach of their parents bringing food." The envy and jealousy that brothers and sisters normally feel for one another inside the home become the emotional norm for the whole society.

Moynihan's information came from the tough-minded sociologist James S. Coleman, whose research showed that among all reasons for the lagging of black children in schools, family structure was the most important. This is set out in Coleman's 1960 report *Equality of Educational Opportunity*. But the idea was ridiculed:

"It was the singular fate of postwar American liberalism that at its peak moment of social optimism, the mid-1960's, a number of studies appeared that argued that social change was going to be far more difficult than anyone had thought. This information was received with equanimity in some liberal quarters but with denial in most. Coleman was viciously attacked in the mode that Hannah Arendt had observed among the totalitarian elites in Europe—the ability to immediately dissolve every statement of fact into a question of motive. Liberalism faltered when it turned out it could not cope with truth. Even the tentative truths of social science." Daniel Patrick Moynihan, "Moved by the Data, Not Doctrine," *New York Times Magazine*, December 31, 1995, p. 25.

"The presence or absence of both parents per se makes little difference": Alvin L. Schorr and Phyllis Moen, *Family in Transition: Rethinking Marriage, Sexuality, Child Rearing and Family Organization* (Boston: Little, Brown, 1983), p. 579.

"Children born at the end of the Second World War": Michael Ventura, "Welcome to the Real World, Kid," *City Pages*, Minneapolis, June 21, 1995, p. 10.

"if the son is released from his struggle with the father": Elizabeth Badinter "In challenging all their fathers' values, the sons unconsciously moved closer to those of their mothers, who are traditionally anti-war, non-competitive, and have no experience of power—other than over their families—or of acting the oppressor. . . . But in reality, the new alliance was based on a misunderstanding. At the very moment when young men were turning their backs on the manly stereotypes and adopting more feminine behavior, women themselves were abandoning some of their millenarian attitudes and taking possession of domains that had previously been the preserve of men. This generation of sons, which had often associated itself with the women's campaign, realized too late that it had been swindled. The ones who had drawn closer to the traditional values of their mothers found it difficult to accept that women were just then distancing themselves from such values. For while these men were trying to build a less aggressive world in which competition would be less fierce, women were now turning out to be formidable competitors. They were no longer merely tenderness and devotion, they were also ambition and egotism. The disarray of the fathers became that of the sons—and so it remains." Elisabeth Badinter, *The Unopposite Sex: The End of the Gender Battle*, trans. Barbara Wright (New York: Harper and Row, 1989), p. 133.

"Mary Pipher, in her study of adolescent girls": Mary Pipher, Ph.D., *Reviving*

Ophelia: Saving the Selves of Adolescent Girls (New York: Ballantine Books, 1994).

"Jack, finding that all his arguments were useless": Iona and Peter Opie, *The Classic Fairy Tales*. The passages that follow are from pp. 221–226.

"Freud in 1899 talked optimistically of cultural progress": Sigmund Freud, *Interpretation of Dreams*, passim.

"the pure culture of the death-instinct": Sigmund Freud, *Civilization and Its Discontents*, trans. James Strachey (New York: W. W. Norton, 1962). Suicide among American adolescents is increasing. The death wish, or death instinct, now has found a way to exhibit itself in the private bedrooms of urban and suburban youth. More and more black teenage boys are killing themselves—12 per 100,000 in 1990, nearly double the rate of 1980. For young white men, the percentage is even higher—now almost 21 per 100,000.

Chapter Three
Swimming Among the Half-Adults

"In the Usenet news group, where digital images": Philip Elmer-Dewitt, "On a Screen Near You: Cyberporn," *Time*, July 3, 1995, p. 38.

Ken Burns, *History of Baseball*, Public Broadcasting System, 1994.

"Adolescents are separating off as a group": Without the acid component being mingled into the lives of the 1960s generation, their moral rebellion may have turned out very differently, more like the sober opposition that the Spanish students gave to Franco over many years. Franco put students in jail for years, and they considered it a fair deal. Franco didn't stop and the students didn't stop. The Spanish students considered their imprisonment and even torture a logical consequence of the rebellion that they embodied, but by 1971 the students in the United States had already arrived at a sibling longing for action with no limitations and no consequence. The parents failed to rescue them, and the antiwar rebellion effectively came to an end.

"An old theme of adolescents," Alan McGlashan, *The Savage and the Beautiful Country*, Boston, Houghton-Mifflin, 1976, p. 46. The implications of Alan McGlashan's remarks and the thoughts of other observers such as Michael Ventura are that we don't have the luxury any longer of ignoring the adolescents.

"For tens of thousands of years tribal people everywhere have greeted the onset of puberty, especially in males, with elaborate and excruciating initiations—*a practice that plainly wouldn't have been necessary unless their young were as extreme as ours*. This is terribly important. It means that when conservatives talk of rock culture subverting the young, when others talk about that same culture liberating the young or when postmodern technologists talk of our electronic environment 'rewiring the software' of new generations—they are all making the same mistake. They fail to understand that a psychic structure that has remained constant for one-hundred thousand years is not likely to be altered in a generation by stimuli that play upon its surfaces. What's really going on is very different: the same raw, ancient *content* is surging through youths' psyches, but adult culture over the last few centuries has forgotten how to meet, guide and be replenished by its force. . . . For about forty years now, the young have generated forms—music, fashions, behaviors—that prolong the initiatory moment. In other words, we cherish and elongate adolescence (or 'initiatory receptivity') as though hoping to be somehow initiated by chance somewhere along the way. For tribal people, the initiatory moment was by far the most intense period of life, lasting no more than weeks, at most about a year. For us, it now lasts decades. And it's as though the pressure to make it last decades increases its chaotic violence. This very extension of the initiatory moment is helping to drive everyone mad. . . . Unlike us, tribal people meet the extremism of their young (and I'm using 'extremism' as a catchall word for the intense psychic cacophony of adolescence) with an equal but focused extremism from adults. Tribal adults didn't run from this moment in their children as we do: they celebrated it. . . . The crucial word here is 'focus.' The adults had something to teach: stories, skills, magic, dances, visions, rituals. In fact, if these things were not learned well, the tribe could not survive. But the adults did not splatter this material all over the young from the time of their birth, as we do. They focused, and were as selective as possible about, what they taught and told, and when. They waited until their children reached the intensity of adolescence, and then they used that very intensity's capacity for absorption, its hunger, its need to act out, its craving for dark things, dark knowledge, dark acts, all the qualities we fear most in our kids—the ancients used these very qualities as teaching tools." Michael Ventura, "The Age of Endarkenment," in *Letters at* 3 AM (Dallas: Spring Publications, 1993).

Many young people grew up even in the patriarchal cultures without any organized practices that we would call initiation. But looking now from the ruins of the patriarchal culture, we see that whatever methods western culture had of passing on knowledge is not working now. Millions of adolescents are coming out of school craving that knowledge, and there are virtually no adults who reach out a hand to them to pull adolescents over into adulthood.

"Men and women in their twenties": Many teachers and art museum curators openly express a wish to destroy the European culture they have not been well introduced to. The Walker Art Center, in Minneapolis, one of the finest contemporary museums, distributed buttons in 1995 that read "In the spirit of Fluxus, Demolish Serious Culture. Walker Art Center."

"hostility to the group's literature": Adolescents in the last twenty years have been shocked by learning the true story of the American past. We used to glimpse the cruelty of great nations only when we heard about Romans overseeing the crucifixion of Jesus, or when we read a history of the Middle Ages, but now we see our past everywhere on television. This knowledge makes a potent stew of guilt and shame. There is a pervasive feeling of unworthiness that is not completely accounted for by our private lives.

Many cultures before us founded their nation by killing all the sheep, cattle, men, women, and children in any town that their particular Moses pointed to; but most national histories have been careful to wrap those facts in resonant tones and pious certainties. All that has evaporated now.

We used to look into the eyes of our mothers and fathers, and their eyes sometimes said that we were worthy. Now we look into the eyes of television, and the eyes reply almost always that we are unworthy. Our unworthiness is supported every day by new revelations. Children, looking at such documentaries, see all. We see in documentaries the criminal acquiescence of our grandparents at best, or the criminal activity of our grandparents at worst. The shock is causing something like a nervous breakdown.

One result is that some educators encourage us to throw away all literature created by men and women who were alive at the time those ugly events occurred.

I am against that. When an individual person has a "nervous breakdown," we don't respond by urging him or her to throw away all the photographs and stories. If a man or woman discovers midway in life that his or her parents were more corrupt than originally thought, that they sexually abused him or her, the woman or man goes into a sort of shock because the soul is not prepared for what it has learned.

In that situation, psychologists may suggest that people undergoing such a shock break off communication with their parents for a while, or move to California for a year, but obviously the person's healing will have to be based on their accumulated history if genuine change is to take place. No one suggests throwing away all the songs the person sang in high school or blotting out all memories of friends and childhood, or renouncing in the same moment their family, their county, their state, their nationality, their race. Everyone knows that that would be madness. Growth can proceed only if people honor that part of their soul that is turned toward the goodness, so to speak, of their ancestors, so that they know there is something essentially worthy in them, for whose sake they go through all this agony.

Why would we want to treat our nation with its shocking past so differently from the way we have learned to treat ourselves? We have to swallow all the dark truths about the Conquistadores and Puritans, the enslaving and murdering of powerless people, and still preserve the common story, so that we do not lose touch with whatever good there was in our ancestors, and with that part of our own soul.

"We have our computers": Virtual reality, touted as an alternative reality, really means no reality at all, or rather it means that the neocortex, outflanked and pressured, creates a place where it can be in control for forty minutes, while the lower brains run everything else in the universe.

The Internet is a perfect creation of the sibling society, particularly in its belief that no codes of literary behavior and no standards are called for, and information can come along fruitfully without any filtering. But civilized proceedings cannot proceed without filters. The great book reviewer Edmund Wilson, for example, was a superb filter. We know that in science, new papers on scientific theory require elaborate filters, or all readers would be overwhelmed. One of the characteristics of the sibling society is its persistent and deeply adolescent hope that we can have a cultural life without filters.

Jon Katz remarks: "America is increasingly a collection of tribal enclaves, each responsive to its own interests but unable or unwilling to step beyond itself on behalf of a common good." That sentence is a very concise description of the sibling society. The opinions, then, that pour onto the Internet with no filtering whatsoever fit into the sibling society principles in that all the individual clans are emphasized, and there is no common story or common good. (In Jon Katz, "Guilty," *Wired*, magazine, Sept. 1995, pp. 128–133, 188.)

Jay Kinney warns about the naiveté of the New Renaissance: "The new political infrastructure of the Net is as handy to Shell Oil as it is to a bedroom publisher of politically incorrect zines." (In Jay Kinney, "Anarcho-Emergentist-Republicans," *Wired* magazine, Sept. 1995, pp. 90–95.)

"Hostility toward the larger group": We could say that the comedienne Roseanne is a model for rude sibling behavior. Maureen Dowd writes in the *New York Times*, September 3, 1995: "There is something disagreeable about turning this Rabelaisian back-lot brat into a feminist ideal. Roseanne stands for things that self-respecting women should disdain: tyrannical behavior, lording it over the help, disguising a love of power as a love of equality. She equates all criticism with misogyny. She takes on the guise of victimhood when it suits her. She promotes herself as a tribune of blue-collar women, while she lives the profligate, plastic-surgeried life of a spoiled star. Even her humor is a religion of grudges."

"People of all ages are making decisions to avoid the difficulties of maturity": The psychologist Takeo Doi reports that this is true of the Japanese as well. The Japanese word *amae* refers to "the behavior of the child who desires spiritually to 'snuggle up' to the mother, to be enveloped in an indulgent love. . . . Takeo Doi goes on to say that the present age is strangely permeated with *amae* is much the same as saying that everyone has become more childish. Or it might be more correct to say that the distinction between children and adults has become blurred. Thanks to the mass communication media, children get to know things so quickly that an increasing number of them are too 'adult' to consider their elders as adults. Indeed, although people talk of the generation 'gap' it might be more appropriate as a description of the present to talk of the loss of any boundary between the generations. It is the same with adults: the 'adult adult' of the past has disappeared and the number of childish adults has increased. And the common element to both adult-like child and childlike adult is *amae.*" Takeo Doi, *The Anatomy of Dependence*, trans. John Bester (New York: Kodansha International, 1981), pp. 8–163.

"Freud maintained that human beings feel a deep hate": Sigmund Freud, *Civilization and Its Discontents.*

"One way to outwit the demands that civilization makes": It appears that neither man nor woman want to be so dependent on each other as they have been in the past. Each gender aims for independence, and that seems natural for us. But as the obligatory dependence between men and women lessens, dependence itself is not lessening, dependence on the state increases.

"I think the Hemlock likes to stand": Emily Dickinson, *The Complete Poems of Emily Dickinson*, ed. Thomas H. Johnson (Boston: Little, Brown, 1960), pp. 256–257.

"Kafka's great story 'The Judgment' ": Franz Kafka, *The Complete Stories and Parables*, ed. Nahum N. Glatzer (New York: Schocken Books, 1983), pp. 77–88.

"Freud gave structure to this turmoil when he pulled in": Sigmund Freud, see *The Psychopathology of Everyday Life*, Standard Edition, vol. 6.

"Won so well he lost": William Stafford, "Brevities," in *Allegiances* (New York: Harper and Row, 1970), p. 55.

"includes a non-respect for the father": Alexander Mitscherlich, *Society Without the Father*, trans. Eric Mosbacher (London: Tavistock Publications, 1969), p. 147.

"A young man studying to be a doctor": Personal communication.

"millions of males may linger passively": Revolutionary activity has already flattened out in the sibling society. Much of the revolutionary impulse in American politics that expressed itself in nineteenth-century populism, in West Coast Wobbly strikes, in Marxist and communist agitators in New York and Chicago, in fierce debates and huge rallies, responded to clear injustice, but some of the emotion rose out of anger against the paternalistic father.

Among the leftists of the thirties, oedipal anger directed at the patriarchal father, who was restrictive and the son of restrictors, fueled much vigorous political engagement. But when in our time the father pulls back his demands and becomes a sibling pal to his son and his daughter, then father-based anger is alchemically changed to confusion, and the fierce shouting at union halls and caucus meetings disappears. The oedipal anger resembled, one could say, that little motor that hung beneath those great airships of the 1930s. The engine was small, compared with the airship, and yet that little motor could send the ship all the way across the country. The unexpected result of the new family arrangements is that there isn't enough focused energy left to start the motor.

"Some of Kurt Cobain's lyrics": Kurt Cobain was a fatherless son who slept under bridges as a boy. We could consider him an example of the pre-oedipal son who couldn't arrive at community. When Janis Joplin sang, her rage flowed parallel to some deep longing for union with another being; but Kurt Cobain's scream took place inside his own echo chamber, his own "recording" studio.

The lyrics of punk rock often had specific targets, but grunge rock tends toward generalized hatred. Cobain said, "Since the age of seven, I've become hateful towards all humans in general only because it seems so easy for people to get along and have empathy." (Quoted in Neil Strauss, "A Cry in the Dark," *Rolling Stone*, June 2, 1994, p. 40.)

"Nauman's 1984 neon sign": See Bruce Nauman's "One Hundred Live and Die," *Bruce Nauman: Exhibition Catalog*, Walker Art Center, ed. Joan Simon.

"At birth, the rhesus monkey, for example, has a brain": Paul Shepard, *The Tender Carnivore and the Sacred Game* (New York: Scribner, 1973).

"These matters came into closer focus when a professor": Louis Bolk, *Das Problem der Menschderwung (The Problem of Human Evolution)* (Jena: G. Fischer, 1926).

"If I wished to express the basic principle of my ideas": Louis Bolk, *Das Problem*, p. 8.

"Neotony": See Stephen Jay Gould, *Ontogeny and Phylogeny*; Paul Shepard, *The Tender Carnivore and the Sacred Game*; and Konrad Lorenz, *Studies in Animal and Human Behavior*, (London: Methuen, 1971).

"Infantilizing is one of the means by which increased brain size": Paul Shepard, *The Tender Carnivore and the Sacred Game*, p. 15, pp. 49–50.

"Man is programmed to learn to behave, rather than": Wilton Marion Krogman, *Child Growth* (Ann Arbor, MI: University of Michigan Press, 1972, p. 2.

"Human exploratory inquisitive behavior—restricted in animals": Konrad Lorenz, cited above, p. 239.

"Thoreau continued doing so all his life": Henry David Thoreau, *The Winged Life: The Poetic Voice of Henry David Thoreau*, ed. Robert Bly (New York: HarperCollins, 1992), p. 81.

"The temple bell stops": Basho, *Basho*, trans. by Robert Bly (San Francisco: Mudra, 1972).

"My heart leaps up when I behold": William Wordsworth, *The Poems*, vol. 1 (New York: Penguin Books, 1977), p. 522.

"Well I call to mind": William Wordsworth, *The Prelude, A Parallel Text*, ed. J. C. Maxwell (New York: Penguin Books, 1971), pp. 50–52.

"Rigorists": Marianne Moore, *Collected Poems* (New York: Macmillan, 1941, 1969).

"Ode to My Socks": Pablo Neruda, *Neruda and Vallejo*, trans. and ed. Robert Bly (Boston: Beacon Press, 1971, 1993), pp. 141–145.

CHAPTER FOUR
THE ADVENTURES OF GANESHA: A HINDU STORY

A full version of the Oedipus story can be found in Robert Graves, *Greek Myths* (New York: Penguin Books, 1975).

"She said to Shiva, 'I want a son'": *Brhaddharma Purana* (2.60.15–18), quoted in Paul B. Courtright, *Ganesa: Lord of Obstacles, Lord of Beginnings* (New York: Oxford University Press, 1985), p. 45.

"Daughter of the mountain, I am not a householder": *Brhaddharma Purana* (2.60.10–14), quoted in Paul B. Courtright, *Ganesa*, p. 42.

"As she was thinking in this way": *Siva Purana* (2.4.13.15–32), quoted in Paul B. Courtright, *Ganesa*, p. 46.

"Siva, who indulges in every form of play": *Siva Purana* (2.5.13.31–35), quoted in Paul B. Courtright, *Ganesa*, p. 64.

"Ganesha struck the great lord with his axe": *Skanda Purana* (3.2.12.15–20; see also *Devi Purana* 111–116; *Mahabhagavata Purana* 35), quoted in Paul B. Courtright, *Ganesa*, p. 63.

"Astonished at this, Siva took his son's head": *Siva Purana*, quoted in Paul B. Courtright, *Ganesa*, p. 69.

"Go in the northern direction": *Siva Purana* (2.4.17.47), quoted in Paul B. Courtright, *Ganesa*, p. 34.

Alain Danielou, *Shiva and Dionysus*, trans. K. F. Hurry (London: East-West Publications, 1982).

"To some extent it is the father's business to be absent": Alix Pirani, *The Absent Father: Crisis and Creativity* (New York: Arkana, 1989), p. 113.

"Restored to proximity with his mother": A. K. Ramanujan, "The Indian Oedipus," in *Indian Literature, Proceedings of a Seminar*, ed. Arabinda Podder, Simla, pp. 127–37, and quoted in Paul B. Courtright, *Ganesa*, p. 103.

"We have been told that Bill Clinton, as a boy of fourteen": David Maraniss, *First in His Class* (New York: Simon and Schuster, 1995), p. 40.

"When a young man in our culture arrives": In the patriarchal society, some people falsified their being in order to get closer to concentrated power. Swift describes such people in his satires, Browning in his monologues, and Eliot in "The Love Song of J. Alfred Prufrock."

In the sibling society, people adopt false selves in order to be more like one another, in order to be invisible, agreeable, and passionless. "Go along and get along." There is very little praise. "People come and go in the Tate, / Saying Michelangelo is not that great."

Some falsify the self to bring it in line with the irresistible sibling unreality. When people talk, they talk of personal failures, but usually avoid other deep anxieties, for example, over the fate of children or of the earth itself. Oprah Winfrey does not offer shows titled "People Who Fought for Wetlands and Lost."

"Everything has come under the antiaura": Lawrence Grossberg, "Is Anybody Listening? Does Anybody Care? On 'The State of Rock,' " in *Microphone Fiends: Youth Music and Youth Culture*, ed. Andrew Ross and Tricia Rose (New York: Routledge, 1994), p. 53.

"When in the *Mabinogion* Culwich": "Culwich and Olwen," in *The Mabinogion*, trans. Gwyn Jones and Thomas Jones (London: Everyman's Library, 1974), pp. 95–136.

"The inexhaustible energies of the cosmos": Joseph Campbell. He mentions this image several times in *The Hero with a Thousand Faces* (New York, Bollingen Foundation, 1949).

"When Mother Teresa came to Brooklyn": *Mother Teresa*, directed by Anne Petrie, available from Mystic Fire Video.

'When I was seventeen years of age": Poor Wolf, "Poor Wolf Speaks," in *News of the Universe*, ed. Robert Bly (San Francisco: Sierra Club, 1980), pp. 259–260.

"There is . . . for those who dare to look for it": Alan McGlashan, *The Savage and Beautiful Country*, p. 46.

"The confrontation between father and son for the mother": A. K. Ramanujan, quoted in Paul B. Courtright, *Ganesa*, pp. 103, 263.

"With the second head comes order and harmony": Paul B. Courtright, *Ganesa*, p. 118.

"Born again into a male world": Paul B. Courtright, *Ganesa*, p. 118.

"The child with the feeling that the pains of maturation": Paul B. Courtright, *Ganesa*, p. 119.

"Flatter than stingrays": Harry Martinson, "Hades and Euclid" (first version), in *Friends, You Drank Some Darkness: Three Swedish Poets*, trans. Robert Bly (Boston: Beacon Press, 1975), pp. 55–57.

CHAPTER FIVE
THE WILD GIRL AND HER SISTER: A NORWEGIAN
STORY

"Once in Norway at a time when animals spoke": George Webbe Dasent, "Tatterhood," in *East o' the Sun and West o' the Moon* (New York: Dover, 1970), pp. 345–353.

"The world tells us what we are to be": Olive Schreiner, *The Story of an African Farm*, quoted in Mary Pipher, *Reviving Ophelia: Saving the Selves of Adolescent Girls*, p. 22.

"In America in the 1990s, the demands of the time": Mary Pipher, *Reviving Ophelia*, pp. 264–265.

"Cayenne told me of a recurring dream in which she was asleep": Mary Pipher, *Reviving Ophelia*, pp. 31–32.

"In *Smart Girls, Gifted Women*, Barbara Kerr explains": Mary Pipher, *Reviving Ophelia*, p. 266.

"Such a wedding happens at the end of the Russian story": Aleksandr Afanas-ev, "Vasilisa the Beautiful," in *Russian Fairy Tales*, trans. Norbert Guterman (New York: Pantheon Books, 1945), pp. 439–447; see also "Snow White and Rose Red," *Grimm's Tales for Young and Old*, pp. 501–06.

"How strange! Both of us": Antonio Machado, *Times Alone: Selected Poems of Antonio Machado*, trans. Robert Bly (Middletown, Conn.: Wesleyan University Press, 1983).

"There lives the dearest freshness deep down things": Gerard Manley Hopkins, "God's Grandeur," in *Poems and Prose of Gerard Manley Hopkins*, ed. W. H. Gardner (New York: Penguin Books, 1984), p. 27.

"Plutarch remarks that Isis is often pictured with cow horns": Ada de Vries, *Dictionary of Symbols and Imagery* (Amsterdam: North Holland Publishing Co., 1974), p. 114.

CHAPTER SIX
WHAT DO DAUGHTERS STAND TO LOSE OR GAIN IN A
SIBLING SOCIETY?

Thomas Verny, with John Kelly, *The Secret Life of the Unborn Child* (New York: Dell, 1981).

"A Western bias of individualism and a 'Lone Ranger' ethic": Jean Baker Miller, "The Development of Women's Sense of Self," *Works in Progress*, No. 12 (Wellesley: Stone Center Working Papers Series, 1984).

"I think that the infant begins to develop an internal": Jean Baker Miller, "The Development."

"Melanie Klein named this gift of hunger, frustration": Melanie Klein, *Envy and Gratitude* (New York: Free Press, 1984), pp. 61–93.

"It is a healthy thing for a baby to get to know the full": D. W. Winnicott, *The Child, the Family, and the Outside World* (Harmondsworth, Eng.: Penguin Books, 1964), p. 62, quoted in Jessica Benjamin, *Bonds of Love* (New York: Pantheon Books, 1988), p. 40.

"Fathers' play with infants differs from mothers' ": Jessica Benjamin, *The Bonds of Love*, p. 102.

"No matter what theory you read, the father is always": Jessica Benjamin, *The Bonds of Love*, p. 103.

"Little girls are seeking the same thing as little boys": Jessica Benjamin, *The Bonds of Love*, p. 108.

"Even today, femininity continues to be identified with passivity": Jessica Benjamin, *The Bonds of Love*, p. 87.

"The only thing women lack is practice in the 'real world' ": Jean Baker Miller, *Toward a New Psychology of Women* (Boston: Beacon Press, 1976), p. 35.

"I do think men are longing for an affiliative mode," Jean Baker Miller, *Toward a New Psychology*, p. 88.

"Women, like men, are by 'nature' social": Jessica Benjamin, *The Bonds of Love*, p. 80.

"The 'real' solution to the dilemma of women's desire": Jessica Benjamin, *The Bonds of Love*, p. 114.

"The deep need is in young girls for certain kinds of open space and solitude": Carol Gilligan and Eva Stern, "The Riddle of Femininity and the Psychology of Love," paper presented at the Seminar on the Psychology of Love, Douglass College, 1986.

"The narcissism of uninitiated women directly fuels": Elizabeth Herron and Aaron Kipnis, personal communication.

"Passion is headed for extinction": Elisabeth Badinter, *The Unopposite Sex*. Passages quoted are from pp. 204–206.

"We are less concerned to dominate and possess the other": Elisabeth Badinter, *The Unopposite Sex*, p. 208.

"In this book, we are arguing that growing up with only one biological": Sara McLanahan and Gary Sandefur, *Growing Up with the Single Parent* (Cambridge, Mass.: Harvard University Press, 1994), p. 60.

CHAPTER SEVEN
WHAT DO SONS STAND TO LOSE OR GAIN IN A SIBLING SOCIETY?

"We know that if the fetus is marked to become male": Anne Moir and David Jessel, *Brain Sex* (New York: Dell, 1992).

"If I were a poet of love": Antonio Machado, *Times Alone*, p. 53.

"Peter Blos . . . remarks that most Freudian analysts prefer to omit": Peter Blos, *Son and Father* (New York: Free Press, 1985), part 1, passim.

"Peter Blos noticed that when he was in long therapy with": Peter Blos, *On Adolescence* (New York: Free Press, 1966).

"The attachment to the father served the little boy": Peter Blos, *Son and Father*, p. 25.

"Janine Chassaguet-Smirgel, the Freudian analyst, sums up much thought": Jessica Benjamin, *The Bonds of Love*, pp. 147–155.

"In the late night listening from bed": William Stafford, "Thinking for Berky," in *The Darkness Around Us Is Deep: Selected Poems of William Stafford*, ed. Robert Bly (New York: HarperCollins, 1994), pp. 37–38.

"Sherwood Anderson said he felt at this age": Sherwood Anderson, "Sophistication," *Winesburg, Ohio* (New York: Viking, 1960).

"A man may go, John Lee says, from experiencing anger": John Lee, personal communication. See also his *Facing the Fire: Experiencing and Expressing Anger Appropriately* (New York: Bantam Books, 1993).

"Martín Prechtel, the writer and teacher of ritual": Personal communication.

"The new equation, male = bad": Elisabeth Badinter, *XY: On Masculine Identity*, trans. Lydia Davis (New York: Columbia University Press, 1995).

CHAPTER EIGHT
DISDAIN AND CONTEMPT FOR CHILDREN IN THE SIBLING SOCIETY

"The parents regress to become more like children": Because parents seem to have, or do have, their faces turned away toward some distant place, the young come to believe they are not welcome, and they respond by deconstructing all the parents' favorite books.

"the young . . . are thrown away": The capitalist or industrial forces early on defeated in England the craftsmen–weavers, needle makers, tinsmiths, wheel makers, dyers, woodworkers, artists. Blake as a craftsman was among that group. By closing the commons, the forces defeated independent workmen who were forced to accept hourly wages or starve. This defeat also amounted to a defeat of women. The cottage wife spun next to her husband, and was his equal; in cottages or farms the wife often contributed as much to the economy as the husband. When the husband left for the factories, the wife had either to become insignificant or to follow the work out of the house. Labor formed unions and for a while held their own. But J. P. Morgan's brutal crushing of the Homestead Strike in 1892 proved to industrial workers that they too could be pushed aside. At the end of this line of people pushed aside by capitalist industrial forces stood the children. Reagan's crushing of air traffic controllers was a contemporary Homestead. The children are the newest in this line of displaced people, who lose clout.

"The work by Bowlby, Winnicott, and Kohut": See John Bowlby, *Attachment* (New York: Basic Books, 1983); C. D. Winnicott, *The Child, the Family, and the Outside World*; and Heinz Kohut, *Self Psychology and the Humanities*, ed. Charles B. Strozier (New York: W. W. Norton, 1985).

"settled for so little from the start that they think a little is a lot": John Lee, personal communication.

"The disappearance of childhood": Neil Postman, *The Disappearance of Childhood* (New York: Vintage Books, 1994).

"Good conversation with grown-ups provides what some researchers": Jane M. Healy, Ph.D., *Endangered Minds: Why Children Don't Think and What We Can Do About It* (New York: Simon and Schuster, 1990), p. 86.

"Nature's imperative is, again, that no intelligence unfolds": Joseph Chilton Pearce, *Evolution's End: Claiming the Potential of Our Intelligence* (New York: HarperCollins, 1992), p. 115.

"The majority of babies born in the United States are placed in full-time day care": *The Parental Leave Crisis*, eds. Edward F. Zigler and Meryl Frank (New Haven: Yale University Press, 1988). See Ken Magid and Carole A. McKelvey, *High Risk: Children Without a Conscience* (New York: Bantam Books, 1988), pp. 139–145.

"The education editor of *The New York Times*," Jane M. Healey, *Endangered Minds*, p. 240.

"You visit some infant care centers," Dr. Susan Luddington-Hoe, quoted in Jane M. Healey, *Endangered Minds*, p. 44.

"After age eleven, it appeared their brains had lost the ability to master": Jane M. Healy, *Endangered Minds*, p. 115.

"It's the end of another day at Proviso West": Karl Bissinger, *New York Times Magazine*, May 29, 1994.

"A study by Dr. Bernia Callenci of NYU": Jane M. Healy, *Endangered Minds*, p. 23.

"A study conducted by the education department at Kent State": Jane M. Healy, *Endangered Minds*, p. 22.

"A comprehensive recent study, supported by the National Institute of Mental Health": Neal Postman and Steve Powers, *How to Watch TV News* (New York: Penguin Books, 1992), p. 147.

"There is a famous experiment with two kittens": Jane M. Healy, *Endangered Minds*, p. 79.

"Scores on the National Assessment of Educational Progress": Jane M. Healy, *Endangered Minds*, p. 26.

"In American universities at large, the general faculty complaint": Joseph Chilton Pearce, *Evolution's End*, p. 20.

"He says that the child whose brain has been impaired": Joseph Chilton Pearce, *Evolution's End*, p. 168.

"In our schools, only 30% can still learn": Joseph Chilton Pearce, *Evolution's End*, p. 169.

CHAPTER NINE
BENJAMIN FRANKLIN'S PIG: ECONOMICS AND OUR HEAVINESS OF HEART

"[It gave] to the weak hope that they too": R. H. Tawney, *The Acquisitive Society* (New York: Harcourt Brace, 1948), p. 30.

"National commerce, good morals and good government": Dean Tucker, quoted in R. H. Tawney, *Religion and the Rise of Capitalism* (Gloucester, Mass.: Peter Smith, 1962), p. 192.

"the State which interferes with property and business destroys": John Locke, *Two Treatises on Government*, book 2, chap. 9, para. 124.

"Enclosure came, and trampled on the grave": John Clare, "Enclosure," in *The Poems of John Clare*, ed. J. W. Tibble (New York: E. P. Dutton, 1935), vol. 1, p. 419.

"Thus God and Nature formed the general frame": Alexander Pope, *Essay on Man*, ed. Maynard Mack (New Haven: Yale University Press, 1951).

"Max Weber in 1904 set up a new tower": Max Weber, *The Protestant Ethic and the Spirit of Capitalism*, trans. Talcott Parsons (New York: Scribner, 1952).

"Remember, that money is of the prolific": Benjamin Franklin, quoted in Max Weber, *The Protestant Ethic and the Spirit of Capitalism*, p. 49.

"At Paddy the Pig's then stand and drink": Thomas McGrath, *Letter to an Imaginary Friend*, parts I and II (Chicago: Swallow Press, 1977), p. 146.

"In 1960 the average pay for chief executives": William Greider, *Who Will Tell the People: The Betrayal of American Democracy* (New York: Simon and Schuster, 1992), p. 397.

"Many orthodox economists routinely assume": William Greider, *Who Will Tell the People*, p. 396.

"A shrug that lets the fragile sequence break": William Stafford, "A Ritual to Read to Each Other," in *The Darkness Around Us Is Deep*, pp. 135–136.

"The abandonment of public institutions in which citizens": Mickey Kaas, "The End of Equality," quoted in Christopher Lasch, *The Revolt of the Elites and the Betrayal of Democracy* (New York: W. W. Norton, 1995), p. 97.

"The United States does not have an automatic call on our resources": William Greider, *Who Will Tell the People*, p. 394.

"Multinational executives work to enhance the company": William Greider, *Who Will Tell the People*, p. 394.

"The market in which the new elites operate": Christopher Lasch, *The Revolt of the Elites*, p. 35.

"[they] are aware of millions of siblings like them": Alexander Mitscherlich, *Society Without the Father*, p. 74.

"There are more than 240 *maquila* plants": William Greider, *Who Will Tell the People*, p. 387.

"Indeed, the *maquiladora* industry boasts of this": William Greider, *Who Will Tell the People*, p. 382.

CHAPTER TEN
TEACHING OUR CHILDREN THAT NOTHING WORKS

"The sibling society can be traced back": Huston Smith sums up Confucian ideals under five key terms. The Confucian ideal society could be considered as the mirror opposite of the sibling society described in this book. The first term is *jen*, which "involves simultaneously a feeling of humanity toward others and respect for oneself, an indivisible sense of the dignity of human life wherever it appears. . . . In private life it is expressed in courtesy, unselfishness, and empathy, the capacity to 'measure the feelings of others by one's own.'. . ." The second is *chun tzu*. "Fully adequate, poised, the *chun tzu* has toward life as a whole the approach of an ideal hostess who is so at home in her surroundings that she is completely relaxed, and, being so, can turn full attention to putting others at their ease. . . . The *chun tzu* carries these qualities of the ideal host with him through life generally. . . . Only as those who make up society are transformed into *chun tzus* can the world move toward peace. . . . The third concept, *li*, has two meanings. Its first meaning is propriety, the way things should be done." It is *comme il faut*. It is wary of excess, and it guards the Five Constant Relationships, "those between parent and child, husband and wife, elder sibling and junior sibling, elder friend and junior friend, and ruler and subject. It is vital to the health of society that these key relationships be rightly constituted. . . . When the meanings of the parents are no longer meaningful to their children . . . civilization is in danger. . . . Three of the Five Great Relations focus on looking up to one's elders." The fourth pivotal concept, *Te*, means literally "power, specifically the power by which men are ruled. . . . No state, Confucius was convinced, can constrain all its citizens all the time nor even any large fraction of them a large part of the time. It must depend on widespread acceptance of its will, which in turn requires a certain positive fund of faith in its total character. . . . Real *Te*, therefore, lies in the power of moral example. . . ." The final concept, *Wen*, "refers to 'the arts of peace' as contrasted to 'the arts of war'; to music, art, poetry, the sum of culture in its esthetic mode. . . . Confucius contended that the ultimate victory goes to the state that develops the highest *Wen*, the most exalted culture. . . . For in the end it is these things that elicit the spontaneous admiration of men and women everywhere." Huston Smith, *The Religions of Man* (New York: Harper and Row, 1958), pp. 159–166.

We all know that such an ideal society has never existed in reality; we are not suggesting that it be set up in the United States. China did experience it in a modified form, and it had its own casts.

"Accountants hover over the earth like helicopters": Robert Bly, "A Dream of Suffocation," *The Light Around the Body* (New York: Harper and Row, 1967), p. 8.

"A sibling culture believes that no truth": The sibling society is, in general, possessed by the thought that truth is spoken only at the edges, by the marginalized, the disenfranchised, the beaten-down. That was an Enlightenment idea, which Voltaire and Rousseau both expressed. When the center of the culture was solid, even stagnant, when the only spiritual voice heard in Europe was the central Roman church, it was wonderfully helpful to give honor to the voices of out-of-the-way visionaries and eccentric rationalists.

But siblings today tend to regard every word spoken by marginalized people as true. This attitude tends to carry all before it in a political debate, or a new historicist conference, and whoever is farthest out at the edges is thought to be the owner of truth. Newt Gingrich's college says we don't need Harvard anymore, and President Clinton tries in a town meeting on television to talk from the margins even though he lives at the dead center. If your arguments have been rejected by four or more institutions, they do not need any evidence at all to be accepted.

The senators who are determined to demolish the welfare system and environmental protection succeed because they paint themselves as being from the margins. That warns us how deadly this idea has become.

"As for the gods, they are, as Michael Meade remarks": Michael Meade, *Men and the Water of Life*.

CHAPTER ELEVEN
LOOKING AT WOMEN'S AND MEN'S MOVEMENTS FROM
INSIDE THE SIBLING HOUSE

Richard Maurice Bucke, *Cosmic Consciousness* (New York: E. P. Dutton, 1940).

"Many who have at last made the discovery": Frederick Douglass, editorial in *North Star*, July 28, 1848, quoted in Miriam Schneir, ed., *Feminism: The Essential Historical Writings* (New York: Vintage Books, 1972), p. 83.

"Now, women do not ask half a kingdom": Sojourner Truth, in Miriam Schneir, *Feminism*, p. 96.

"patriarchal structures have dissolved in many fields": "The relationship between man and woman is part of a general power-system that controls the relations of men among themselves. This explains why in the beginning the first attacks on patriarchy were made by men and not by women. . . . Even if women were its ultimate beneficiaries, the ideological upheaval introduced by the French Revolution, the most decisive of all revolutions in the Western world, dealt a mortal blow to every power imposed by the grace of God. . . . Begun in the eighteenth century in the democratically-inclined countries, patriarchy's death throes lasted almost two hundred years, not without experiencing moments of extreme remission in some countries. . . . In most Western democracies, the patriarchal system has received the *coup de grace* in the last two decades. A minute dot on the line of human evolution, the nineteen-eighties have transformed the relations between men and women in a large part of the world, although we have still not fully realized the fact.

The death of patriarchy is the result of a double upheaval: the father has lost his prestige, and Eve has dealt herself a new hand. The eighteenth and nineteenth centuries dispossessed the father of his divine sponsorship, the twentieth century will finally deprive him of his moral authority and the exclusivity of his economic power." Elisabeth Badinter, *The Unopposite Sex* pp. 115–130.

"the abolition of the monogamous family": Friedrich Engels, *Origin of the*

Family (1884), quoted in Josephine Donovan, *Feminist Theory* (New York: Continuum Publishing, 1992), p. 75.

"To break up that relic of the patriarchal age": Charlotte Perkins Gilman, *The Home* (Urbana: University of Illinois Press, 1903), p. 38.

"All the same, it was not until the twentieth century that equality": Elisabeth Badinter, *The Unopposite Sex*, p. xii.

"Marion Woodman titled one of her books": Marion Woodman, *Addiction to Perfection* (Toronto: Inner City Books, 1983).

"American men are taking their manhood back": Jane Tompkins, *West of Everything* (New York: Oxford University Press, 1992), p. 33.

"There is no such thing as deep masculinity": Michael Kimmel, ed., *The Politics of Manhood: Pro-Feminist Men Respond to the Men's Movement* (Philadelphia: Temple University Press, 1995), p. 159.

Alan Alda, "What Every Woman Should Know About Men," in *Men's Lives*, ed. Michael S. Kimmel and Michael A. Meissner (New York: Macmillan, 1989), pp. 294–295.

Barry Glassner, "Men and Muscles," in *Men's Lives*, pp. 310–320.

Gary Alan Fine, "The Dirty Play of Little Boys," in *Men's Lives*, pp. 171–179.

Joseph Pleck, "Prisoners of Manliness," in *Men's Lives*, pp. 129–137.

Barbara Ehrenreich, "A Feminist's View of the New Man," in *Men's Lives*, 1pp. 34–42.

"Honey, I'm going to take the leadership of the family": *The Seven Promises of a Promise Keeper*, ed. Al Janssen and Larry K. Weeden (Colorado Springs, Co.: Focus on the Family, 1994).

CHAPTER TWELVE
EXULTATION IN THE MIDST OF FLATNESS

"There is a story out of Africa": Laurence van der Post heard it from the Bushmen, and there are a number of separate versions.

"Arsenic lobsters": Federico Garcia Lorca, "Play and Theory of the Duende," in *Deep Song and Other Prose*, trans. and ed. Christopher Maurer (New York: Directions, 1980).

"The damage to brain-labor": Neal Postman, *Amusing Ourselves to Death: Public Discourse in the Age of Show Business* (New York: Penguin Books, 1985).

"The average child in the United States": Joseph Chilton Pearce, *Evolution's End*, pp. 165–167.

"Mourning": Georg Trakl, in *Twenty Poems of Georg Trakl*, trans. James Wright and Robert Bly (Madison, Minn.: Sixties Press, 1961), p. 57.

"There is a wire stretched": Federico Garcia Lorca, "Dance of Death," in *Lorca and Jimenez: Selected Poems*, trans. Robert Bly (Boston: Beacon Press, 1973), pp. 151–157.

"Exultation is the going": Emily Dickinson, *The Complete Poems of Emily Dickinson*, ed. Thomas H. Johnson (New York: Little, Brown, 1960), p. 39.

"Do not seek too much fame": Traditional, West African; in Robert Bly, James Hillman, and Michael Meade, ed., *The Rag and Bone Shop of the Heart* (New York: HarperCollins, 1992), p. 498.

"It so happens I am sick": Pablo Neruda, "Walking Around," translated by Robert Bly, *Neruda and Vallejo: Selected Poems* (Boston: Beacon Press, 1971, 1973, new edition, 1993), pp. 29–31.

"The fact is this": Ortega y Gasset, *Revolt of the Masses* (New York: W. W. Norton, 1932), p. 54.

CHAPTER THIRTEEN
THE DIFFICULTY OF UNDERSTANDING MYTHOLOGY IN
THE SIBLING CULTURE

"In the play Amy didn't want to be": William Stafford, "First Grade," in *The Darkness Around Us Is Deep*, p. 102.

"I would like to kiss you": Rumi, *The Essential Rumi*, trans. Coleman Barks (New York: HarperCollins, 1995), p. 37.

"The great Russian children's writer Kornei Chukovsky": Kornei Chukovsky, *From Two to Five*, trans. Miriam Morton (Berkeley and Los Angeles: University of California Press, 1968).

"We'll take an example of a symbolon embedded in a story": Jacob and Wilhelm Grimm, "Hans My Hedgehog," in *Grimms' Tales for Young and Old: The Complete Stories*, pp. 375–379.

" 'They pretend,' as I hear, 'that the verse of Kabir": Henry David Thoreau, *The Winged Life*, p. 46.

"One women's magazine published a long article accusing me": Sharon Doubiago, "Enemy of the Mother: A Feminist Response to the Men's Movement," *Ms.*, March–April 1992, pp. 82–85.

CHAPTER FOURTEEN
WHAT IS VERTICAL THOUGHT?

"That is no country for old men": W. B. Yeats, "Sailing to Byzantium," *The Poems of W. B. Yeats* (New York: Macmillan, 1983), pp. 193–194.

"That were to shirk": W. B. Yeats, "Man and the Echo," in *W. B. Yeats: The Poems*, ed. Richard Finneran (New York: Macmillan, 1983), p. 345.

"How blessed is the man who like Hafez": Hafez, "When the one I love," trans. Robert Bly, in *The Soul Is Here for Its Own Joy*, p. 238.

"Even if an artist creates a spiritual work": Randall Jarrell praised Wallace Stevens's vertical gaze, and contrasted it with the literature of leveling: "Throughout half this century of the common man, this age in which each is like his sibling, Stevens has celebrated the hero, the capacious, magnanimous, excelling man; has believed, with obstinacy and good humor, in all the heights which draw us toward them, make us like them, simply by existing." Review of *The Collected Poems of Wallace Stevens*, *Yale Review* 63, no. 3 (March 1955): 351.

"The hermit's hill has always been dear to me": Giacomo Leopardi, trans. Robert Bly. For the original, see *The Penguin Book of Italian Verse* (ed. George Kay, Baltimore: Penguin, 1958), p. 272.

"Mankind owns four things": Antonio Machado, "Fourteen Poems Chosen from 'Moral Proverbs and Folk Songs,' " in *Times Alone*, p. 113.

"I do not complain of suffering for Love": Hadewijch of Antwerpt, "Knowing Love in Herself," trans. Oliver Davies, in *The Soul Is Here for Its Own Joy*, p. 119.

"The captain walks on the planks of fearful things": Rumi, trans. Robert Bly, unpublished.

"If someone insults you": Margaret of Navarre, "Wind Will Blow It All Away," trans. Robert Bly, in *The Soul Is Here for Its Own Joy*, pp. 228–229.

"My friend, I went to the market and bought": Mirabai, "It's True I Went to the Market," in *The Soul Is Here for Its Own Joy*, p. 191.

"The soul, like the moon": Lalla, trans. Coleman Barks, in *The Soul Is Here for Its Own Joy*, p. 198.

"I am not I": Juan Ramón Jiménez, trans. Robert Bly, in *Lorca and Jiménez*, p. 77.

"In the night that was dark": Saint John of the Cross, "The Dark Night," trans. Robert Bly, in *The Soul Is Here for Its Own Joy*, pp. 203–204.

CHAPTER FIFTEEN
THE SNAKE THAT WANTS TO EAT ALL ITS BRIDES: A
SWEDISH STORY

"The Wurm story": Andrew Lang, *The Pink Fairy Book* (New York: Dover, 1967), pp. 301–314.

"Seeing the snowman standing all alone": Richard Wilbur, "Boy at the Window," *Things of This World* (New York: Harcourt Brace Jovanovich, 1952, 1980).

"The sleep of reason produces monsters": Words written by Goya on one of his *caprichos*.

"When you're dealing with a person who is doing violence": Orland Bishop, personal communication.

"A person who is cursed always goes to the house of a person": Malidoma Somé, personal communication.

EPILOGUE

"When Euclid set out to measure Hades": Harry Martinson, "Hades and Euclid" (first version), in *Friends, You Drank Some Darkness*, pp. 55–57.

"No single individual . . . will be able to arrest," Soren Kierkegaard, *The Present Age*, translated by Alexander Dru, (New York: Harper and Row, 1962).

"If you don't know the kind of person I am," William Stafford, "A Ritual to Read to Each Other" in *Stories That Could Be True: New and Collected Poems* (New York: Harper and Row, 1977), p. 52.

"The [person] with the clear head," Ortega y Gasset, *Revolt of the Masses* (New York: W. W. Norton, 1932), p. 170.

"to pull adolescents across the border": Michael Meade has been organizing a series of week long conferences in the inner cities which include a potent mixture of adolescents and adults. Bob Roberts has instituted an impressive project in Louisiana in which young men coming out of prison to a halfway house receive help from older men—most of whom have been convicts themselves—with drug treatment, family counseling, individual and group counseling sessions, and job placement. The cost to put a man through the ninety-day program is $3,200. Without such treatment, or with standard state treatment, 75 percent of convicts in Louisiana are arrested and incarcerated again; the cost of the tracking, arresting, arraigning, trial preparation and trial can easily reach $100,000. Roberts's men have a return rate of 4.5 percent. The project has been funded by the New Orleans Business Council, and recently by the U.S. Department of Justice under Janet Reno. Currently the project has ten full-time and two part-time staff. Roberts can be reached at 1010 Commons Street, Suite 1460A, New Orleans, Louisiana, 70112, Onadje Benjamin is active in Alabama. Harris Breiman of Woodstock, New York, helps to organize men's sessions in maximum security prisons in upstate New York. A long-time worker with troubled men is Johnny Ray Youngblood, pastor of St. Paul's Community Baptist Church in Brooklyn.

"And gathers jewels of feelings for others," Ansari, trans. Robert Bly, in *The Soul Is Here for Its Own Joy* (Hopewell, NJ: Ecco Press, 1995), p. 13.

The Seventh Father of the House story can be found in Asbjornsen and Moe, *Eventyr*, Ofdendal Forlag, Oslo, Norway, various editions.

Bibliography

Adams, Paul L., and Judith R. Milner. *Fatherless Children*. New York: John Wiley and Sons, 1984.

Afanas-ev, Aleksandr. *Russian Fairy Tales*. Translated by Norbert Guterman. New York: Pantheon Books, 1945.

Ainsworth, Mary. *Infancy in Uganda*. Baltimore: Johns Hopkins University Press, 1967.

Alda, Alan. "What Every Woman Should Know About Men." In *Men's Lives*, edited by Michael S. Kimmel and Michael A. Meissner. New York: Macmillan, 1989.

Anderson, Sherwood. *Winesburg, Ohio*. New York: Viking Press, 1960.

Andrews, V. C. *Flowers in the Attic*. New York: Simon and Schuster, 1979.

Angel, Ronald. *Painful Inheritance: Health and the New Generation of Fatherless Families*. Madison: University of Wisconsin Press, 1993.

Aronwitz, Stanley. *Education Under Siege*. South Hadley, Mass.: Bergin and Garvey, 1985.

Badinter, Elisabeth. *The Unopposite Sex: The End of the Gender Battle*. Translated by Barbara Wright. New York: Harper and Row, 1989.

———. *XY: On Masculine Identity*. Translated by Lydia Davis. New York: Columbia University Press, 1995.

Bank, Stephen P., and Michael D. Kalm. *The Sibling Bond*. New York: Basic Books, 1982.

Barfield, Owen. *History, Guilt, and Habit*. Middletown, Conn.: Wesleyan University Press, 1979.

Barsamanian, David, and Noam Chomsky. *Chronicles of Dissent*. Monroe, Me.: Common Courage Press, 1992.

Basho. *Basho*. Translated by Robert Bly. San Francisco: Mudra, 1972.

Bellah, Robert N., et al. *Habits of the Heart: Individualism and Commitment in American Life*. Berkeley: University of California Press, 1985.

Benjamin, Jessica. *Bonds of Love*. New York: Pantheon Books, 1988.

Bensen, Leonard. *Fatherhood: A Sociological Perspective*. New York: Random House, 1968.

Biller, Henry. *Fathers and Families: Paternal Factors in Child Development*. Westport, Conn.: Auburn House, 1993.

Bissinger, Karl. *New York Times Magazine*, May 29, 1994.

Blankenhorn, David. *Fatherless America: Confronting Our Most Urgent Social Problem*. New York: Basic Books, 1995.

Bloom, Allan. *The Closing of the American Mind*. New York: Simon and Schuster, 1987.

Blos, Peter. *On Adolescence: A Psychoanalytic Interpretation*. New York: Free Press, Collier-Macmillan, 1962.

———. *The Son-Father Relationship from Infancy to Manhood: An Intergenerational Inquiry*. New York: Free Press, Collier-Macmillan, 1985.

———. *Son and Father: Before and Beyond the Oedipus Complex*. New York: Free Press, Collier-Macmillan, 1985.

———. *The Young Adolescent*. New York: Free Press, Collier-Macmillan, 1970.

Blum, Harold, ed. *Female Psychology: Contemporary Psychoanalytic Views*. New York: International Universities Press, 1977.

Bly, Robert. *Leaping Poetry: An Idea with Poems and Translations*. Boston: Beacon Press, 1975.

———. *The Light Around the Body*. New York: Harper and Row, 1967.

Bly, Robert, ed. *News of the Universe*. San Francisco: Sierra Club, 1980.

———. *The Soul Is Here for Its Own Joy: Sacred Poems from Many Cultures*. Hopewell, N.J.: Ecco Press, 1995.

Bly, Robert, James Hillman, and Michael Meade, eds. *The Rag and Bone Shop of the Heart*. New York: HarperCollins, 1992.

Bok, Derek. *Higher Learning*. Cambridge, Mass.: Harvard University Press, 1986.

Bolk, Louis. *Das Problem der Menschderwung (The Problem of Human Evolution)*. Jena: G. Fisher, 1926.

Boose, Lynda E., and Betty S. Flowers, eds. *Daughters and Fathers*. Baltimore: Johns Hopkins University Press, 1989.

Bourne, Randolph, *The Radical Will: Selected Writings*. Edited by Olaf Hanson. Berkeley: University of California Press, 1977.

Bowlby, John. *Attachment*. New York: Basic Books, 1983.

———. *A Secure Base: Parent-Child Attachment and Healthy Human Development*. New York: Basic Books, 1988.

Brandon, David Lynn. *Daughters and Parents: Past, Present and Future*. Monterey, Calif.: Brooks/Cole, 1979.

———. *The Father: His Role in Child Development*. Monterey, Calif.: Brooks/Cole, 1974.

Bucke, Richard Maurice. *Cosmic Consciousness*. New York: E. P. Dutton, 1940.

Burns, Ailsa, and Cath Scott. *Mother Headed Families and Why They Have Increased*. Hillsdale, N.J.: Erlbaum, 1994.

Chomsky, Noam, and David Barsamian. *Chronicles of Dissent: Interviews with David Barsamian*. Monroe, Me.: Common Courage Press, 1992.

Chomsky, Noam, and Edward S. Herman. *The Washington Connection and Third World Fascism from the Political Economy of Human Rights*. Vol. 1. Boston: South End Press, 1979.

Chukovsky, Kornei. *From Two to Five*. Translated and edited by Miriam Morton. Berkeley: University of California Press, 1968.

Clare, John. *The Poems of John Clare*. Vol. 1. Edited by J. W. Tibble. New York: E. P. Dutton, 1935.

Cottle, Thomas J. *Like Fathers, Like Sons: Portraits of Intimacy and Strain*. Norwood, N.J.: Ablex, 1981.

Coupland, Douglas. *Generation X: Tales for an Accelerated Culture*. New York: St. Martin's Press, 1991.

Courtright, Paul B. *Ganesa: Lord of Obstacles, Lord of Beginnings*. New York: Oxford University Press, 1985.

Danielou, Alain. *Shiva and Dionysus*. Translated by K. F. Hurry. London: East-West Publications, 1982.

Dasent, George Webbe. "Tatterhood." In *East o' the Sun and West o' the Moon*. New York: Dover, 1970.

Degler, Carl. *At Odds: Women and the Family in America from the Revolution to the Present*. New York: Oxford University Press, 1980.

Deutsch, Helene. *A Psychology of Women: A Psychoanalytic Interpretation*. Vols. 1 and 2. New York: Grune and Stratton, 1944, 1945.

Dickinson, Emily. *The Complete Poems of Emily Dickinson*. Edited by Thomas H. Johnson. Boston: Little, Brown, 1960.

Dinnerstein, Dorothy. *The Mermaid and the Minotaur: Sexual Arrangements and Human Malaise*. New York: HarperCollins, 1977.

Doi, Takeo. *The Anatomy of Dependence*. Translated by John Bester. New York: Kodansha International, 1981.

Donovan, Josephine. *Feminist Theory and the Intellectual Traditions of American Feminism*. New York: Continuum, A Frederick Ungar Book, 1992.

Doubiago, Sharon. "Enemy of the Mother: A Feminist Response to the Men's Movement," *Ms.*, March–April 1992.

Dowd, Maureen. *New York Times*, September 3, 1995.

Ehrenreich, Barbara. *Fear of Falling: The Inner Life of the Middle Class*. New York: HarperPerennial, 1990.

———. *"A Feminist's View of the New Man."* In *Men's Lives*, edited by Michael S. Kimmel and Michael A. Meissner. New York: Macmillan, 1989.

Eliot, T. S. *Collected Poems*. New York: Harcourt, Brace, 1936.

Elmer-Dewitt, Philip. "On a Screen Near You: Cyberporn." *Time*, July 3, 1995.

Elshtain, Jean Bethke. *Public Man, Private Woman: Women in Social Political Thought*. Princeton, N.J.: Princeton University Press, 1993.

Elson, Miriam. *Self Psychology in Clinical Social Work*. New York: W. W. Norton, 1986.

Fair, Charles. *The Dying Self*. Middletown, Conn.: Wesleyan University Press, 1969.

Faludi, Susan. *Backlash*. New York: Doubleday, 1991.

Fields, Suzanne. *Like Father, Like Daughter: How a Father Shapes the Woman His Daughter Becomes*. Boston: Little, Brown, 1983.

Fine, Gary Alan. "The Dirty Play of Little Boys." In *Men's Lives*, edited by Michael S. Kimmel and Michael A. Meissner. New York: Macmillan, 1989.

Fishel, Elizabeth. *The Men in Our Lives*. New York: William Morrow, 1985.

Freud, Sigmund. *Civilization and Its Discontents*. Translated and edited by James Strachey. New York: W. W. Norton, 1959.

———. *Group Psychology and the Analysis of the Ego*. Translated and edited by James Strachey. New York: W. W. Norton, 1959.

Friedman, Robert, and Leila Lerner. *Toward a New Psychology of Man: Psychoanalytic and Social Perspectives*. New York: Guilford Press, 1986.

Gaines, Donna. *Teenage Wasteland: Suburbia's Dead End Kids*. New York: HarperCollins, 1991.

Garcia Lorca, Federico. *Lorca and Jimenez: Selected Poems*. Translated by Robert Bly. Boston: Beacon Press, 1973.

———. "Play and Theory of the Duende," in *Deep Song and Other Prose*. Translated and edited by Christopher Maurer. New York: New Directions, 1980.

Gilder, George F. *Sexual Suicide*. New York: Bantam Books, 1975.

Gilligan, Carol, and Eva Stern. "The Riddle of Femininity and the Psychology of Love." Paper presented at the Seminar on the Psychology of Love, Douglass College, 1986.

Gilman, Charlotte Perkins. *The Home*. Urbana: University of Illinois Press, 1903.

Glassner, Barry. "Men and Muscles." In *Men's Lives*, edited by Michael S. Kimmel and Michael A. Meissner. New York: Macmillan, 1989.

Golding, William. *Lord of the Flies*. London: Faber and Faber, 1962.

Gopnick, Adam. "Read All About It." *New Yorker*, December 12, 1994.

Gorer, Geoffrey. *The American People: A Study in National Character*. New York: W. W. Norton, 1948.

Gould, Stephen Jay. *Ontogeny and Phylogeny*. Cambridge, Mass.: Harvard University Press, 1977.

Goulter, Barbara, and Joan Minninger. *The Father-Daughter Dance*. London: Routledge, 1994.

Graves, Robert. *Greek Myths*. New York: Penguin Books, 1975.

Greider, William. *Secrets of the Temple*. New York: Simon and Schuster, 1987.

———. *Who Will Tell the People: The Betrayal of American Democracy*. New York: Simon and Schuster, 1992.

Grimm, Jacob and Wilhelm. *Grimms' Tales for Young and Old: The Complete Stories*. Translated by Ralph Manheim. New York: Anchor Press / Doubleday, 1977.

Griswold, Robert L. *Fatherhood in America*. New York: Basic Books, HarperCollins, 1993.

Hamburg, David. *Today's Children*. New York: Times Books, 1992.

Hamilton, Marshall. *Fathers' Influence on Children*. Chicago: Nelson Hall, 1977.

Hammer, Signe. *Passionate Attachments: Fathers and Daughters in America Today*. New York: Rawson Associates, 1982.

Healy, Jane M. *Endangered Minds*. New York: Simon and Schuster, 1990.

Hendin, Herbert. *The Age of Sensation*. New York: W. W. Norton, 1975.

Henry, Jules. *Culture Against Man*. New York: Random House, 1963.

Hiebert, Ray E., and Carol Reuss, eds. *Impact of Mass Media*. New York: Longman, 1985.

Hillman, James, ed. *Facing the Gods*. Irving, Tex.: Spring Publications, 1980.

Hoffer, Eric. "A Time of Juveniles," *Harper's*, June 1965.

Holtz, Geoffrey T. *Welcome to the Jungle: The Why Behind Generation X*. New York: St. Martin's Press, 1995.

Hopkins, Gerard Manley. *Poems and Prose of Gerard Manley Hopkins*. Edited by W. H. Gardner. New York: Penguin Books, 1984.

Hudson, Liam, and Bernadine Jacot. *The Way Men Think*. New Haven, Conn.: Yale University Press, 1991.

Illich, Ivan. *Towards a History of Needs*. New York: Bantam Books, 1977.

Irigaray, Luce. *Thinking the Difference for a Peaceful Revolution*. Translated by Karin Montin. New York: Routledge, 1994.

Janssen, Al, and Larry K. Weeden, eds., *The Seven Promises of a Promise Keeper*. Colorado Springs, Co.: Focus on the Family, 1994.

Jarrell, Randall. Review of *The Collected Poems of Wallace Stevens, Yale Review* 63, no. 3 (March 1955).

Jensen, Derrick. *Listening to the Land: Conversations About Nature, Culture and Eros*. San Francisco: Sierra Club Books, 1995.

Jonas, David, and Doris Klein. *Manchild: A Study of the Infantilization of Man*. New York: McGraw-Hill, 1970.

Jones, Gwyn, and Thomas Jones, *The Mabinogion*. London: Everyman's Library, 1974.

Jordan, Judith, ed. *Women's Growth in Connection: Writings from the Stone Center*. New York: Guilford Press, 1991.

Kafka, Franz. *The Complete Stories and Parables*. Edited by Nahum N. Glatzer. New York: Schocken Books, 1983.

Katz, Jon. "Guilty." *Wired*, September 1995.

Kierkegaard, Soren. *The Present Age*. Translated by Alexander Dru. New York: Harper and Row, 1962.

Kilpatrick, William. *Why Johnny Can't Tell Right from Wrong and What We Can Do About It*. New York: Simon and Schuster, 1992.

Kimbrell, Andrew. *The Masculine Mystique*. New York: Ballantine Books, 1995.

Kimmel, Michael S., ed. *The Politics of Manhood: Pro-Feminist Men Respond to the Men's Movement*. Philadelphia: Temple University Press, 1995.

Kimmel, Michael S., and Michael A. Meissner, eds. *Men's Lives*. New York: Macmillan, 1989.

Kinney, Jay. "Anarcho-Emergentist-Republicans." *Wired*, September 1995.

Klein, Melanie. *Envy and Gratitude and Other Works* 1946–1963. New York: Free Press, 1975.

Koestler, Arthur. *The Ghost in the Machine*. New York: Macmillan, 1968.

Kohut, Heinz. *Self Psychology and the Humanities*. Edited by Charles B. Strozier. New York: W. W. Norton, 1985.

Kotlowitz, Alex. *There Are No Children Here: The Story of Two Boys Growing Up in the Other America*. New York: Doubleday, 1991.

Kozol, Jonathan. *Savage Inequalities: Children in America's Schools*. New York: HarperPerennial, 1992.

Krogman, Wilton Marion. *Child Growth*. Ann Arbor: University of Michigan Press, 1972.

Lamb, Michael E. *The Father's Role: Applied Perspectives*. New York: John Wiley and Sons, 1986.

Lang, Andrew. *The Pink Fairy Book*. New York: Dover Press, 1967.

Lasch, Christopher. *Culture of Narcissism*. New York: W. W. Norton, 1979.

———. *Haven in a Heartless World: The Family Besieged*. New York: Basic Books, 1979.

———. *The Minimal Self: Survival in Troubled Times*. New York: W. W. Norton, 1984.

———. *Progress and Its Critics*. New York: W. W. Norton, 1991.

———. *The Revolt of the Elites and the Betrayal of Democracy*. New York: W. W. Norton, 1995.

Lawrence, D. H. *Psychoanalysis and the Unconscious*. New York: Viking Press, 1960.

Leach, William. *Land of Desire*. New York: Vintage Books, Random House, 1993.

Leeuw, Gerardus van der. *Sacred and Profane Beauty: The Holy in Art*. Translated by David E. Green. New York: Holt, Rinehart and Winston, 1963.

Lee, John. *Facing the Fire: Experiencing and Expressing Anger Appropriately*. New York: Bantam Books, 1993.

Lehman, David. *Signs of the Times: Deconstruction and the Fall of Paul de Man*. New York: Simon and Schuster, 1991.

Leonard, Linda Schierse. *The Wounded Woman*. Athens, Ohio: Swallow Press, 1982.

Lewis, Charlie, and Margaret O'Brien. *Reassessing Fatherhood: New Observations on Fathers and the Modern Family*. London: Sage Press, 1987.

Lindblad-Goldberg, Marion. *Clinical Issues in Single Parent Households*. Rockville, Md.: Aspen, 1987.

Locke, John. *Two Treatises on Government*.

Lorenz, Konrad. *Studies in Animal and Human Behavior*. London: Methuen, 1971.

Lowenfeld, Harry and Yala. "Our Permissive Society and the Superego." *Psychoanalytic Quarterly*, **39**, 1970.

Macedo, Donaldo P. *Literacies of Power*. Boulder, Col.: West View Press, 1994.

Machado, Antonio. *Times Alone: Selected Poems of Antonio Machado*. Translated by Robert Bly. Middletown, Conn.: Wesleyan University Press, 1983.

MacLean, Paul. "Man and His Animal Brains." *Modern Medicine*, March 2, 1964.

———. *A Triune Concept of the Brain and Behavior*. Edited by D. Campbell and T. J. Boag. Toronto: University of Toronto Press, 1973.

Magid, Ken, and Carole A. McKelvey. *High Risk: Children Without a Conscience*. New York: Bantam Books, 1988.

Maine, Margo. *Father Hunger: Fathers, Daughters and Food*. Carlsbad, Calif.: Gurze Books, 1991.

Maraniss, David. *First in His Class*. New York: Simon and Schuster, 1995.

Marcuse, Herbert. *Eros and Civilization: A Philosophical Inquiry into Freud*. Boston: Beacon Press, 1966.

Martinson, Harry. "Hades and Euclid." In *Friends, You Drank Some Darkness: Three Swedish Poets*. Translated by Robert Bly. Boston: Beacon Press, 1975.

Mause, Lloyd de. *Reagan's America*. New York: Creative Roots, 1984.

McGlashan, Alan. *The Savage and Beautiful Country*. Boston: Houghton Mifflin, 1967.

McGrath, Thomas. *Letter to an Imaginary Friend*. Parts 1 and 2. Chicago: Swallow Press, 1977.

McLanahan, Sara, and Gary Sandefur. *Growing Up with a Single Parent*. Cambridge, Mass.: Harvard University Press, 1994.

McLuhan, Marshall. *The Mechanical Bride*. Boston: Beacon Press, 1969.

Mead, Margaret. *Coming of Age in Samoa*. New York: Mentor Books, 1949.

———. *Male and Female*. New York: William Morrow, 1949.

——. *Sex and Temperament in Three Primitive Societies*. New York: Mentor Books, 1950.

Meade, Michael. *Men and the Water of Life: Initiation and the Tempering of Men*. San Francisco: Harper San Francisco, 1993.

Miedzian, Myriam. *Boys Will Be Boys*. New York: Doubleday, 1991.

Miller, Jean Baker. "The Development of Women's Sense of Self," *Work in Progress*, No. 12. Wellesley, Mass.: Stone Center Working Paper Series, 1984.

——. *Toward a New Psychology of Women*. Boston: Beacon Press, 1986.

Mirabai. *Mirabai*. Translated by Robert Bly. Penland, N.C.: Squid Ink, 1993.

Mitscherlich, Alexander. *Society Without the Father*. Translated by Eric Mosbacher. London: Tavistock Publications, 1969.

Moir, Anne, and David Jessel. *Brain Sex*. New York: Dell, 1992.

Moore, Marianne. *Collected Poems*. New York: Macmillan, 1941, 1969.

Moore, Robert. *King, Warrior, Magician, Lover*. San Francisco: Harper San Francisco, 1990.

Moynihan, Daniel Patrick. "Moved by the Data, Not Doctrine." *New York Times Magazine*, December 31, 1995.

Moynihan, Daniel Patrick, *The Negro Family: The Case for National Action*. Westport, Conn.: Greenwood Press, 1981.

Nauman, Bruce, ed. Joan Simon, *Bruce Nauman: Exhibition Catalogue*. Minneapolis: Walker Art Center, 1994.

Neely, Richard. *Tragedies of Our Own Making*. Urbana: University of Illinois Press, 1994.

Nelson, John. *Healing the Split: Integrating Spirit into Our Understanding of the Mentally Ill*. Albany: State University of New York Press, 1994.

Neruda, Pablo. *Neruda and Vallejo: Selected Poems*. Edited by Robert Bly. Boston: Beacon Press, 1971, 1993.

Nurbakhsh, Dr. Javad. *The Psychology of Sufism*. London: Khaniqahi-Nimatullahi Publications, 1992.

Opie, Iona and Peter. *The Classic Fairy Tales*. New York: Oxford University Press, 1974.

Ortega y Gasset. *Revolt of the Masses*. New York: W. W. Norton, 1932.

Orwell, George. *The Orwell Reader*. Edited by Richard Rover. New York: Harcourt Brace Jovanovich, 1956.

Osherson, Samuel. *Finding Our Fathers: The Unfinished Business of Manhood*. New York: Free Press, Collier-Macmillan, 1986.

Ostrovsky, Everett S. *Children Without Men*. New York: Collier Books, 1962.

Paglia, Camille. *Sex, Art and American Culture*. New York: Vintage Books, Random House, 1992.

———. *Sexual Personae: Art and Decadence from Nefertiti to Emily Dickinson*. New Haven, Conn.: Yale University Press, 1990.

———. *Vamps and Tramps*. New York: Vintage Books, Random House, 1994.

Parke, Ross D. *Fathers*. Cambridge, Mass.: Harvard University Press, 1981.

Pearce, Joseph Chilton. *Evolution's End: Claiming the Potential of Our Intelligence*. San Francisco: Harper San Francisco, 1992.

Pipher, Mary, Ph.D. *Reviving Ophelia: Saving the Selves of Adolescent Girls*. New York: Ballantine Books, 1994.

Pirani, Alix. *The Absent Father: Crisis and Creativity*. New York: Arkana/Viking Penguin, 1989.

Pleck, Joseph. "Prisoners of Manliness." In *Men's Lives*, edited by Michael S. Kimmel and Michael A. Meissner. New York: Macmillan, 1989.

Polakow, Valerie. *Lives on the Edge: Single Mothers and Their Children in the Other America*. Cambridge, Mass.: Harvard University Press, 1993.

Pollitt, Katha. "Bothered and Bewildered." *New York Times*, July 22, 1993.

Pope, Alexander, ed. Maynard Mack. *An Essay on Man*. New Haven: Yale University Press, 1951.

Postman, Neal. *Amusing Ourselves to Death: Public Discourse in the Age of Show Business*. New York: Penguin Books, 1985.

———. *The Disappearance of Childhood*. New York: Vintage Books, 1994.

———. *Technopoly: The Surrender of Culture to Technology*. New York: Alfred A. Knopf, 1992.

Postman, Neil, and Steven Powers. *How to Watch TV News*. New York: Penguin Books, 1992.

Rashbaum, Beth, and Olga Silverstein. *The Courage to Raise Good Men*. New York: Viking Press, 1994.

Reich, Annie. "Early Identifications as Archaic Elements in the Superego." *Journal of the American Psychoanalytic Association*, **2**, 1954.

Ross, Andrew, and Tricia Rose, eds. *Microphone Fiends: Youth Music and Youth Culture*. New York: Routledge, 1994.

Rotundo, E. Anthony. *American Manhood: Transformations in Masculinity from the Revolution to the Modern Era*. New York: Basic Books, 1990.

Rumi. *The Essential Rumi*. Translated by Coleman Barks. New York: Harper-Collins, 1995.

Sapolsky, Robert. "Ego Boundaries, or the Fit of My Father's Shirt." *Discover* 16, no. 11, November 1995.

Schneir, Miriam, ed. *Feminism: The Essential Historical Writings*. New York: Vintage, 1992.

———. *Feminism in Our Time*. New York: Vintage Books, 1994.

Schorr, Alvin L., and Phyllis Moen. *Family in Transition: Rethinking Marriage, Sexuality, Child Rearing and Family Organization*. Boston: Little, Brown, 1983.

Sharpe, Sue. *Fathers and Daughters*. London: Routledge, 1994.

Shepard, Paul. *The Tender Carnivore and the Sacred Game*. New York: Scribner, 1973.

Shulman, Shmuel. *Father-Adolescent Relationships*. San Francisco: Jossey-Bass, 1993.

Sidel, Ruth. "But Where Are the Men?" In *Men's Lives*, edited by Michael S. Kimmel and Michael A. Meissner. New York: Macmillan, 1989.

Smith, Huston. *The Religions of Man*. New York: Harper and Row, 1958.

Snarey, John R. *How Fathers Care for the Next Generation*. Cambridge, Mass.: Harvard University Press, 1993.

Somé, Malidoma Patrice. *Of Water and the Spirit*. New York: G. P. Putnam's Sons, 1994.

Stafford, William. *Allegiances*. New York: Harper and Row, 1970.

———. *The Darkness Around Us Is Deep: Selected Poems of William Stafford*. Edited by Robert Bly. New York: HarperCollins, 1994.

Stanley, Lawrence. *Rap: The Lyrics*. New York: Penguin Books, 1992.

Steiner, George. *In Bluebeard's Castle: or Some Notes Towards a Redefinition of Culture*. London: Faber and Faber, 1971.

Stivers, Richard. *The Culture of Cynicism*. Oxford: Blackwells, 1994.

Strauss, Neil, with Alec Foege. "A Cry in the Dark." *Rolling Stone*, June 2, 1994.

Sykes, Charles. *A Nation of Victims*. New York: St. Martin's Press, 1992.

Tawney, R. H. *The Acquisitive Society*. New York: Harcourt, Brace, 1948.

———. *Religion and the Rise of Capitalism*. New York: Penguin Books, 1947.

Theweleit, Klaus. *Male Fantasies. Vol. 1: Women, Floods and Bodies*. Translated by Stephen Conway. Minneapolis: University of Minnesota Press, 1987.

Thoreau, Henry David. *The Winged Life: The Poetic Voice of Henry David Thoreau*. Edited by Robert Bly. New York: HarperCollins, 1992.

Tiger, Lionel. *Men in Groups*. London: Marion Boyars, 1984.

Tocqueville, Alexis de. *Democracy in America*. Translated by George Lawrence. New York: HarperPerennials, 1988.

Tompkins, Jane. *West of Everything: The Inner Life of Westerns*. Oxford, Eng.: Oxford University Press, 1992.

Trakl, Georg. *Twenty Poems of Georg Trakl*. Translated by Robert Bly and James Wright. Madison, Minn.: Sixties Press, 1961.

Turnbull, Colin. *The Mountain People*. New York: Simon and Schuster, 1972.

Ventura, Michael. "Welcome to the Real World, Kid," *City Pages*. Minneapolis, June 21, 1995.

———. *Letters at Three AM: Reports on Endarkenment*. Dallas: Spring Publications, 1993.

———. *Shadow Dancing in the USA*. Los Angeles: Jeremy Tarcher, 1985.

Verny, Thomas, with John Kelly. *The Secret Life of the Unborn Child*. New York: Dell, 1981.

Vidal, Gore. *United States*. New York: Random House, 1993.

Vogt, Max. *Return to Father: Archetypal Dimensions of the Patriarch*. Dallas: Spring Publications, 1991.

Vries, Ada de. *Dictionary of Symbols and Imagery*. Amsterdam: North Holland Publishing Co., 1974.

Warner, Marina. *Six Myths of Our Time*. New York: Vintage Books, Random House, 1995.

Weber, Max. *The Protestant Ethic and the Spirit of Capitalism*. Translated by Talcott Parsons. New York: Scribner, 1952.

Weston, William J., ed. *Education and the American Family*. New York: New York University Press, 1989.

Wiehe, Vernon R. *Sibling Abuse: Hidden Physical, Emotional and Sexual Trauma*. Lexington, Mass.: Lexington Books, 1990.

Wilbur, Richard. *Things of This World*. New York: Harcourt Brace Jovanovich, 1952, 1980.

Winnicott, D. W. *The Child, the Family, and the Outside World*. Harmondsworth, Eng.: Penguin Books, 1964.

Wolin, Steven and Sybil. *The Resilient Self*. New York: Villard Books, 1993.

Woodman, Marion. *Addiction to Perfection*. Toronto: Inner City Books, 1983.

Wordsworth, William. *The Poems*. Vol. 1. New York: Penguin Books, 1977.

————. *The Prelude, A Parallel Text.* Edited by J. C. Maxwell. New York: Penguin Books, 1971.

Yeats, W. B. *W. B. Yeats: The Poems.* Edited by Richard Finneran. New York: Macmillan, 1983.

Zanardi, Claudia, ed. *Essential Papers on the Psychology of Women.* New York: New York University Press, 1990.

Acknowledgments

I have brooded over the ideas in this book for some years; and I have bene-
fited greatly from conversations with friends and working companions. Saul
Galin helped me from the start. Gioia Timpanelli, Michael Meade, Martín
Prechtel, John Lee, Marion Woodman, Carl Faber, Judith Weissman, Michael
Ventura, Owen Christianson, Donald Hall, and Thomas R. Smith have been
immensely generous with thoughts and insights. More recently I am grateful
for discussions with Paul Courtright, James Hillman, Robert Moore, Ernst
Benker, Frank Pittman, Eric Beesmeyer, Harris Breiman, Eric Storlie, Andrew
Dick, Larry Luck, James Lenfesty, Aaron Kipnis, Malidoma Somé, Lewis
Hyde, Dr. James Stoeri, and Mary Helen Hopponen. My editor at Addison-
Wesley, William Patrick, has given fervent help throughout. I've also bene-
fited by discussions with participants at the 1995 Conference on the Great
Mother, the 1995 Minnesota Men's Conference, and the 1996 Asilomar Con-
ference, particularly the criticisms and suggestions brought forward by Mar-
ianne Lust, John Mickelson, Rita Shumaker, Fran Castan, Mark Clemons,
Wendy Martyna, Nils Peterson, Tina Stallings, Theodore Harris, William
Tweed Kennedy, and Lizzy Camp.

Claire Peacock prepared the bibliography. Thomas Smith prepared the
footnotes. Two of my daughters, Mary Bly and Bridget Bly, read relevant
sections with penetrating comments; and Noah Bly helped me to stay on
the point. My greatest gratitude is to my wife Ruth Bly, who talked over the
major ideas in the book with keen interest, saved me from many extremes,
and did some superb editing.

Copyright Acknowledgments

Index